MESSAGE MACHINE

MESSAGE MACHINE

How Communications Will Make
You An Unstoppable Founder

JAG SINGH & OLIVER AUST

EDITORIAL
Authors: Jag Singh & Oliver Aust
Editor: Gabriella Williams
Designers: Bianca Amorim, Daniel Iowe

PUBLISHED BY
Eo Ipso Communications GmbH
Friedrichstraße 68, 10117 Berlin, Germany

ISBN: 978-3-9821088-4-1

www.messagemachine.io

ALSO BY OLIVER AUST

How to Speak Like a CEO: How Successful Leaders Communicate (2019)

Mastering Communications: How CEOs and Executives Can Build a Great Reputation in the Digital Age (2019)

Unignorable: Build Your Personal Brand and Boost Your Business in 30 Days (2020)

Business Leader to Thought Leader in 9 Steps (ebook, 2021)

www.oliveraust.com

CONTENTS

FOREWORD

For more than fifteen years, I've been running a fundraising workshop attended by every company that comes into Techstars. That's over 3,000 companies, with founders from different parts of the world. Many of these companies have grown tremendously and returned a ton of value to their shareholders. Dozens have become unicorns.

The focus of that workshop surprises founders each time. It isn't at all about teaching them secret negotiation tactics, or about presenting convincing metrics. Entrepreneurs know how to do those things already. Instead, I've always focused on communication skills.

In this book you're holding, Jag and Oliver have perfectly captured this idea in a much broader sense. If any entrepreneur can learn and improve their skills to become an unstoppable founder, then they owe it to themselves to do so. And this book will help them to strive for excellence in communications. The communication skills of company founders often reflect the way their businesses communicate with the outside world. That's why this is an important subject.

I also love that our two authors come from vastly different and diverse backgrounds. They've lived through and seen failures as well as successes. The result of those experiences is a shared approach to communications. It's one that people from all walks of life will appreciate.

I've always strongly believed that if you can be a better communicator, then you can be a much better fundraiser. Or salesperson. Or spouse. Read on, and enjoy.

David Cohen

David Cohen is the Founder and Chairman of Techstars. David is an investor in thousands of startups globally via Techstars, the worldwide network that helps entrepreneurs succeed, including 20 unicorn companies that are collectively worth several hundred billion dollars.

FOREWORD

Introduction

FROM COMMUNICATIONS LAST TO COMMUNICATIONS FIRST

If you are building a startup, you will probably face an existential crisis sooner rather than later. Almost all of them could be avoided with better communications. "**As a company grows, its biggest challenge always becomes communication**," says Ben Horowitz, the co-founder of Andreessen Horowitz.

Our mission with this book is to spare founders the agony of an existential crisis through stronger communications that lead to growth, be it in terms of revenue, jobs, valuation or real-world impact. Few companies crush these goals. Startup history is littered with great teams with fantastic products and services who could not figure out fast enough how to get noticed, build trust or simply sell their product. As a result, they can't scale, exit or make an impact. **If you don't communicate, you don't exist.**

What exactly do we mean by communications? We use the term in its broadest sense to encompass any way in which a business interacts with its internal, external and financial stakeholders. This includes interactions with employees and applicants, potential investors and shareholders, customers, regulators and the public.

This can happen one-to-one, one-to-few, one-to-many, through conversations, media and social media, materials such as pitch decks, brand identity and even the pricing of the product. The plural *communications* refers to the various disciplines that are relevant for founders, such as internal, external, and financial communications. The singular describes your personal *communication*.

Becoming an Unstoppable Founder

Excellence in communications has never been more critical for founders. It impacts everything a startup does and is the underlying reason why so many ventures fail, as we will see shortly. There are also more startups, exits and ecosystems today, but not more attention. Audiences are increasingly fragmented. It is much harder to get noticed by the right people for the right reasons. Harder, but not impossible.

Imagine the best version of yourself as a communicator. Someone who can lead, inspire and persuade others with words. Written, spoken, online, on stage, in front of a camera – it doesn't matter. You are perceived as charismatic and have the ability to create a permanent impression on people in any situation. And you save a lot of time in the process.

Now imagine your company as a well-oiled communications machine, where there is total clarity in everyone's mind about what you do and why, and how to attract customers, investors and top talent. You have a great team that crushes your marketing, investor relations, and conversations with customers. The leadership inspires everyone on the team. We call this kind of organization a Message Machine. A Message

Machine is an organization that has mastered communications and uses these skills strategically to achieve its overall business objectives.

The founders and startups at this level are unstoppable. They are not content to reach the *ok plateau* of decent communications. They turn communications from biggest challenge to biggest opportunity. The most successful founders embrace the fact that communications is their master skill. We think of founders like Melanie Perkins, the CEO and co-founder of the graphic design platform Canva, who often describes herself as a natural introvert. Despite being rejected by over a hundred investors, Perkins still found a way to convince the right ones. Today her company is unique not just because of the amount of money it's raised, but also because it's actually profitable. The skills and tactics such founders employed to become better communicators are the same ones we apply to help you build your Message Machine.

When we make references to public figures or well-known companies, we hope they inspire you and show you what is possible. We don't suggest that you compare yourself to where they are today. Instead, we'd rather you work on improving your own skills and track your progress over an extended period of time.

This book will show you how to become an unstoppable founder through communications. It will show you how you move from fact-telling to story-telling and how you can ensure everyone in the company tells the same story. You will learn how to persuade and how to handle fierce conversations. You will see clearly what needs to be done in marketing, hiring, PR, and fundraising, and how you can get everyone focused on that. You will also be certain who to task or hire to lead these efforts. You will know what the number one quality of a CMO is, what the perfect pitch looks like and what attracts A-players to apply and stay in your company. That, and much more.

Everything is Rooted in Communications

We've written this book for founders and those working alongside them, focusing on companies that have already raised some money and set themselves up on the path for growth. When you build or join a startup, you expect to exert control over your career. You're not working at some large, faceless corporation. You seek out responsibility, and want to fine-tune your way to success. You accept the risks associated with working in fast-changing environments. We believe that you can reduce these risks significantly, and deliver top-tier performance, by improving communications.

We have reviewed thousands of pitches. We've mentored, advised and interviewed hundreds of startup founders. We've invested in over a hundred companies, with a few even hitting that elusive unicorn status. We've even built several companies ourselves. In witnessing all this success and failure, we can point to three key reasons why early-stage startups fail: the team falls apart; the team isn't able to figure out, build and deliver what customers want; or the team is unable to raise money. Founders who are strong communicators avoid the main reasons why most startups fail. They are much more likely to build an effective team, raise money and deliver what customers want.

Once a team has worked closely together for a considerable amount of time – and is able to deliver what its customers want – it enters the 'scale-up' phase, where a different set of challenges arise that can all lead to failure. Avoiding these requires leadership, marketing, communicating strategy, hiring and fundraising. In other words, **all the key tasks of a startup founder require high proficiency in communications**. According to former Y Combinator president Sam Altman, a startup CEO should spend 95% of their time making sure strategy is happening: "You just have to relentlessly say, 'This is what we are doing, this is why, and this is how we're going to do it.' And that part – the communication and evangelizing of the company vision and goals – is time-wise by far the biggest part of the job."

These challenges demonstrate that as your startup grows, your company's communications and your own communication skills as a founder have to grow in step. Your vision can only become reality through and with other people. True, communications aren't everything, but without strong communications nothing else matters. Too often, communications are an afterthought at the beginning, until a startup hits a wall due to a lack of customers, unenthusiastic investors or a rudderless team. "Communication is the most important skill any entrepreneur can possess," as Richard Branson says. Successful founders embrace the fact that communication is their master skill. They even start to enjoy it because it makes such a positive difference.

Communications tie it all together, and **poor communications are the underlying reason why startups fail.** This means that communications are not just another priority.

WHY STARTUPS FAIL

Early Stage

- A team falls apart
- A team isn't able to figure out, build and deliver what customers want
- A team isn't able to raise money

Scale-up Phase

- The company's leadership isn't able to attract and retain talent
- The leadership fails to align the team on strategy and to empower them to take ownership
- The company fails to find enough paying customers
- The company cannot position itself as the category leader in the customers' minds
- The company fails to defend itself against new entrants
- The company doesn't convince enough investors to back the opportunity

They should be your number one priority because they impact all other priorities in your business. This only becomes more important as your company grows. As you prepare to enter additional markets, you need to continue to professionalize communications, be it marketing, employer branding, or preparing for an exit.

Companies Don't Rise Above the Communication Skills of Their Founders

If communications are the engine that drives high-growth ventures, how do you approach the topic? You are in a race against time and extremely busy. You need the fastest, most time-efficient way to become a master communicator and turn your company into a Message Machine that paves your way towards unicorn status, real-world impact or successful exit.

Speed follows mindset. "Successful founders transition from a *communications last* to a *communications first* mindset," as leading executive coach Bettina Hausmann puts it. Once you make that mental shift, you take action, iterate fast, ask the right people for advice, and commit to learning what is necessary to succeed. And, you are comfortable with being uncomfortable while doing it.

Communication has two dimensions: the founders' personal communication skills and the company's capacity in communications. Both are crucial to driving a company's culture, reputation and bottom line. What's striking is that generally **companies don't rise above the communication skills of their founders**. If the founders are mediocre communicators with a mediocre understanding of how to build a Message Machine, it puts a hard limit on growth. Or worse.

Firing someone is always a hard decision. But such a decision can be made even harder by doing it in a cold and callous manner, even if your company is winning accolades publicly. Vishal Garg, the founder of online mortgage broker Better.com, reinforced his position as one of the poster boys for bad CEO communications when he fired 900 people, shortly before Christmas 2021, via a video-conferencing call. He'd already made headlines the previous year for calling some of his employees 'dumb dolphins'. Nevertheless, his company had been ranked by LinkedIn as the hottest startup to work for in 2020 and 2021, and had also received a $750 million cash infusion from investors just the day before he fired nearly 10% of all employees. Many top executives resigned in protest shortly afterward, and after widespread condemnation on social media, Garg temporarily stepped down as CEO. The company had to fire several thousand more employees when the financial markets turned sour a few months later, and its plans to go public were also shelved.

Garg eventually apologized for his actions: "I failed to show the appropriate amount of respect and appreciation for the individuals who were affected, and for their contributions to Better. I own the decision to do the layoffs, but in communicating it, I blundered the execution. In doing so, I embarrassed you." We would argue it was all too late.

On the other hand, **great communications accelerate growth.** Founders who become better communicators unlock the potential of their companies. They hire an excellent team that can challenge and support their leaders to become even better communicators. The founders and the team then motivate each other to excel. After the initial push, the Message Machine Flywheel keeps spinning and they get better and better results for themselves and the business. Competent leaders promote and protect the business. Bevel, the male grooming products brand now owned by the multinational consumer giant Procter & Gamble, is a great example. The founder, Tristan Walker, set it up with a singular purpose to make health and beauty simple for people of color. Many suffer issues of skin irritation as a result of having curly hair. Walker frequently talks about communicating with customers in ways that they haven't experienced before, by being "really rich in authenticity and culture. There's such a wide-open opportunity to build something very special for an audience that had to suffer from this issue for way too long, and we keep repeating this to investors, employees and customers."

Understanding these two dimensions – personal and company – allows you to approach communications strategically and holistically. You and your team can then master all mission-critical skills through deliberate practice, expert guidance and day-to-day usage. These skills include pitching, investor relations, marketing, PR and internal communications. Each of them in turn consists of a number of micro-skills. In the case of pitching, for instance, these include presentation skills, telling an equity story, and non-verbal communication. We are not talking about hacks here. This is how skill acquisition works.

To unlock growth, it is crucial to understand the following principle: **all communications are audience-specific**. While there is always a sender and a receiver, effective communication is not a one-way street. This is often forgotten when companies blast out social media posts, internal memos or customer information, believing the job is done when the send button is hit. "We are changing the world through digital experiences.

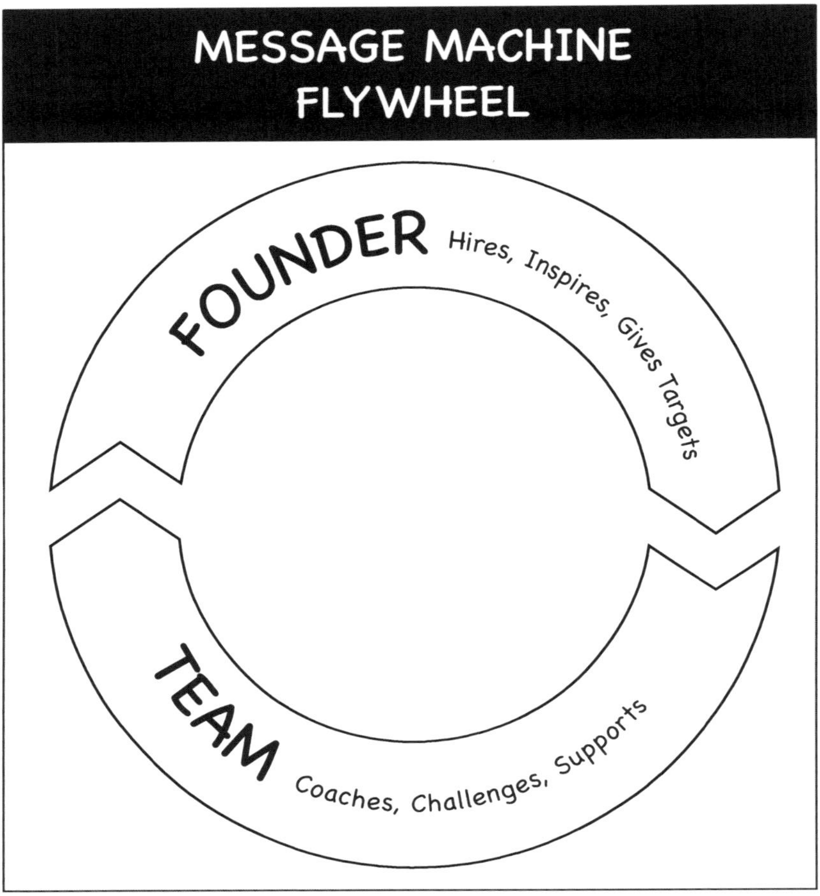

Our creative marketing and document solutions empower everyone," one company informed the world, probably still waiting for a response.

Effective communication always feels like a one-to-one conversation with an individual who is made to feel special, not a one-to-many. It also takes the context and the situation into account. Approaching communications as conversations and audiences as partners gives you a big advantage. As a founder, you communicate pretty much every day with the three types of audiences that matter to your business: your internal, financial and external stakeholders. Internally you communicate up (board/directors), down (employees) and at your level (co-founders and the rest of the leadership team). Your financial target audiences include investors (people you want to invest) and shareholders (people already invested). Externally, there are talents, customers and prospects, regulators and legislators, as well as intermediaries through which you can reach them, i.e. the media, social media and other channels. Underpinning all communications is a layer of psychology, which we'll outline in the first chapter.

Start with Your Personal Communication Skills

That's a lot of audiences to think about, so where do you start? You start with *yourself.* As a founder, the best place to start building a Message Machine with high-growth potential is to level up your own communication skills. Once you understand the fundamental skills and principles in this book and how to apply them, you can implement them in your own organization. Starting with yourself does not mean doing it on your own, though. The best way to blitzscale your master skill is to have a great team around you, both internally and externally.

All of this has a huge effect on the way a company runs. A company's approach to communications and its processes that were put in place by early-stage teams tend to carry on once the company matures. Even after the founding team may have left, many of the markings in the DNA of a company can be traced back to what happened when it was just a small team working toward product-market fit. Path dependency is real, so getting this right from the start has huge benefits.

To be clear, anyone can become a master communicator, regardless of background or innate ability. This does not mean being a polished speaker on stage. That view of communications is way too narrow. We are talking about founders who stay true to themselves and amplify their best traits as opposed to emulating someone else. And they use these skills to build highly successful companies.

Richard Branson is not a great speaker and tends to be awkward in interviews. Instead, the Virgin founder has used stunts to attract publicity globally. Elon Musk – an equally awkward interviewee – shot a Tesla into space and completely revolutionized how auto companies market their cars by going direct to buyers. Steve Jobs went from being terrified of media interviews to being an excellent public speaker (although he remained an abysmal communicator internally). Almost every inspirational founder went from terrible communicator to master communicator – in their own way. They unlocked the growth of their ventures by working on their own skills and understanding of communications.

In working with hundreds of founders over the years, we have realized that those who are naturally gifted and extroverted don't necessarily become the best communicators. Introverts tend to listen more, prepare better and work harder to improve, and often become better communicators as a result.

Both of us certainly have been on a journey as communicators. When Oliver was first interviewed by a reporter in 2005, he didn't even realize it at first. He thought they were just having coffee. Five years and hundreds of interviews later, he gave ten BBC TV and radio interviews in a single day during the volcanic ash crisis that grounded Europe's air traffic. Jag's journey from CTO to CEO wasn't an easy one. He still has nightmares about his first presentation to the Board. He didn't know it at the time, but his "five step plan to world domination" was shot down – not because of the content, but because the Board actually wanted a "three step plan to steady the ship." The very nervous and slightly shifty new CEO wasn't really conveying confidence.

The Key Principles of Communications

Communication matters to all founders, but the challenges become increasingly apparent after the seed round. Internally, as the team grows beyond 15 or 20 you create hierarchies and organizational structure to avert chaos and stay sane. While these changes are necessary, you no longer know everyone in the company, and the impromptu buddy-buddy approach of the early days doesn't fly anymore. Before you know it, you have an HR manager, codes of conduct and team members with widely diverging expectations. Instead of leading, you find yourself managing. Your most important shareholders are no longer friends or family members, but professional VCs who live inside Excel spreadsheets and have to answer to their own investors. Externally, there is more pressure than ever to find customers and keep up the momentum.

Despite the importance of communications for a company's success, there is surprisingly little systematic advice out there for founders. Sure, there are plenty of books, courses and blog posts on every other aspect of building a company – except for "its biggest challenge", communications. Similarly, there is a lot of material for early-stage founders and post-IPO businesses, but little advice for the post-seed to pre-IPO years. We were both searching for the seminal book or at least some decent resources on communications during that phase, to little avail. The material is not part of the MBA curriculum either. The real knowledge tends to be with company builders, VCs and people like us who have been in the trenches and learned the lessons the painful way.

Covering all aspects of communications is a lot of ground to cover in a single book. We aim to pull it off by focusing on principles. You may have heard about **the hierarchy of communications: the most basic level is data, above that comes information, then knowledge, and finally wisdom at the top**. Principles fall into the wisdom category. They trump data, information and knowledge. That's why they are so powerful. This book gives you the most important principles in one place. Principles are marked in bold throughout the text. At the end of the book, you can find the complete list. We combine the key principles with the most relevant tactics and methods. As a founder, you expect principles to be actionable, and rightly so. What we won't do is pretend there is a neat five-step process for post-seed companies or give you tools or hacks that will be outdated in six months. What you read in this book is real and timeless advice, not the latest shiny method.

We will be throwing a lot of terms around, so let's quickly clarify what we mean. If you put your offer on a banner online or a billboard in the street, that's advertising. When people remember you and tell your story, that's branding. When you talk to prospects about the advantages of working with you, that's sales. And if you followed a plan to execute all of it, that's marketing. Marketing gets your message out. It generates leads, and the act of closing a customer is referred to as sales. PR is not part of marketing. Rather PR creates a public record of your company, which is important for a host of reasons. Strategic communications refers to a strategic, systematic approach to communications, as opposed to focusing on tactics and channels. More on these later.

How This Book Is Structured

The structure of this book follows these fundamental insights: communications are audience-specific and they consist of a number of skills. These skills can be learned. In the first chapter, to lay the foundation, we discuss how human psychology impacts communications.

Building a Message Machine starts with the founders and their mindset. In Chapter 2, we show you how you can become a founder who communicates with impact and how you turn that into fundraising success. In fact, fundraising is such a decisive skill for founders that it is a recurring theme throughout the book rather than a topic we cover in one chapter.

In Chapter 3, we introduce the prerequisites for 'message-market fit,' which covers the positioning and message discipline required to strive for and maintain communication excellence as your company grows. We also provide you with the parameters you need to estimate your own company's message-market fit from the early stage to the growth phase.

COMMUNICATIONS SKILL SET		
	Founder	Startup
General	Storytelling, presenting and speaking with impact, interpersonal communication	Messaging, crisis communications
Internal	Inspirational leadership, articulating strategy, coaching	Company culture, internal communications
External	Thought leadership, media interviews	Branding, marketing, PR, employer branding, political communication
Financial	Pitching, investor and shareholder communications	Fundraising, investor relations
Psychology		

Chapters 4 through 6 deal with your primarily external challenges, and we'll walk you through the communication principles required to build an iconic and long-lasting brand, attract better customers in higher numbers, and scale your visibility to heights previously unimaginable.

We discuss company culture and the all-star team you'll be working with to power this Message Machine in Chapter 7. In Chapter 8, we build on some of the previous chapters to dissect how you can be an employer of choice through state-of-the-art internal communications and employer branding.

As companies grow and new challenges arise, Chapter 9 gives you the knowledge to protect yourself, both in a business or organizational crisis and in a time of crisis like an epidemic or recession. Finally, in the conclusion, we show you how you can turn the principles in this book into immediate action. We also provide additional materials on https://messagemachine.io.

If all of this seems like a lot right now, don't worry. We will guide you through every aspect and will do our best to make the principles and insights accessible and actionable, so that you can focus on becoming an unstoppable founder.

Chapter 1

REVEALING THE HIDDEN PSYCHOLOGY OF COMMUNICATIONS

Communications can be planned, but they can't be controlled. That's what makes them so fascinating and so scary at the same time. Both of us became fascinated decades ago by how much political communications, in particular election campaigns, are designed with the individual psychology of voters in mind. On the surface, campaigns are about the country and the big issues. In reality, they address the concerns and hopes of individual voters. In the early days, political campaigners learned a lot from advertising professionals. Later, marketers would apply insights that well-funded political campaigns gained. So in the late 1990s, Oliver went to London to study politics and become a "spin doctor." He talked his way into a party headquarters and their rapid rebuttal unit, as well as a London mayoral campaign, learning the ropes of political communications.

In the early 2000s, Jag accidentally (and rather conveniently) fell out of love with the world of mathematics and into the world of politics. It started with a suggestion from a medical doctor that he find an outlet to channel his teenage anxiety and hormones, by working on her husband's mayoral campaign.

It wasn't long after this that he found himself working on John Kerry's 2004 presidential campaign, directing hundreds of staffers across an entire state. A few years later, he'd written the most widely used algorithm to determine a person's political preferences based on their web browsing behaviors.

The fascination with the hidden psychology of communications has stayed with us to this day. As humans are at the center of all communications, we believe having a deeper understanding of the ultimate drivers of what we say and do is crucial for anyone in leadership positions. Neuroscience delves even deeper into the human mind, discovering biological and chemical processes in the brain and nervous system. It can tell us why (certain) stories such as the hero's journey work universally and which narratives work better than others. It also explains why non-verbal cues have such an effect on us, and what that means for our body language. All of this applies to your internal, external and financial communications.

Up to 98% of what our brains are doing is subconscious, including a number of levers that are hugely important for communications. Understanding how the brain is wired therefore increases the chances of a pitch, brand or message working as intended. And that can be the difference between getting funding or not, winning or losing customers, and attracting talent or repelling them. In this chapter, we will give you a brief overview of the concepts that make your communications impactful, before we show you how to use these ideas to take your personal communication to the next level in Chapter 2.

Clarity

Clarity trumps complexity – because our brains are attracted by order and drawn away from confusion. Thinking requires energy, and our brains are constantly trying to conserve energy. If your brain reckons that it would have to burn too many calories to process the information, what does it do? Nothing, it moves on. Hence the "simplicity paradox": the less you tell people, the more they understand.

As TechCrunch put it in a recent article entitled *Startup founders. Consider your language. Keep it simple*: "You understand that a complicated word sometimes is more precise than a simple word. Remember that you also have a duty to your audience. The problem is not that they cannot understand. They can. A sixth grader can read complicated texts. But it takes a lot of energy."

The business world is full of jargon and empty phrases. One company that apparently didn't consider their audience's energy stated that "if half the battle is identifying what the challenges are, the ball is very much in the brand's court to action the second half." We can only guess what it means, but it could probably be said in a few simple words. In fact, too complicated is the prime reason why most business communications are ineffective. This includes pitches, websites, marketing materials, internal memos – you name it. It also explains why most employees don't understand their company's strategy.

That was certainly the problem with General Motors, the world's largest car manufacturer for decades and owner of countless mediocre brands all over the world. If there was a strategy, it wasn't clear to GM's hundreds of thousands of employees before the company went bust in 2010 and American taxpayers floated their $50 billion bailout. "Lack of internal communications killed General Motors. For 35 years, GM couldn't implement a culture of teamwork, feedback, and internal communication, and they failed," one observer noted. Oliver's only attempt at a corporate career happened to be at General Motors, one that he quickly abandoned for what his boss at the time called a "risky startup". Today, we know that company as easyJet.

Regardless of your audience, keep it simple. Clarity shows that we've put our audience first. A clear message shows that we've made an effort to make ourselves understood. When founders forget this, and they do, language becomes dehumanized. Audiences don't like corporate speak or the feeling that they are listening to a message-bot. Employees, investors and customers simply switch off. At Google, any additional feature or other complication has to go through an "audition" and extensive testing. That's because "more points equal less simplicity," as Marissa Mayer put it when she was the company's director of consumer web products.

Hold on to your humanness, your plain language, your common sense. It is a competitive advantage, for you personally and for the business. Don't tolerate salesy, corporate or otherwise incomprehensible language in your startup. If you don't find something interesting or compelling, don't think for a second that people out there who don't work for your company will. This applies regardless of whether you operate in a direct-to-consumer market (DTC), the business-to-consumer market (B2C) or the business-to-business market (B2B). In every case, your communications should be H2H, human-to-human, whether they are consumers, investors or employees.

This also affects buying decisions. Buyers are suffering from information overload and display shorter attention spans than ever. Since Steve Jobs first envisioned the Apple App Store in 1983, the number of available apps on the market has gone from 1 in 1997 to more than 5 million apps available across the Google Play and Apple App Stores. The same is true for everything from toothpaste to enterprise software.

This has led to an increase in cognitive load, meaning there is too much information for anyone to hold in their working memory. Naturally our brains filter out most of what we see and hear, especially anything that does not appeal to us immediately. We opt for solutions to our problems that grab our attention and are easy to understand. "If you confuse, you lose," as marketing heavyweight Donald Miller puts it.

Beware of the fallacy that *my customers/investors/employees know exactly what I'm talking about,* so it is okay to speak in jargon. Avoiding clarity is a really bad idea. Firstly, this ignores the *curse of knowledge*. This term describes the mistaken belief that others know what we know. They usually don't. Secondly, even if they do know what you know, they do not appreciate you adding to their cognitive load.

They may also conclude that you don't fully understand what you are talking about, because **clear thinking precedes clear communication**. Investors demand clear and concise pitch decks for a reason. They deduce from a pitch deck how much clarity founders have about their venture and if they can communicate it well enough to persuade their audiences, as we will see in the next chapter.

You have heard the quotes by Leonardo Da Vinci, Albert Einstein, Mark Twain, Coco Chanel, Steve Jobs and countless other smart people that all say the same thing: keep it simple.

Value

Customers, investors or talent decide to do business with you or work for you if they value what you offer them. This is about what *they* value, not what *you* value. They lead busy lives and have a heavy cognitive load. If they encounter you, your company or your product, they will ask themselves: "So what?", or "What's in it for me?" This even has an acronym – WIIFM – that has been used in sales and marketing circles for decades. It reminds those professionals that they must answer this question clearly, because **no one cares about the company or product. People care about what they get out of it**. It's about the benefits, not the features.

The worst thing you can do to call a customer's attention is to yell "Hey! Look at all our bells and whistles." As Juan Andrade of Rebank correctly puts it: "We stopped talking about our product because nobody cared. We saw a 10x improvement as soon as we tripled down on communicating how we will help them progress."

Spanx's communications don't focus on its product either. Instead, the company and founder Sara Blakely talk about their mission: To help women feel great about themselves and their potential. Similarly, on the surface SoulCycle offers workouts on a stationary bike. Except that the focus of the brand is on community ("Your Soul Fam is waiting"), enjoying physical activity ("a 45-minute cardio dance party on a bike") and self-improvement ("We move people to move the world. Because we move people to move themselves. Physically. Mentally. Emotionally.")

There's a difference between what your customers value and what your investors perceive to be valuable. We often remind founders who are about to embark on a fundraising exercise to emphasize what is in it for the investors, rather than what customers would value in their product. Jens Lapinski, one of Europe's most active angel investors, puts it in a clever way: "Don't pitch me the product. Sell me a way to make lots of money. None of your existing investors care what company you end up building ... just as long as it's a unicorn."

It sounds obvious, yet it is one of the most common pitfalls for startups. We are all used to seeing the world through our own eyes. However, building a startup requires us to see the world (and our company and product) through the eyes of others. Not once, but every day, whether we are talking to investors, the team or customers. This is called empathy.

While investors see value in higher returns, customers and talents value whatever alleviates their pain or fulfills their desires. It's important to have this reflected across all forms of communication, from product demos given to customers, to the offer letters sent out to prospective hires.

Connection

People want to feel connected to others. It is a basic human desire. As a leader, you want to connect with your internal, external and financial audiences at every opportunity. For instance, when you hold a talk or give a presentation, look directly at the audience and meet the gaze of a few individuals before you start. Or if you're speaking to just one person, take a couple of seconds and try to make note of the color of their eyes – it's a trick that many successful politicians have employed on the campaign trail. Timely eye contact, appropriate touching and non-verbal cues such as smiling are indicators of self-esteem and sincerity, which foster connections between people. That's why we in the Western world usually shake someone's hand, look them in the eye and smile the first time we meet them. It releases oxytocin which drives both connection and generosity.

Every conversation or piece of communication has two dimensions: the explicit content dimension and the relational dimension. This involves what is being said and what that means for your relationship with the other person. The first is about the information and the message. Inexperienced leaders sometimes come across as if only the facts mattered. The second is about connection. It entails how we make the other person feel, whether we connect or repel someone. Take a simple sentence such as "Could you get this done by tomorrow?" The content is clear, but the way it is said – tone of voice, facial expression, non-verbal cues – will determine whether it comes across as a friendly ask or an order. For example, tilting your head is perceived as more empathetic whereas a straight head makes you come across as more authoritative and firm. You can also add verbal cues like using someone's name in a conversation (or in a marketing email). As a founder, you want to pay attention to the relational dimension of every conversation. Incidentally, this is one of the first principles Goldman Sachs executives are taught in their training.

Listening is a crucial part of connecting, because it allows us to understand the other side's values, emotions and fears. We don't build connections by monopolizing a conversation. Once we understand, we can empathize and address the other person's points.

We as **humans put a lot of value on authenticity in communications**. This is particularly true today. We live in a time that values authenticity – being real – highly. Plus, the startup world has been burned by Adam Neumann, Sam Bankman-Fried, Elizabeth Holmes and the Wirecard gang. As an authentic leader, you will find it easier to connect with investors, customers, your co-founders and the team. Authenticity means that what you believe, say and do is consistent. You walk the talk. Of course, what is perceived as authentic differs from culture to culture. Whenever you find yourself in a different cultural context or professional setting, be mindful of the inherent expectations of those around you.

For instance, a journalist starts with the most interesting aspect of a story and expects you to give her the news straight away. You don't connect by withholding information. You may need to take a markedly different approach when communicating with engineers or if you find yourself in settings that require in-depth analysis and context setting. Engineer-heavy cultures prefer a communication methodology that Tom Tungusz, a former Google product manager turned VC, calls "the scientific method, verbalized." Recalling his experiences at Google, "when pitching a new product, I detailed the observations, product hypotheses, experimental design, results and conclusion in that order. The discussion focused mainly on the experimental design and the biases in the results and the implications for the conclusion." This is an entirely natural approach for him that helps to connect with his audience of engineers, but certainly not for other settings. Communication frameworks like the SCQA (Situation, Complication, Question and Answer) method are very important in business writing and used to structure information in a way that captures a reader's attention.

Like an authentic speaker, authentic brands build an emotional connection with their community. And top talent wants to work for authentic companies that share their values. Great communicators understand the value of being authentic, and convey that authenticity continuously.

Fear and Scarcity

As mentioned, if you don't communicate, you don't exist. Even if you are in *stealth mode,* you are communicating. You are signaling to investors that "we are building something super cool and if you are a legitimate investor you absolutely must learn more". Yet the real reason some founders avoid speaking about their project is fear. Fear is an instinctive human reaction to a perceived risk or danger. We can learn to channel fear by programming the nervous system to motivate ourselves, instead of succumbing to the desire to protect ourselves. Nothing hinders a founder's ability to communicate more than the fear of rejection, or the fear of looking bad. As RuPaul once quipped, "**Your fear of looking stupid is making you look stupid.**" We keep saying communication skills can be learned, and becoming a better communicator is very much about trying to stay in a 'growth mindset.'

Stanford psychologist Carol Dweck coined the dual concepts of growth and fixed mindsets in her book *Mindset: The New Psychology of Success.* She found that those with growth mindsets viewed intellectual capacity and talent as traits that are entirely possible to improve through effort. Those with fixed mindsets would view those same traits as permanently unchangeable. A growth mindset also identifies failure as a stronger motivator than success.

The good news: You can work on identifying and isolating your triggers, and both nurture and harness them over a period of time in order to stay in a growth mindset.

We also tend to value items and opportunities that are difficult to obtain, or scarce. We're familiar with these as marketing concepts like Black Friday sales, limited editions, artificial scarcity or expiring offers. If this triggers the anxiety associated with potentially losing out, then you're essentially using the *fear of missing out* (FOMO) tactic.

Just like in the political world, the investment ecosystem is a powder keg that's driven by the *fear of looking bad.* A complaint most founders have about investors is that they're essentially always "playing it safe." This is simply because it's easier to pass on a company than to justify a bad investment decision to their peers (in an investment committee), their investors or even to the public. Your task as a founder is to communicate in ways that play to your strengths, and to the investor's fear of missing out.

FOMO is used in marketing, hiring and also in fundraising. If you're a startup founder, you've probably already tried to convince an investor that they may be losing out on a big opportunity for themselves or their portfolio if they don't act quickly. In those instances, what you really need to sell to investors is the opportunity for them to invest in *this* opportunity, *right now.* You also have to project credibility and trust. This requires meticulous planning and careful consideration of communications during the fundraising process, which we'll cover in more detail in the next chapter.

Tread carefully, though. This concept has a sharp double edge. Trying to trigger fear of missing out tends to alienate people in any context, most clearly demonstrated in fundraising blunders where only one investor takes the bait. This is also where the fear of looking bad might come into play for them. In order for FOMO to really work on investors, you really must have more than one of them interested, at the same time. We've seen several startups falter because they weren't able to secure multiple investment term sheets from investors within the same time period. Jag remembers one particularly memorable #epicfail where a startup claimed to have an oversubscribed Series A round, and asked for improved terms to be offered. Jag called their bluff, declined, and wished the founders luck. It was an instinctive bet that the founders didn't really have other investors lined up, which then led to the founders credibility being called into question. The company failed soon after.

The other scenario that we've seen play out is when founders approach a new investor with an incredibly tight deadline – some investors have complained of getting pitched for the first time only a mere 24 hours prior to a fundraising close. Most experienced investors will say "no" immediately. It can be seen as manipulative and is therefore a red flag for investors. This is the opposite of what you want to achieve, namely to build meaningful relationships of trust with people who you want to be on this journey with you for years to come. It's way better to be honest about what you know and what you don't. This doesn't mean that FOMO can't work in your favor when you receive your first term sheet and all of a sudden other investors want to join the party. But conscious attempts to trigger it tend to backfire.

Differentiation

Scarce or not, any successful personal brand, professional brand or business needs to be different from their competitors. People only notice who or what is different. This is true for products, companies and founders.

As a thought leader, you aim to be the authority on one topic. Like Lubomila Jordanova. On holiday in Morocco, she was shocked by the amount of plastic waste spoiling nature. She started collecting waste but felt overwhelmed. What could the causes of this waste be? Already an avid animal lover, she started to dig deeper, investigating pollution and noticing the correlation to other issues. Understanding that there must be a better way, Lubomila decided to dedicate her life to protecting the environment through business, as this allows her to scale solutions and make more of an impact. Realizing that apocalyptic, abstract statistics do not work, she now focuses her communication strategy on straightforward, positive messages, combined with a sense of urgency. Whenever she presents an environmental problem, she also brings a scalable solution. Today, the co-founder of Plan A and of Greentech Alliance is an Obama leader, MIT Under 35 Innovator and a LinkedIn Top Voice. She is making a real impact in greentech, in part thanks to her distinct voice as an environmentalist who is embracing business and technology.

What is true for founders is also true for startups. **Creating a meaningful distinction between you and the competition is what branding and marketing is all about**. Your "ability to compete is dependent upon the ability to differentiate from competitors," confirms Harvard Business School marketing professor Youngme Moon. This not only makes you memorable, but also tells your customers why they should buy from you instead of your closest competitor – your unique selling proposition. The height of differentiation is to own one word or an entire category, like Google and search. We explore these topics in Chapter 4.

Scarcity and differentiation influence the way you communicate as a business and market your products. You want to think about communications on a spectrum going from bespoke and individualized on one side to mass communications on the other. This often correlates with pricing. The less scarcity there is and the lower your product is priced, the less bespoke your communications have to be. For instance, as a food delivery service, you may opt for outdoor advertising in cities, whereas as a luxury brand, you go for more bespoke options like exclusive events.

The key take-away here is that your brand – personal, company and product – as well as your communications, have to be different from your competition. If you as a founder or your startup are exchangeable, then what is the point? That differentiation should be obvious and easy to grasp, like the Museum of Ice Cream. Not content to offer a sugary treat, MOIC helps you rediscover the kid in you by offering a sensory explosion like no other ice cream parlor. The concept has taken off, and MOIC has expanded into Asia.

You'll also need a 'different' solution if you're pursuing category creation and design, which we will talk more about in Chapter 3: Achieving and Maintaining Message-Market Fit. We often point to Octopus Energy, a British renewable utilities company specializing in sustainable energy, as a great example in that regard. Jag first encountered the founder and CEO, Greg Jackson, when they both worked in the political communications space over a decade ago. Jackson's – and by extension Octopus Energy's – obsession with customers is visible across all forms of communications. Is it not just limited to the CEO's Twitter presence, where he frequently responds to customers and media enquiries. Customers dialing in to the company's call centers are delighted with hold music that is targeted to their age group. In case you were wondering, Jag had "...Baby One More Time" by Britney Spears, while Oliver got "Ride On Time" by Black Box.

The website, at the height of the European energy crisis in 2022, clearly and directly told potential customers that they'd probably be better off staying with their current energy supplier. The company's agile use of segmentation technology, coupled with a superior communications strategy, has helped it mount a challenge against its larger energy rivals. Wired Magazine gave it a ringing endorsement by asking, "Why can't all utility companies be like this?"

But you can be as different as you like – none of that matters if you, your business or product aren't trusted.

Trust

Companies move at the speed of trust. Your investors, customers and employees need to trust you so that your company can stay on a high-growth trajectory. The people in your leadership team and in the whole organization also need to trust each other for the same reason. What is true for people is also true for products. If your software is vulnerable to cyber attacks, the delivery and logistics service you use is unreliable, the promises you've made to investors are beginning to unravel, or your sales team bends the truth, not enough people – customers or investors – are going to buy.

While trust is key to any founder or business, it may also seem elusive. Fortunately, it is not. As behavioral scientist and best-selling author Jon Levy outlined in his book *You're Invited*, today we understand that three conditions need to be fulfilled for someone to trust you:

1. Competence: you are good at what you do
2. Integrity: you tell the truth
3. Benevolence: you care about the other person

If the company and whoever is doing the sale are competent, truthful and genuinely interested in helping prospects, the door is wide open. If not, it may be in trouble, because customers have bullsh*t detectors. They intuitively understand when companies do not have their best interests at heart – like telecommunications companies. Ironically, they are hard to get on the phone and have often been found to charge unfair or inexplicable fees by government watchdogs. Unsurprisingly, they are among the least trusted businesses by consumers.

The three pillars are not equal though. Customers can forgive the occasional lapse of competence – we all make mistakes after all – but they will find it hard to excuse selfishness or a lack of integrity.

Putting it all together, the trust formula is:

Trust = competence + integrity + benevolence

Trust is a two-way street. For your customer, investor and colleagues to trust you, you must also trust them – their intelligence, competence and good faith. They will sense that you trust them and will repay you by extending their trust to you in turn.

Of course, it does take time to build trust (and one wrong move can destroy it). To build and project trust, you need to be visible, as we can't trust what we don't know. Humans trust and like the familiar. **No visibility, no trust.** This familiarity bias is why companies spend money on PR, sponsoring and advertising. That's why brands create as many touch points as possible for a specific audience, online and offline. We like to buy what's familiar from people like us.

That is the reason why social proof is so important. Prospects want to see real customers, and ideally people like themselves. You wouldn't promote skateboards by showing a guy in a suit. Prospects use social proof to avoid buyer's remorse. A wrong buying decision makes a customer feel bad. Worse, they may look like an idiot in front of their co-workers or friends. To overcome the anticipation of buyer's remorse, you can offer a 100% money back guarantee. You can alternatively provide endorsements and case studies to show that your product does what it says on the landing page. And you want to make sure you send the right messages after a buying decision. It reassures the customer that they made the right decision.

Techstars, an investment firm where Jag worked for several years, found an effective way to eliminate objections from founders who are reluctant to give away equity. Techstars is an operational investor that supports founders on their entrepreneurial journey and runs accelerators in cities all over the world. In 2014, they introduced the *Equity Back Guarantee* (EBG) that has afforded startups the option to reduce, or even eliminate, Techstars' shareholding at the original price paid for the shares.

In one fell swoop, the EBG meant that Techstars was able to signal extreme confidence in its own offering to startups, whilst also differentiating itself from other accelerators. As a true VC, Jag would like to take this opportunity to congratulate himself for maintaining a record of zero startups triggering that EBG option, out of the forty or so he invested in for Techstars. We will talk more about trust when we introduce the concept of message-market fit in Chapter 3.

Framing

Frames are concepts that shape how we see the world. Italian food. First class. Cat videos. A word or phrase activates a certain frame in your mind. If you hear the word "startup", it activates a frame which contains ideas, information and connotations about startups. To many people, startups are full of hope, promises and exciting opportunities – to others, the term implies a lack of profitability and stability. The word "scale-up" activates the imagery of more mature and solid footing, in comparison, though fewer people will be generally familiar with it.

In every conversation, you want to hold the frame. Framing is extremely powerful, because humans aren't necessarily rational. Political operators have long understood this, which is why different political camps use different terms for the same thing: freedom vs fairness, pro-choice vs pro-life, red tape vs consumer protection.

Words matter because they activate frames. To persuade someone or change someone's mind, activate the right frame. How you frame your message influences the emotional response of your listeners. This is relevant for many aspects of communications, from the positioning of your company, to marketing, to the daily conversations you have with your team. For instance, if you want your direct reports to take on new responsibilities, you can just tell them to do so. If your team values personal growth and career advancement, you can also frame it as an opportunity to learn new skills and emphasize the value this will bring to the company. The second option would be more effective, assuming you are serious about empowering your team.

Words can trigger different frames for different people. We often see startups excitedly talking to investors about their "pilots" with corporations that could turn a test project into a recurring contract. They do this to signal that there could be a match with a large company, and that they are reducing the barriers to a large corporation saying yes. This is almost definitely a good thing, if an executive in a largely bureaucratic company is able to say yes to a trial of the product without needing to involve other managers or enter into a discussion about long-term pricing. But to an investor evaluating two companies – one with customers, and the other with "pilots" on the books, then this activates a different frame, since pilot projects rarely lead to long-term contracts. It positions the company as an early-stage startup that is likely also lacking stability in its sales forecasts.

If framing is the process of building and managing frames, then reframing is the process of intentionally shifting a conversation from one frame to another. You are changing the conversation to grounds that are more favorable for you. Female and other under-represented founders will recognize that reframing can be a useful tactic to deploy when implicit and unconscious biases are at play. It's common knowledge that women usually get asked more prevention-oriented questions by both male *and* female investors, like "How much of this are you actually doing in-house?" or "How do you prevent users from getting bored with your product?" A comparable male founder would likely be asked a promotion-oriented question, like "What kind of team will you need to build this into a billion-dollar company?"

In those situations, you want to shift the dynamics. Instead of coming from a position of defensiveness, think of how you might respond with power or strength. You can also easily draw this strength from your opponent, using humor. Our ability to influence others arises out of our own self-confidence as well as our willingness to use these strengths in interpersonal communication. But remember, the goal is not just to tell your story, but to tell the *best* story whilst *also* acknowledging ways to defuse bias and handle objections.

The most successful founders, like politicians, learn how to subtly reframe by first recognizing the orientation of the questions they're being asked, rejecting their premise, and then taking the opportunity to answer the spirit of the questions. The biggest mistake founders make is appearing to evade the questions entirely. If asked a question like "How long will it take you to get to profitability?" that is obviously prevention-oriented, then we recommend channeling your inner politician to answer the question by also including positive frames about the company's growth prospects. This is done by using a bridging technique, or ABC for Acknowledge, Bridge, Communicate, as in: (A) *We expect profitability next year (B) but there is another important aspect here. (C) We expect to double the number of users over the next three months.*

Clarity, value, connection, scarcity, differentiation, trust and framing – the psychological concepts covered in this chapter will help you persuade your audience and avoid costly mistakes, if you apply them consistently and regularly. **Repeat what is important so it sticks**. We will come back to these levers throughout the book and will also introduce some more. If you want to dive deeper, Robert B. Cialdini's *Influence* and *The Catalyst* by Jonah Berger are excellent starting points.

In the next chapters we will build on the insights gained in this chapter and show you how to put them into action – starting with supercharging your personal communication skills. Let's dive in.

THE PSYCHOLOGY OF COMMUNICATIONS

Clarity ⇨	Keep it simple and avoid complexity. Confuse and you lose.
Value ⇨	Tell people what's in it for them.
Connection ⇨	Focus on the content AND the relationship.
Fear & Scarcity ⇨	Become a bold and honest communicator.
Differentiation ⇨	Ensure your business and brands are different.
Trust ⇨	Make building trust a priority in every communication.
Framing ⇨	Activate the right frame to persuade people.

Chapter 2

POWERFUL FOUNDER COMMUNICATION: FUNDRAISING AND BEYOND

In a startup, the founders are at the center of everything, according to entrepreneur, investor and author Brad Feld. Great communicators build great companies. There is nothing more powerful than an inspiring founder who communicates with courage, passion and clarity.

Take, for example, NextDoor CEO Sarah Friar. She is a passionate advocate for a kinder world where everyone enjoys a neighborhood they can rely on. Not content to just increase user numbers, she encourages app users to meet in real life as well and build communities from the bottom up.

Or Rod Drury, the founder and former CEO of Xero, the leading international cloud accounting solution for small businesses. "For me, what gets me out of bed in the morning, is our vision at Xero. We want to make small businesses more productive. That in turn will drive the economy. I'm always telling people I'm in this for better schools and hospitals. That's what a growing small business economy will give us. I know we can make a difference and that's why I'm in it for the long haul." Sarah and Rod are passionate leaders who inspire others to engage with their companies and their causes.

We emphasized in the introduction that startup communications have two dimensions: the founders' personal communication skills, and their role in the company's internal, external and financial communications. Both shape the culture, reputation and bottom line of a startup. In this chapter, we give you the most important skills needed for powerful founder communication. Mastering these skills will significantly increase your chances of success when fundraising, and will also help you in any other situation you encounter as a founder.

Inspire to Do Inspiring Work

Bad communication ends a lot of good things, so you want to ensure that your skills grow at least as fast as your company grows. When a company grows faster than the communication skills of the founders, this area quickly becomes a startup's biggest challenge. That's because expectations and demands increase exponentially as you scale. You don't want that to happen. You want to be ahead of the game.

"Developing original ideas and communicating those ideas effectively is the single greatest skill you can build today to own your future," states the bestselling author of *Talk Like TED*, Carmine Gallo. The return on time invested is particularly high for founders, because it enables them to communicate the company's why, raise money and create a higher-performing team, culture and company. Reputation precedes revenue. And your reputation depends above all else on your ability to effectively communicate your company's purpose, strategy and offer to customers, employees and shareholders.

While you want your company to become a well-oiled Message Machine, as a founder you want to avoid a top-down, one-dimensional communication style. Despite the use (and overuse, in our opinion) of war metaphors in the startup world, you are not a military general sending orders to your troops. Simply telling people what to do and expecting them to execute it like a machine does not work in a startup environment. The risk is that team members will either leave or disengage, and the company won't go anywhere. Smart people joining startups want to be inspired to do great work, not told what to do.

The late Zappos co-founder and CEO Tony Hsieh understood this and made "Build Open and Honest Relationships With Communication" a core value of the company. Before his tragic death, he built a workplace culture and structure that empowered all employees and respected their individuality. Hsieh believed strongly in the value of customer service, and ensured that customer service agents could do right by the customer. Amazon acquired Zappos in 2009 in a deal valued at approximately $1.2 billion.

Yet you still sometimes hear people talk about communication skills as "soft". This implies that they are less important than "hard" technical, financial or operational skills. This has always been a misguided way to think about leadership, as even a casual glance at history, politics and business reveals. Today, it is completely outdated as a mental model.

Communication is a hard skill for founders – how else would you turn your strategy into reality if not by persuading customers, investors and your team? Your vision can only become reality through other people. This was confirmed by a 2022 Harvard Business School study which showed that when companies search for top leaders today, especially new CEOs, they "prioritize one qualification above all others: strong social skills," including the ability to listen and communicate well. Today's leaders are highly attuned to their audiences and quick to adapt to any context or situation.

Fast Tracking Mastery

The world rewards courageous communicators who stand for something. Amazing things happen when the leadership of a startup shifts from a *communications last mindset* to a *communications first mindset*. We've witnessed increases in trust, retention, brand equity and revenue when founders bring true strategic alignment to the team and continuously evangelize about the company and its mission. This has to be done in the right way, though.

The typical pitfall is when founders lecture instead of connecting with their audiences. They speak at people instead of with people. As a result, their audiences tune out and become disengaged. In contrast, successful communicators always put the audience at the center of their thinking. Instead of 'What is my message?' they ask 'How can I get my message across to this particular audience?' Great communicators always focus on the audience and use the power of different formats and channels to their advantage. Their communication style adapts to the situation, be it a board meeting, a 'town hall' with employees or a social media post. They have internalized that people won't understand their strategy if they don't communicate it well. They know how to show up on social media, what the fundamentals of media interviews are and how to take charge in a crisis. Regardless of the situation, they are always their true self. They bring their personality and their personal story. But how do you get there? How do you become such a master communicator?

It is a journey that can take years. But, it is possible to fast-track it. If you are like most founders, you are an interesting person with a great story and tons of passion. Stay true and honest to yourself while you work on professionalizing your communications. Keep the startup spirit alive and avoid becoming boring or interchangeable as your business grows. Practically, you focus on the 20% of communication skills that give you 80% of the benefit and engage in deliberate practice to perfect them. Fortunately, the communication skills that are essential for fundraising are also the ones you use on a daily basis throughout your founder's journey, so you get two for one. The five skills that we emphasize are:

1. Communicating with clarity
2. Listening to understand
3. Telling engaging stories (your own and your company's)
4. Speaking and presenting with impact
5. Leading difficult conversations to positive outcome.
   Let's tackle each of these now.

MESSAGE MASTERY 1: COMMUNICATING WITH CLARITY

We have already introduced the importance of clarity. However, communicating innovation and new ideas is hard, especially in a high-pressure pitch situation. “The single biggest problem in communication is the illusion that it has taken place,” quipped Irish author George Bernard Shaw. The main reason: a lack of clarity. What happens if an announcement, email or presentation at an all-hands meeting isn’t clear? People will be confused, tune out or keep doing things the way they did them before. Mission not accomplished.

A lack of clarity is found everywhere. Let’s look at a company’s North Star, which tells the world why you exist, what you do and how you do it. A North Star (or whatever term you prefer) usually encompasses the following:

1. Your vision (or purpose), mission and values: Why does your company exist and what problem does it solve? While early-stage companies are often pilloried as being delusional about their grand vision, the ability to articulate a bold and inviting vision is actually relevant at every stage of a company’s lifecycle.
2. Your business ambition (or strategy): How do you plan to make your vision and mission happen? What’s your key metric? You should be able to tell anyone your ambition in one sentence.
3. Your unique value proposition: What is unique about your offer? Why should anyone buy from you instead of buying from your competitors?

Needless to say that these basic building blocks must be clear and easy to remember. If they are, you will find it easier to convince investors, top talent and customers. Clarity among the fundamentals will also make all other aspects of your founder communication more effective. While important to provide clarity, your North Star should not be set in stone while you build your startup. As it will evolve over time, you need to give yourself and the team the emotional license to explore alternatives and pivot if necessary.

Communicating clearly is hard, and a lot of founders struggle with it. If you find your points difficult to get across, it's a sign that they lack clarity. This is often due to a lack of training and deliberate practice. In other cases, messages have never been properly tested for clarity, or the fundamental building blocks like the North Star have never been written down. Or they have been forgotten, maybe because they were too generic, ambiguous or complicated and therefore hard to remember. The result is the same: the team has no clarity on what to do. It is your role as a founder to be the guardian of clarity in your startup. Powerful founder communication is clear and straightforward.

Often it is just a matter of going over a text or presentation once more to make it powerful. James Clear, one of the world's most successful non-fiction authors ("Atomic Habits"), points out that "you can't double your intelligence in one hour, but you can use one hour to write something twice as clear. And ideas that are easy to read and easy to understand will make you seem smarter. **The better you communicate, the more intelligent you appear.**" You may think that you do not have that hour. If you think effective communication is a time-waster, try scaling a company where no one is clear about what the founders want. Besides, you don't have to do it all on your own. Your own team and wider network can act as sparring partners and help you to craft the right words.

To gain clarity when preparing a presentation, talk, email or all-hands, start by answering these questions:

1. What is my objective?
2. Who is my audience?
3. What do I want them to know, feel and do?
4. How can I best deliver my key message?
5. When is the right time?

Too often, speakers and presenters think their job is to give information. Sure, that's part of it. It covers the content dimension, but not the relational dimension of communication. It also neglects that audiences can't retain a lot of information, so powerful founder communication is about inspiration, not merely information. Using the above questions as guidelines helps you avoid this trap. They remind you to always give something of value to your audience. Your audience trusts you with their time and gives you their attention. They rightly expect something from you in return, be it an idea, an insight or a solution to a problem they face. You'll also find it easier to keep someone's attention if they know the general direction your story is heading. You want to give them the answer to the underlying question: "why must I care?"

It definitely helps to pick the right format. Sure, it can be a written piece or a presentation. You can also mix it up with interactive sessions, videos and audio formats that feel fresh and different. One advantage of this is that you reach all of the audience's sensory channels including sight, sound and touch. For instance, a memorable presentation relies on speech, visuals and the written word as well as props or physical objects for people to touch.

Regardless of the format, **focus on one idea**. The aim is to transfer one idea from your head into the heads of each member of the audience. What is the one point you want to make? Ultimately you want the audience to remember your most powerful idea. Make this idea your headline. The headline or title is prime real estate and should not be wasted on stating the topic. Then repeat it several times. A common pitfall is including too much information and too many ideas, like when you see paragraphs of bullet points in a presentation. Keep your communication simple so that it's memorable.

MESSAGE MASTERY 2: LISTENING TO UNDERSTAND

There are only two sides to a conversation: either you speak, or you listen. Both are crucial, and you want to achieve excellence in both. The way someone listens can change the entire outcome of any relationship-building exercise. As Kevin Kelly, the co-founder of Wired, put it: "Speak confidently as if you are right, but listen carefully as if you are wrong." It's also necessary to understand the distinction between listening and hearing. Think of hearing as collecting data with your ears. Think of listening as the analysis that happens in your brain. **Hearing is passive. Listening is active.**

Listening is the result of curiosity, a crucial trait for any problem-solving entrepreneur. Shilpka Gautam, the CEO and founder of climate fintech SALT, said: "At the heart of every conversation and leadership style should be curiosity. Curiosity makes you ask questions. Curiosity makes you listen. Curiosity makes you eager to understand problems as an entrepreneur. Curiosity helps you see where your team might need you to do things differently. Curiosity helps you see gaps from a go-to-market perspective. Curiosity helps you understand your customers better."

When you're truly listening, you pay attention to facts, context, body language and emotions, and sometimes even what *isn't* being said. Imagine an investor asking you whether you really believe your product is good enough to win market share. Of course, she wants an answer to her question, but she also wants to see how you respond. Are you confident and reassuring or defensive and dismissive? Do you listen at all? This is listening to understand in action – understanding the facts and gaining an understanding of the other person at the same time.

Learning to listen requires an understanding of what the other person is looking for. When investors ask about product-market fit, they're actually wanting to know the founder's maturity and level of experience with the product and market, rather than a number or score. When a product manager is asking about product-market fit, they're likely expecting a response with a mention of a Net Promoter Score (NPS) and details on how customers are currently engaging with the product.

What is true for one-on-one conversations also applies when you listen to a few colleagues in a meeting or to a large group. To read the room, you observe, listen consciously rather than talk too much, contextualize what is being said and then guide the conversation to your desired outcome.

An effective way to guide a conversation is through asking the right questions and then going back into listening mode. Asking the right questions can change the outcome of a conversation because, let's face it, founders are penalized for asking the wrong questions. Especially in conversations where the power dynamics may be imbalanced, like with investors. **There is such a thing as a stupid question.** Asking the wrong questions can reveal naivety or misjudgement. Asking a Series B investor which metrics your business should really be tracking would set off alarm bells. That investor is expecting to buy shares in a company that is ready to scale, and is growing rapidly. *Not ready to look after my money*, may be their conclusion.

There is a better way. For instance, asking a potential investor for references from portfolio founders, as well as enquiring how much capital the fund has deployed and how their decision-making process works, would immediately demonstrate an understanding of how venture capital really works. Asking an experienced product manager about the way they solved a peculiar or specific problem previously shows that you've actually given some thought to how they may use their experience within your company. But it only works if you then listen attentively rather than thinking about the next question to ask. It's a skill to understand what people really mean with their answers.

The interplay between listening and questioning, and also using the right questions in specific situations can be a powerful technique to help solve problems, build consensus on a course of action, or even as a negotiating tool. Different question types serve different purposes. Some questions guide the flow of conversation, others help us to reach closure, and some help us build stronger relationships and get to know each other better.

Questions are often used in a structured question-funnel to gather information and requirements. You're essentially trying to elicit an answer that you can follow up on, to ask for either more clarification or further detail, such as "What are your concerns and worries about these numbers?" Such questions frame the issue (*I understand you believe there is reason to be concerned*) and leave a broad range of possibilities.

Open, closed, hypothetical, leading, reflective – these are just some of the many different types of questions, and you can combine them in even more ways. If you're trying to get to the root of a simple problem, you might consider using the exceptionally straightforward '5 whys' technique, designed by Sakichi Toyoda, the founder of Japanese car manufacturer Toyota. You essentially drill down to the root cause of a problem when you encounter it by asking "Why?" five times. Another question-based approach to gathering data across different stages of the problem solving process involves constantly asking "so what?" Consistently asking "so what?" helps you to get the most information out of a simple fact or statement. It also helps ensure you're only surfacing the most important elements to convey the right message within a conversation.

In situations where another person is aggressive or defiant, responding to a strong objection with an equal or similar force is counterproductive. Deflective questions can help you transform a negative situation into a more collaborative problem-solving one. These can range from the simple "Do you really believe that to be true?" to "Would you mind giving me more context? I'd love to understand it a bit more" to the politician's favorite answer, "I'm sorry, I can't hear you over the crowds of supporters." It's why political operators love gaggle-like situations where press reporters are shouting over each other, which leads to an opportunity for the politician to provide an off-the-cuff remark that they almost certainly spent weeks preparing. The point is that pros think strategically about their question-funnel so they can frame important conversations and then listen carefully. Over time, this becomes more automatic.

To get the right answers we must ask the right questions, and to turn answers into positive outcomes, we must listen to understand.

MESSAGE MASTERY 3: STORYTELLING

Two friends struggle to pay the rent. Given that hotel rooms are hard to come by in San Francisco during conferences, they decide to put air mattresses on the floor and rent them out to earn some extra cash. The idea appeals to budget-conscious travelers. Brian Chesky and Joe Gebbia think they are onto something and turn their idea into a business called airbedandbreakfast.com. They launch it at South by Southwest in 2008. Far from being a huge success, the idea bombs and they only get two bookings.

The founders are running out of cash. Investors ignore them. They rack up $20,000 in credit card debt. Brian Chesky loses 20 pounds. The situation is hopeless. But they have one final card to play. In a last-ditch effort, Airbnb seeks admission into Y Combinator. Its founder Paul Graham is skeptical of the unproven idea, but is impressed by the founders who raised some much-needed cash by selling Obama and McCain branded cereal boxes during the 2008 US presidential campaign. He decides to invest, but still struggles to get other investors interested. Months later Airbnb expands into a few new geographical markets, and junior members of investment firms start talking it up to the senior partners, who then come on board. Today Airbnb is a global brand, millions of customers book via the platform, and its founders are billionaires.

The Airbnb story works because it's dramatic. It starts with the heroes facing a crisis, then things get worse and worse until – finally – they get better. In the process, they are being transformed and have learned something life-changing. Change is bloody hard, and it leads to a complete transformation of the founders and the hospitality industry.

"Every great founder can really tell a great story. If a founder doesn't have it, it's harder to get funding, attract employees, or get attention," said Jeff Jordan, general partner at Andreessen Horowitz and former CEO of OpenTable.

Founders therefore want to move from fact-telling to storytelling, from rational narrative to something that moves people. Telling stories is extremely powerful because humans have evolved to tell and remember stories. They are how we process information and make sense of the world. In fact, our brains are "story-processors", not "logic-processors," according to NYU psychology professor Jonathan Haidt. They are how we transfer ideas to one another and drive each other to take action, which is how humans came to rule the planet. The most important theme in storytelling is human connection. In the Airbnb story, the founders are friends who also lived together. More importantly, human closeness is the essential differentiator between their business and hotels.

Your Story is Your Strategy

Stories work because they are emotional, and emotional is the opposite of boring. They include tension, conflict and challenges, which keep listeners hooked. Stories trigger hefty doses of neurochemicals in your brain. Since the mission of the brain is control, as Will Storr writes in *The Science of Storytelling*, great storytellers create moments of unexpected change, which are endlessly fascinating to us. These turns of events put our brains on high alert, as they could signal either danger or opportunity.

In business, stories are more engaging than any other form of communication. "Storytelling is the most underrated skill," said Ben Horowitz in an interview with Forbes. "Companies that don't have a clearly articulated story don't have a clear and well thought-out strategy. **The company story is the company strategy.** The story must explain at a fundamental level why you exist. Why does the world need your company? Why do we need to be doing what we're doing and why is it important?"

To those who believe that the product is all that matters, he replies: "You can have a great product, but a compelling story puts the company into motion. If you don't have a great story it's hard to get people motivated to join you, to work on the product, and to get people to invest in the product."

In his view, **the CEO is the chief storyteller**. "The CEO must be the keeper of the story. The CEO is responsible for getting the story right, that it's up to date, compelling, and can move the hearts of men and women. That's the fundamental responsibility of the chief executive. The mistake people make is thinking the story is just about marketing. No, the story is the strategy. If you make your story better you make the strategy better."

Stories bring your brand and your company to life; they win your customers' hearts and minds. When we think of a brand, we often imagine all the stories behind it: the origin story, the story of the founders and how the idea for the product came about. Knowing the structure and the principles allows you to use storytelling in many different situations: from pitching to selling, to presenting to your team, to speaking on stage. Stories are an asset for B2B companies like Shopify and a game-changer for B2C companies like Airbnb.

As a founder, you want a personal signature story. Jannes Fischer, the founder of German proptech startup Zenhomes, often recounts how he helped his grandparents with their rental apartments and noticed that there were no digital solutions to make this process easy for private landlords. So he built one himself, which became a market-leading property technology company in Germany that he successfully sold to a listed company a few years later. Telling an audience how you wanted to help your grandparents elicits emotion, the key to great communication. "Emotion is the fastest path to the brain," as Carmine Gallo puts it. Every founder has a great story, it just needs to be brought to light.

Your signature story weaves your own journey and your company's together. It should not be self-referential or salesy, but make a larger point in a way that your audience can relate to. Start with a short version and add elements and details until it resonates. An experienced coach or mentor can support you in this. "An extraordinary life will require an extraordinary story," writes entrepreneur M.J. DeMarco. "Whenever hardships, failures, and struggles are encountered, you are simply drafting the story."

Build Sh*t and Tell Stories

Your company also needs a story, a story in which your customer is the hero. This story can be used on your website, in conversations, in your marketing and sales materials and in campaigns. This serves two purposes. Firstly, customers pay more attention to stories than to information. Secondly, your story humanizes your businesses, so that your marketing does not feel like marketing. Instead, it builds trust. Your personal story and your brand story explain what you personally and your startup stand for. Don't just recount what happened. Talk about something bigger that's at stake. This is where it becomes interesting for the outside world. Not all stories resonate, so what distinguishes a powerful story from one that falls flat?

Stories traditionally follow a three-act structure of set-up, conflict and resolution. In recent years, Donald Miller has popularized a more business-tailored approach in his book "Building a Storybrand" that entails seven steps:

1. A character (= your customer)
2. Has a problem
3. And meets a guide (= your company)
4. Who gives them a plan
5. And calls them to action
6. That helps them avoid failure
7. And ends in success

The crucial insight is that in the hero's journey, **the customer is the hero, never the company**. The company is the guide that helps the customer become a hero. If you use these steps, you can craft a powerful story in no time. You don't have to write a lengthy tale. Cover each element in one or two clear sentences to keep it punchy. The result is a story that resonates and can be used by everyone in the company to explain what the company does to employees, investors and the media. A compelling brand story connects everything and fills your company with life and meaning. It's the story that gives the word Patagonia meaning and triggers emotions and associations, not the logo or the clothes.

We recommend you internalize this seven-step storytelling technique and **include at least one story in all of your talks, interviews and presentations to make them more impactful**. Every startup has stories to tell. Even in the early stages of a venture, you can tell stories about personal experiences, milestones, customers and the problem your business solves.

Most stories in a business context apply the hero's journey. There are several other relevant plots such as 'The Quest,' 'Overcoming the Monster' and 'Voyage and Return,' as Christopher Booker analyzed in *The Seven Basic Plots: Why We*

Tell Stories. These offer alternatives for advanced storytelling. Meta is on a quest: *There is something that needs to be done, and we are on a quest to get it done.* Tesla is overcoming the metaphorical monster: *There is a big opportunity, we made a plan, we're now killing that monster.* Actually, they are targeting two monsters: the auto industry and climate change. Netflix's story is one of voyage and return: We built a movie rental business, we even offered ourselves to Blockbuster for $50mil but they declined, so we then built a streaming service that's worth 2000x more.

According to Gerrit McGowan, who coaches founders and specializes in the neuroscience of building startups, "founders have only two tasks: To build sh*t and tell stories." Your pitch should also include storytelling because that is what humans – and investors are humans – respond to. However, a pitch story is different from the usual company story. We are talking about aligning your pitch with a narrative that triggers the right neurochemicals in your listener to justify an investment in your startup.

A pitch always starts with 'the problem.' This early climax releases cortisol which increases attentiveness. A problem signals that there is something that warrants our attention. If you nail the problem, you can trigger adrenaline. And that's really useful because adrenaline subsequently triggers generosity. Provide the solution next. Thanks to the release of dopamine, solutions make us feel good, which enhances memory. Use character-driven stories to establish a bond between listeners and storytellers. They trigger oxytocin for more empathy and connectivity. As you can see, the right equity story can release a whole cocktail of neurochemicals that can work to your advantage.

You can inject some humor into your pitch to drive happiness and feelings of peace. The release of endorphins has an energizing, positive effect. But: This can be tricky to pull off. If you don't come across as competent and appropriate, humor backfires. Confident, appropriate humor increases likeability and status, whereas nervous, inappropriate humor makes an investment less likely. McGowan compares using humor in a pitch to a boxing match: "You want to see that all the punchlines land. Don't swing and miss."

MESSAGE MASTERY 4: SPEAKING AND PRESENTING WITH IMPACT

As your company grows, there will be more demands on your time, in particular to present or speak to the team, the media, on stage or on podcasts. At first you are delighted about the attention it brings your company, but it quickly becomes overwhelming. Some founders then go from saying yes to most opportunities to saying no to almost everything. Don't overcomplicate it. Say yes to the things that move the dial, and no to all others. And if you say yes, use every opportunity to make an impression on your internal, external or financial audiences.

As a founder, it is not your job to inform; your job is to inspire. And that requires passion: If you are passionate about your idea, then others will buy into that passion and into your idea. Facts and figures will only persuade if they serve as evidence for your key message or big idea. The audience will switch off if you rattle off numbers or if your speech drags on.

As a founder, you interact with your audiences every day, so you need to be able to craft powerful speeches and stories within minutes rather than hours. Here's how: You start with a clear idea about the point you want to make. Don't choose a topic like "the future of proptech"; choose a message such as "why proptech is entering a golden age". Now you can develop your outline on a single page. It really helps to follow a template like the crystal structure, as it will prompt you to write down the key elements of your talk. This method was refined by top communications coach Bettina Hausmann and is based on the diamond structure which has been around for a long time.

As shown in the visual, on the top of the page is your headline, which needs to reflect your point or key message. At the top of your crystal is your hook. We live in a three-second world, as Brendan Kane pointed out in *Hook Point*, meaning you need to grab the audience's attention within a few seconds. They will immediately decide whether to keep listening or do something else. Always start with a bang. This can be a story that draws people in and develops an emotional connection. It can also be a question or a broad claim. It has to be something that demands attention and that gives the audience the opportunity to follow a storyline.

The middle of a talk or presentation can be conversational and free-flowing. Limit yourself to three points that underline your key message. Depending on how much time you have, each point should be made memorable by a story or a fact. The only numbers you include should be 'killer facts' that will highlight a point you are making or that the audience will remember. In your conclusion, come back to your main point and close the loop you opened in your introduction. For instance, if you use a provocative question as an attention hook at the beginning, answer it at the end. If you create a knowledge gap at the start,

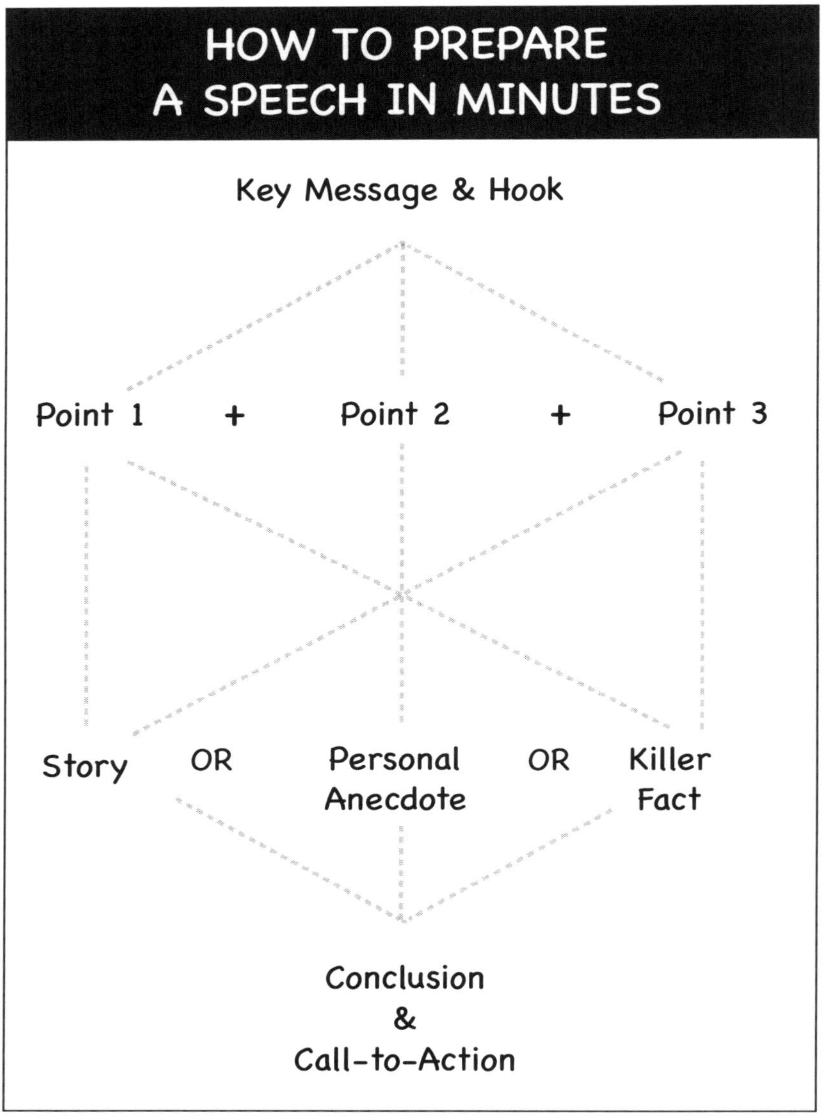

close it. Otherwise you leave your audience disappointed. Your closing should include a call-to-action.

The crystal allows you to visualize the whole talk in your head and forces you to be very clear about the one point you want to get across and how you will bring it to life. Once you have that plan on a page, you can rehearse and prepare. Keep your talks and speeches short and sweet. Research suggests that we can listen to a single speaker for a maximum of fifteen minutes before we lose interest – and that's for the best speakers and the most interesting topics. You want to deliver a powerful message, not a lecture. In terms of language, keep it simple. Stick to conversational language, as if you were explaining your idea to just one friend or colleague. If you are speaking to an international audience, ensure that non-native speakers can follow along.

Your Signature Talk

You can take it to the next level as a speaker by creating your own TED-style signature talk. It serves as an inspirational speech for internal and external audiences. Your personal or your brand story may feature, but they should not be the focus. A signature talk should instead address an issue or question that your audience cares about. Some have even used a TEDx talk to get their venture off the ground. In 2012, Boyan Slat shared the findings of his research on the TEDx stage of his home town of Delft in The Netherlands. The virality of his talk coincided with his 2013 launch of The Ocean Cleanup, attracting the support of a global audience and setting the company on a path to raise over $40 million. Their goal: remove 92%

of plastic contamination from the ocean. Keep in mind that it takes practice before such a talk feels completely natural. After all, TED talks are honed and rehearsed for six months before the speaker goes on stage.

On a TED stage or in any other situation, consider how visionary or down-to-earth you want to appear. If your cruising altitude is too high, you may seem aloof, unapproachable and out of touch with the audience. If your cruising altitude is too low, you may come across as a manager rather than a leader, and therefore may not develop the gravitas and clout you need to move the organization forward. Managers tend to talk about their area of expertise. The right cruising altitude for a founder, however, is to focus on the big picture in an inspirational and passionate manner.

There are some big differences between an in-person gathering, a virtual meeting and a hybrid format. In real life, a leader is on stage or stands out in some way, and the audience tends to listen. On Zoom, a leader looks the same as everyone else on the screen, and no one can really tell who is listening. That means you need to be even more inclusive and consciously connect with as many people as possible to lead well. Personal stories and questions that combine warmth and competence come across as charismatic. Hybrid is even more challenging than virtual. Often the attention and energy stay in the room and the colleagues online are all but forgotten. What works for us is to include a deliberate element in the meeting to connect with the folks online, such as asking each person online a brief question at the very beginning.

Virtual and hybrid settings require us to think meetings through from beginning to end. Winging the running of meetings never worked, and it works even less in a remote world. The underlying challenge for leaders is to nurture a team when remote work is here to stay. This requires investing in team building and culture to avoid teams falling apart. Successful founders manage to create these rare moments when the whole team is together – virtually and in person – and then work towards cohesion.

… and Signature Presence

In addition to your signature talk, you also want a signature presence that is confident but not cocky. Because both what you say and how you say it matter. "A strong idea cannot stand alone. It needs to be accompanied by strong cues," as body language expert Vanessa van Edwards puts it in her book *Cues*. Many smart people make this classic mistake: they focus too much on *what* they say, not *how* they say it. Your body language, your voice and the subconscious cues you send in a high-stakes situation like a pitch will either support or undermine your message. To convince investors and others, you want the body language of a leader who is worth backing. But what does that mean?

"**Highly charismatic people exhibit the perfect blend of warmth and competence**. They immediately signal trust and credibility," writes van Edwards, building on earlier work by Amy Cuddy and others. "We see them as friendly and smart, impressive and collaborative." Unfortunately some people have an imbalance between these two traits. People who score high on competence but low on warmth find it harder to build rapport and relationships of trust. Those who are higher in warmth but lower in competence are trustworthy but not necessarily impressive – not a great combination when looking for investment.

Energy is vital in leaders. Audiences respond well to speakers who are excited about sharing their ideas. **Be an energy-giver, not an energy-taker.** This is not about role play but rather tapping into your genuine energy. That excitement will provide the fuel, whether you are speaking to investors, your team or customers. If necessary, change your inner state before you speak. For instance, find a ritual that gives you a boost of energy and do that each time before you give a talk. That can be your personal superhero pose, jumping up and down or clicking your fingers. Whatever works for you. Don't hold back! Low-energy speakers are boring. Low energy kills even the best speech and the most refined delivery. *If you don't feel excited, why should I?*, the audience will wonder. Actually, your delivery needs to feel over the top to be just right. That's because stages, cameras or screens are energy filters. You need to inject additional energy to make up for that loss of energy. That's why a deliberate change of your mental state is necessary before you speak. This "flipping the switch" reminds you to amp up the energy and deliver for your audience.

If "everything feels like a chore and a never-ending struggle," we recommend the book *Energize* from award-winning life coach Simon Alexander Ong. It explores practical methods relating to the art and science of energy management, a stark contrast to the potentially toxic 'hustle and grind' culture that is so pervasive in the startup world.

In terms of body language, be dynamic. You should record yourself giving a speech and analyze your body language. Most of us may feel silly when we adapt our movements to keep attention. It may feel over the top, but it will appear natural when you are on stage.

The good news is that nonverbal communication is a skill, not talent or fate. It can (and should) be improved in the same way that verbal communication can be improved – by deliberate training. When you practice, the camera is your friend. Work with a coach or mentor and review the recordings together to hit the sweet spot of competence and warmth. Yes, it's uncomfortable at the beginning. But you will appreciate how fast you progress.

Speaking and presenting with impact applies to ALL forms of communication, whether it's a Whatsapp audio message you leave a journalist or a Loom demo recording. Or even the first message you send your significant other after your first date. Jag remembers passing on a company's investment after one of the founders left him a voice note in response to a question he'd posed about the company's distribution strategy. The contents of the message made the founder come across disorganized and unsure of their own strategy. The fourteen-minute rambling stream-of-consciousness message would have been a little bit more tolerable were the founder also not standing near what seemed to be a construction site.

Audience expectations with regard to both verbal and nonverbal communications rise with the maturity of the business, so it's not a skill that you master once and be done with it. Charismatic leaders continue to hone their skills.

MESSAGE MASTERY 5: LEADING DIFFICULT CONVERSATIONS TO POSITIVE OUTCOMES

Your business succeeds or fails one conversation at a time. Difficult conversations happen all the time in a startup. That's why founders' interpersonal skills matter so much. You may have to let someone go, tell the Board that you've missed your targets and argue about strategy with your co-founders. And that's just Tuesday.

What feels like a pain is actually a competitive advantage that startups have. "The biggest difference I see between high-growth startups and large corporations is around communication and conflict," said Stanford lecturer and author of *The Creator's Code: The Six Essential Skills of Extraordinary Entrepreneurs*, Amy Wilkenson. "There is an intense amount of conflict in startups and it's communicated very directly, right in your face. There is no time to waste if you believe your company will not exist in six months." **Direct communication equals speed**. (This does not mean that it's a good idea to bulldoze people though.) Those working in large corporations lack that sense of urgency and don't speak as openly as a result. Instead, they drive for consensus, which slows everything down.

Of course, candid feedback and difficult conversations only work to a startup's advantage if they are constructive and don't burn bridges. Feedforward instead of feedback. While each conversation is different, there are some general principles that help you turn around a tricky conversation:

1. Have real conversations and confront the real issues: "While many fear 'real,' it is the unreal conversations that should scare us to death," writes Susan Scott in *Fierce Conversations*. "You will accomplish your goals in large part by making every conversation you have as real as possible."
2. Be present and listen: The conversation you are having at the moment is the most important in the world. And if it isn't, perhaps you shouldn't be having the conversation.
3. Consider who you are talking to and how you talk to them: Someone from a different background, culture or generation is likely to have a different communication style. Be mindful of that and adapt your delivery if appropriate.
4. Take responsibility for your emotions: The stakes are high, and you are under a lot of pressure. It is completely normal to occasionally let your anger get the better of you. Except: don't. Unpredictable or moody leaders come across as toxic, and smart people leave toxic environments. The business suffers. Teams don't achieve great things if they are worried about what Founder X will say to them in the next meeting. Yes, people should feel uncomfortable at work – but only because the tasks are challenging. They should never feel uncomfortable for who they are or because their manager has had a shitty day.

When it comes to conversations with employees, don't believe that they work *for* you. They work *with* you, and you help each other in different ways. Being the boss doesn't fly very far or high these days. Be a leader, coach and role model, and witness how your reputation and company grow.

Bad communication often leads to unhealthy friction that can escalate into ongoing frustration on all sides. Once again, don't avoid a difficult conversation, but turn it around and bring it to a positive conclusion.

Avoiding Founder Fall Out

The most important (and the most difficult) conversations are those among the leaders of organizations, often the founding team. A lot of founders have fallen out, losing momentum externally and trust internally. And if you have self-made problems, your investors would rather spend their time on other high-performing companies. In addition, how leaders communicate amongst themselves has huge repercussions on company culture, internal communications and the general atmosphere of the organization. We have attended management meetings where the CMO and the CTO were shouting at each other for not doing their jobs properly. Word got out and instead of fixing problems together, their teams were busy blaming each other for a lack of growth.

An easy way for any investor to pass on an investment opportunity is when co-founders disagree in a pitch meeting, sometimes on the tiniest details. When those disagreements surface in a public setting, it implies that there aren't already structures in place for disagreements. Declan Kelly, the General Partner of Foreword Ventures, recalls a dinner with three co-founders at a startup with several dozen staff. They'd met him to discuss a potential investment into their company. "I started with my favorite probing question: Who's your next hire on the leadership team?, and they each gave a different answer. It would have been great if they just left it at that and suggested postponing the discussion until after dinner, but they went for it right away. Two of the co-founders were brothers, and let's just say I learned a whole new vocabulary of curse-words that night. The company went on to raise lots of money (not from me!), but ultimately failed a few years later. It transpired that their employees never had faith that the co-founders would resolve disagreements in a cordial and constructive manner." This is a serious matter. A dysfunctional leadership team cannot lead a company to success. It is often the root cause of failed startups.

There are two questions that almost every investor we know hates to evaluate: *Which founding teams are likely to fall apart?* and *What will make a founding team stay together?* The first question is easy to answer for early-stage companies, as practically all early-stage teams will break up in one way or another. How they manage that falling out is what makes them a real company. The second one is why the leadership of the two most successful startup accelerators, Y Combinator and Techstars, frequently recommend that founders get help from coaches and mentors as early as possible.

Patrick Lencioni, in his insightful book *The Five Dysfunctions of a Team*, dissects what can go wrong within a team:

1. Absence of trust amongst team members. As such, team players are not open about their weaknesses

and mistakes, thereby making it difficult to build a foundation of trust.

2. Fear of conflict in the team. When teams lack trust, they will not be able to engage in an unfiltered and genuine exchange of ideas. Rather, they resort to veiled discussions and spiteful comments.
3. Lack of commitment from the team players. Because the team members have been unable to air their opinions in healthy debate environments, they are then rarely ready to commit to decisions.
4. Avoidance of accountability by team members. Without commitment, there is no accountability. As there is no plan of action, the team will hesitate to call out their peers on actions and behaviors that may seem counterproductive.
5. Finally, inattention to results. If no one is holding anyone to account, individual team members will put their own needs above the needs of the team as a whole.
6. Additionally, we would add lack of communication in general to Patrick Lencioni's five reasons. It is the overarching problem. Many leaders find communication difficult, partly because they fear being wrong, vulnerable or out of control. Running remote companies makes this even more complicated.

Conflict avoidance is at the root of the behavior Lencioni describes. It is a type of people-pleasing behavior that typically arises from a deep-rooted fear of upsetting others. People who respond to conflict this way often expect negative outcomes and find it difficult to trust the other person's reaction. The answer is to create psychological safety, i.e. the shared belief that the team is safe for interpersonal risk-taking and that speaking your mind does not have negative consequences for you personally. This is a process and requires turning around the problems identified by Lencioni. If we phrase his advice in a positive way, the six secrets to a functional, cohesive leadership team are:

1. People trust one another
2. Team members engage in unfiltered conflict around ideas
3. They happily commit to decisions and action plans
4. They hold one another accountable
5. They collectively focus on the achievement of results
6. They openly communicate with each other – a lot!

Ideally the founders agree on these principles – trust, commitment, accountability, focus and open communication – on day one and build the organization accordingly. The second best day to do it is today. Take an honest look at the interactions among the leadership team. If you still see potential to improve communications within the team, tackle it as a priority. It will make the whole company more effective if the leadership is in sync.

Often outside facilitation can help steer the kind of difficult conversations this requires. Jag has at times even recommended marriage counselors and couples therapy to some of the later-stage founders in his portfolio, since many of the ingredients required to make a marriage work can also be applied to a founding team. Arguments aren't something you want to avoid at all costs – rather, it's healthy debate that you want to strive for.

WITH GREAT SUPERPOWERS COME GREAT FUNDRAISING ABILITIES

In 2021, venture capitalists globally invested an average of a billion and a half US dollars every day. That money only flowed because a company found traction with investors, usually as a result of customers finding attraction in the marketing. What this figure does not tell you is that investors generally speak to about 100 startups before pulling the trigger to make one investment. Even once a VC's investment committee agrees to fund a company, there is still a chance of the company failing the due-diligence process, or for the investors to get cold feet if they sense a shift in the market and aren't convinced of the company's ability to navigate choppy waters.

Given these odds, investors tend to be inherently more skeptical than the average population – it's their job, after all, to find the best opportunities to make lots of money. When asked what he looks for in a compelling pitch, Y Combinator co-founder and former president Sam Altman said: "Are they good communicators? If someone cannot communicate clearly, it's a real problem." And influential investor Chris Sacca says founders must be great storytellers. "It's how you raise money. It's how you recruit people to your company. It's how you retain them. It's how you talk to the press. It's the cornerstone of everything we do in business."

Winning Over Skeptical Investors

A team that doesn't get along or disagrees about the direction of the company is a red flag for investors. They sense it and will not write the check. But even with a tightly-knit founder team, there will be plenty of challenging conversations every time you decide to raise money. Jag raised his company's Series A round at the height of the 2007-2008 Great Financial Crisis, and also learned painful lessons in defusing bias with effective communication. He argues that it is also where he really learned to develop his sense of humor.

The key to closing a round is to use the psychological levers outlined in Chapter 1 - including value, connection, differentiation, trust and framing - and combine them with the five Message Mastery skills discussed in this chapter. Then you use all of these skills and insights to deliver a tightly controlled narrative. Once you communicate with exceptional clarity, can identify and understand your audiences, persuade them with stories, speak and present with impact and lead difficult conversations to positive outcomes, you can win over even skeptical investors. Your personal communication skills matter a great deal in getting funded. When it comes to overcoming biases, you can change the conversation with the Acknowledge, Bridge, Communicate (ABC) framework that we covered under the subject of 'Framing' in the first chapter of this book.

Tristan Walker, the founder of Bevel, whom we first mentioned in the Introduction to this book, often talks about this background as a way to highlight the opportunity. "As a black man, I have a different hair type. I have a different skin type.

And those needs should be respected. As I walk down retail aisles, I deserve not only products that work for me, but also a design experience that doesn't make me feel like a second class citizen."

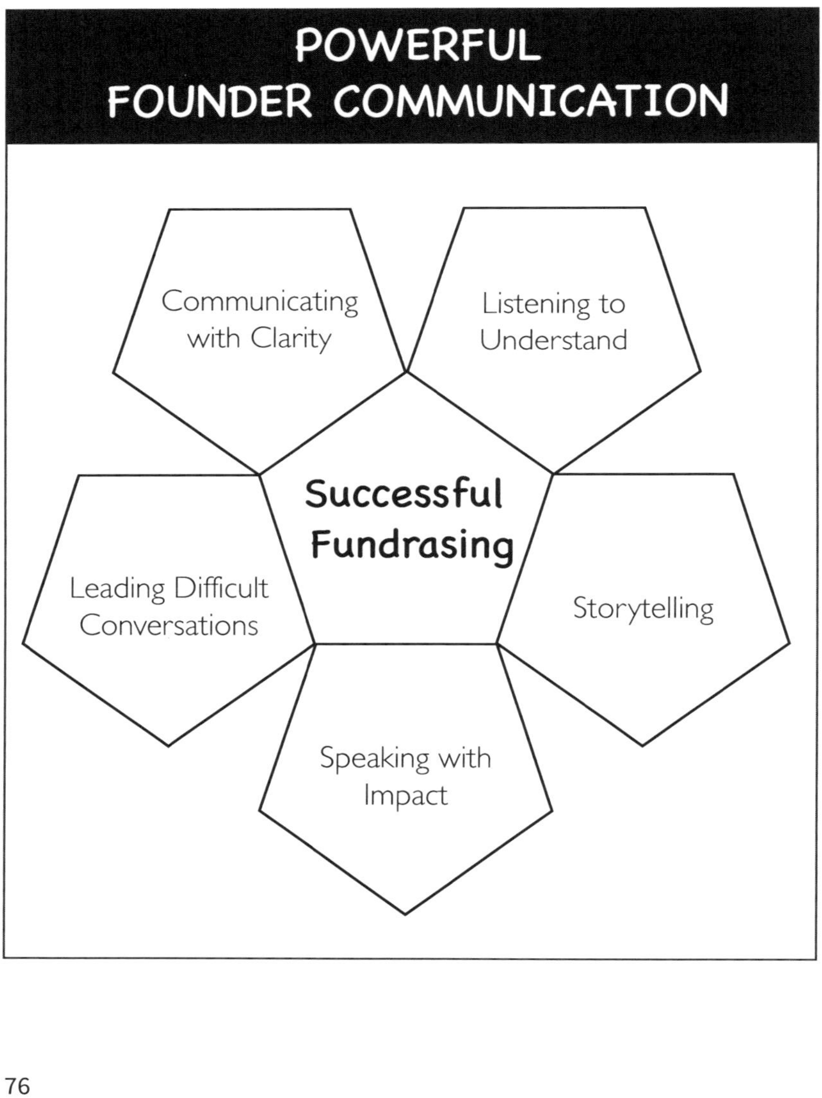

There is a dangerous and pervasive myth that the great founders of our time have only ever needed a one-sentence pitch in their back pocket to unlock an untold amount of charm to audiences, and this couldn't be further from the truth.

The aim of any pitch is to communicate the right amount of information to the audience in order to induce them to take a specific action. You fine-tune your pitch depending on the level of expertise your audience has on a specific subject. In that sense, the perfect pitch can be one sentence, but it can also just as much be several sentences that take 45 seconds to say out loud. Sometimes, the perfect pitch requires visual aids or a prop. Sometimes, further information is necessary that cannot easily be presented—be it in the form of clarifying conversations or additional text.

Of course, your pitch deck also plays a role, but since you have already raised money and there is plenty of information available already, we won't dwell on it here. Suffice to say: **Your pitch deck is as strong as your thinking is clear.** As Gil Dibner, a General Partner at Angular Ventures puts it, "It's not that I, as a VC, require you to have a deck to pitch me. It's that 9 times out of 10, you, as a founder, need to have a deck to give your most effective pitch."

Unlike participants in the public markets, investors in private markets are usually making decisions based on very little verified information, in rather non-transparent settings that are marked with high degrees of risk. Hence it's not only facts and metrics that matter in a pitch. The pitch is everything from the words on the page to the language used in the presentation, the slides on the wall and the body language of the presenter. It could also no longer just be the founder who's pitching. We talk more about this in the context of message alignment and discipline in Chapter 3. And the specific way a pitch is delivered matters just as much as what is being said.

Ideally, your investors today will also be your investors tomorrow. In addition to financing your venture, they have the network to open doors to your best advisors and talent, and the motivation to be your most convincing advocates, especially in a fundraising context. Investors usually spend significant amounts of their time cultivating relationships with investors who are further downstream and likely to invest in their portfolio at later stages. The best Series A investors will be very familiar with Series B and C investors, which means targeted and consistent communication with your existing investors plays a significant role in keeping them onboard and tapping into such an invaluable resource.

As a strong communicator, you are now in a position to turn your startup into a fast-growing Message Machine. Yet, there is one missing ingredient needed to raise funds and win over customers. As companies mature, message-market fit becomes crucial for fundraising and revenue-growth – at times, even more than product-market fit. This is where we turn next.

Chapter 3

SUCCEEDING WITH THE MESSAGE-MARKET FIT METHOD

***Build it and they will come* does not work.** Your target audience cares about its own needs, problems and feelings, not about you or your product. It is your job as a founder to make them care. If you do, a path to scaling opens up. That's why **every successful company needs to achieve both product-market fit (PMF) and message-market fit (MMF).**

Product-market fit describes the stage of a startup where you have developed an attractive product that serves a particular type of customer. But any business needs customers, and customers need to be persuaded that your product or service is the best solution to their problem. That's where your messaging comes in.

Message-market fit means that the words you use to convince your target audience resonate and make them want to invest in you, work for you or buy from you. You attract the people who really want to be part of your journey, your brand, your product. You feel it when you are talking to prospects or investors and they nod and want to know more. You notice that customers are not haggling over the price and recommend your brand to colleagues. This is the message-market fit nirvana:

you've managed to enter a conversation already taking place in the heads of your audience.

Messaging Frames Your Company

Messaging allows people to make sense of your company or product by giving them a frame of reference. By framing your company or product in the best possible way, you can make it appear exceptional. This can save you a lot of marketing dollars and gray hairs (and makes your investors happy).

In fact, what is considered to be a marketing or sales problem is often an issue with a startup's positioning or messaging. So if your growth isn't what you expected, it is crucial to first go back to your positioning and messaging and optimize it before you throw money at a new campaign.

Never forget: **all communications are audience-specific** and depend on the context. Different messages are designed to convince A-players, potential business partners and investors to work with you or invest in you. The basic idea and story are the same, but your messaging needs to be flexible enough to allow tailoring for each audience. Because customers want a solution to a problem they face right now and talent want to understand why they should work for you instead of any other company in the universe.

Investors buy into the future potential of your business, but they also want to see that you have your messaging figured out. They know how hard it is to get noticed and to persuade an ever-increasing number of buyers to part with their money. That's why you need to show in your pitch that you have achieved message-market fit, especially after your seed round. Message-market fit is something you absolutely need to maintain, once you have it. That does not mean it stays stable though. Messaging inevitably evolves over time as your market changes, customer behavior fluctuates and your offer expands. Constant optimization helps you to retain customers and to counter rising customer acquisition costs. After all, you are only a startup if you win new customers, fast. And that requires continuous improvement of both your product and your messaging.

The founders of SumUp went from small shops to independent cafés to convince small merchants to try their payment device. The message was straightforward: our card reader is simple, easy to use and affordable. It makes taking payments so much easier. Today, the London-based fintech is a unicorn with a significant presence on several continents. Since SumUp now offers a whole range of financial services, the messaging had to change too: "Business made simple" is the tagline, still aimed at the same audience of small merchants who just want the financial stuff taken care of.

When Messaging Goes Badly

At the other end of the spectrum, we find startups whose messaging has gone down spectacularly badly. German startup Pinky Gloves developed single-use pink plastic gloves for women to dispose of used menstrual products. Things started well. In 2021, the two founders managed to secure funding from a well-known investor on the German version of Shark Tank. The backlash came hard and fast. The messaging was poor, as the founders claimed many women would stay home during their period due to a lack of a product such as theirs. But the real problem was the messengers. Both the founders and the investor were men. In the absence of problem-founder fit and the presence of terrible messaging, their idea turned into a laughing stock. "Our product and its communications wasn't thought through," they admitted. #pinkygloves became #pinkygate, and the two founders threw in the towel.

Timing also matters. Airbnb launched their 'floating world' marketing campaign in 2017, which included an image of a water-themed house sitting on the surface of water. The copy included, "Stay above water," and "live the life aquatic with these floating homes." Harmless right? Well, this campaign launched on August 28, 2017, when Hurricane Harvey was engulfing Houston.

From financial services to personal hygiene, messaging matters regardless of the sector you are in. It's as true for a coffee shop as it is for Web3 ventures where "messaging is the biggest challenge," as investor Chris Dixon pointed out. "There are a lot of misunderstandings around it, some of it is self-inflicted by the community. You have a lot of people who react negatively to crypto, which can lead to overzealous regulatory behavior."

In a startup, everything depends on selling, and selling depends on the right messaging. That's because customers only know how good your product is *after* they buy it. So to create demand for your product, you must find an effective way to communicate its unique value. "If you want success, be unique," as Net-a-Porter founder Natalie Massenet put it.

If your messaging works, as it does for SumUp, everything else gets easier. It's the difference between pushing a boulder up a hill and letting it roll down a hill. To achieve that, you not only need to know your customers, but really understand what is going on inside their heads. Specifically, you need to know what causes them pain. After all, our primary instinct as humans is to move away from pain and toward whatever makes the pain go away.

Many startups see some initial traction but hit a plateau after a while where growth slows down. It's a common problem as a company reaches beyond its initial customer base. If we really boil it down, there are only two possible reasons for this. Either your product does not appeal to enough people, or your message is not resonating. If your product isn't competitive, you want to fix that asap. It is absolutely crucial that your product or service is excellent. With very few exceptions (think Tamagotchi), the best communications in the world won't turn a turd into a success story. This can happen at any point: a startup can have product-market fit and then lose it. It can also have message-market fit and then lose it.

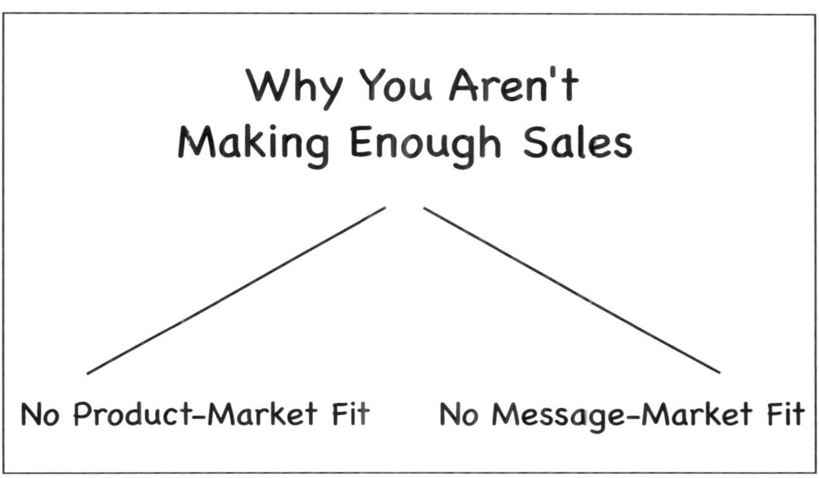

If your messaging falls on deaf ears at any point, it is probably because it is confusing, boring or otherwise ineffective. You may have also targeted the wrong people. Or you have targeted the right people, but you are looking for them on the wrong channels. We will tackle your channel strategy in Chapter 5. Our main concern right now is to get your messaging right, because if you don't, nothing else matters.

We see this a lot: a startup has a promising product, but it doesn't sell fast enough to scale or to satisfy its investors. Its dream customers don't understand the product or how it is relevant to them, so they won't even try it. If that problem isn't fixed, the company will eventually run out of runway. The good news is, this is a fixable problem, and it requires two steps. First, you need to nail your positioning. This gives you the right answers. Second, your messaging gives you the right words and puts your positioning into action.

THE RIGHT POSITIONING

The foundation of your messaging is your positioning. To determine their positioning, companies like to use positioning statements. These are a tool that aims to answer the central questions underpinning sales, marketing and brand building. The formula goes like this:

(product name) is a (product category) for (target audience) that (core benefit) by (unique differentiator) without (customer pain point).

For Google it may read like this:

Google is a search engine for everyone who uses the internet that helps people quickly find relevant information by having the best algorithms that deliver the fastest and most relevant results without clutter.

This approach is helpful to capture and clarify your current thinking. Since this format is hard to remember, does not trigger the best possible answers, and (let's be real) is too boring to convince anyone, you will need to go a step further. Effective positioning goes deeper and is more actionable.

In her book *Obviously Awesome,* April Dunford offers an improved approach to nail product positioning. Her process, which starts with the audience instead of the product, centers around six questions:

1. Competitive alternatives: What would your customers use, if you did not exist?
2. Unique attributes: What's special about your product?
3. Value: What value does your product unlock? How can you prove it?
4. Target audience: Who cares most about that value?
5. Market category: What is the best frame of reference to make your value obvious to target customers?
6. Trends: What makes your product relevant right now?

The answers to these questions can be captured in a one-page positioning canvas. (If you have several products, you want a positioning canvas for each of them.) This makes it memorable and easy to distribute throughout the organization. We are not going to go through each of the steps, as product positioning is a wide-ranging topic in itself and beyond the scope of this book. However, we want to shed some light on three out of the six elements above that are incredibly relevant from a messaging perspective: your uniqueness and value; your target audience; and your category.

Define Your Uniqueness and Value

"Strong positioning is centered on what a product does best," according to April Dunford. You want to isolate what makes you different and better. Specifically, her advice is to list all of the capabilities you offer that the alternatives do not. Your unique attributes can unlock value for a particular group of people. As discussed in Chapter 1, prospects will always wonder "What's in it for me?" In addition, you need third-party proof that your product does what it says in the sales deck. Your own opinion is irrelevant in the eyes of your prospects.

While your product may have numerous unique features, you want to focus on a small number to cut through. That number can and often should be one – your strongest, most unique attribute. Given that noisy world we live in where human attention is a scarce commodity, **focusing on your biggest differentiator can be very powerful**, provided your audience cares about it. Oliver lives near a place that has the best cinnamon buns in town. All their marketing and branding focuses on this delicious treat. The place is heaving because they manage to combine value (most delicious) and uniqueness (cinnamon buns). The other bakeries in the area offer much more choice but no clear differentiation. The same is true for the startup world, where unicorns like Uber, Ola, Grab, Airbnb and Wise have built on the 'sharing economy' model to combine value (cheaper and faster) and uniqueness (community).

Who is Your Target Audience?

We all think the world has been waiting for our company. The reality is, and we can't stress this enough: no one cares. In a highly competitive marketplace, **no one cares about you, your company or your product**. Of course there are exceptions, but, let's face it, nothing will ever be truly, completely new and so innovative that the world sees it only once. And even in that case, when you have invented the new thing, the northern lights on the product horizon, the Taj Mahal of services (congrats btw!), don't be fooled. Your product or service will be copied and put out on the market by others in a millisecond. Even if you patent and protect it. In any case, your message cannot stay for very long: *Hey, look at this, this is the newest, hottest, never ever seen before thing.* **You have to make them care.**

Before you can nail your positioning, you need to understand who cares most about your unique product and the value you create. Who owns the problem you solve, or feels it most intensely? That is your target. Think about real-life people, not just artificial avatars or personas. Try to get into their heads and think like them. Maybe you have had the same problem and figured out a way to solve it.

Consider your target customers' demographics (i.e. who they are; procurement manager, female, based in San Francisco,

30-ish) and – equally important but often neglected – their psychographics. The latter refers to what they feel. For instance, investment managers who may feel nervous about a pitch because their VC's investment committee rejected a string of companies they proposed.

If you truly know who your audience is, you can get an understanding of their internal and external pain points. You can then tell them how your product (or company) will make their pain go away. Pain killers (must have!) are easier to sell than vitamins (nice to have), especially in lean times.

Your customers usually have an external and an internal pain point, just like the hero in any story has an external challenge (evil villain) and an internal struggle (*am I good enough?*) to overcome before they transform into a better being. In a business context, external pain points are often related to financial pressures. *My company's sales are down this quarter!* is an external pain point. *My boss is breathing down my neck and my promotion is at stake* is an internal pain point. The latter are about the person and what drives or bothers them, not the company. These are often the more powerful motivators, although they are often not even mentioned by either side in the sales process. Understand these internal and external dynamics and you can craft messaging that hits a nerve.

People buy pain killers, not because they want to have them, but because they need them. **Customers don't buy what you are selling, they buy the outcome** – a problem solved, pain gone away. You'll remember in Chapter 2, we talked about investors in a very similar way – they want to buy the opportunity, not your product. One of the most famous quotes in marketing comes from Harvard Business School Professor

Theodore Levitt: “People don’t want to buy a quarter-inch drill. They want a quarter-inch hole!” Sounds plausible, but actually that’s not true either. Customers don’t want a hole in the wall. They want a picture on the wall. You may sell razor blades, but people buy a clean-cut look. People who buy life insurance don’t want life insurance (they will be dead when it pays out); they want security for their families.

Salesforce, for instance, is selling software. But the customers are not really buying a CRM. They are buying more sales. That’s why sales is part of the name. Everything they do is centered around the message *We help you sell more*. So even though they’re providing software, what their customers are really buying is revenue. And that’s how their brand and their company and the product are measured. Salesforce nailed its message early. The same principle applies to your startup. You center your message on the bigger issue or problem that your company tackles. Because that is what motivates your target customers to buy your product.

Once you have clarity about your customers and what they are buying from you, you can position your company or product in the most effective way. For that, you also need to grasp the market as well as the competitive landscape.

Market Category

Which market category you choose provides a frame of reference for your target market. You have three options: you can try to dominate an existing category; target a subcategory; or create a new category from scratch. Each of these has advantages and disadvantages.

An existing category may be crowded, but needs little explanation. Potential customers already understand why they need the kind of product you offer. Your focus would be on convincing them that your offer is significantly better. Email existed already, but Gmail went to market with the promise to improve it. The second option, dominating a subcategory, allows you to be more focused on your best-fit customers. Superhuman did not set out to convince everyone to switch email clients, but focused on one subcategory: email for busy high performers. You may also be able to build a better product because of your relentless focus on a subcategory that is secondary for the big guys.

The third option is to create and own an entire category, to occupy a space in your buyers' minds. Smartphones? Apple. Professional network? LinkedIn. Buy anything online? Amazon. Slack, for instance, did not attempt to improve email, but created a new category: a messaging program designed for the workplace. Category leadership is extremely powerful. However, companies following this approach need to educate people and explain why their offer is necessary in the first place. This can be challenging. Even if you dominate a category, you have to protect and continuously develop it. For years, Skype was synonymous with video calls. Now it has mostly been replaced. Grow with your category or become irrelevant.

So what should be your approach? Al and Laura Ries, in their (still relevant) 1998 book *22 Immutable Laws of Branding*, introduced the Law of Contraction: "A brand becomes stronger when you narrow the focus. A powerful branding always starts by contracting the category, not expanding it." Similarly, Peter Thiel pointed out in *Zero to One* that a startup should strive to dominate a niche and grow from there. Fast-growing startups are a master of one, not a master of none. That "one" can be a new niche or an existing subcategory.

Only expand once you dominate that part of the market. If you expand, it has to be gradual and logical. Google jeans? Starbucks software? Facebook fragrance? You don't need market research to know that these are stupid ideas. Yet the world of branding is littered with brand extension failures like Colgate frozen dinners and Harley-Davidson perfume.

Your positioning leads you to the right answers. Your messaging gives you the right words. Together they underpin your branding and marketing. It is not a one-way street though. Your marketing gives you valuable feedback on your positioning and messaging and tells you how to evolve. At easyJet, the early marketing simply stated that you could fly cheaply to a certain destination. At some point that stopped working, partly due to its own success. The public had internalized that flights had become more affordable. In response, the airline's messaging evolved to give people specific reasons to travel beyond a low price. The positioning also changed from "low-cost" to "best value-for-money" when the market became more crowded. Let's now turn your positioning into the right messaging.

NAILING YOUR MESSAGING

Your messaging brings your positioning to life. Many startups craft a Unique Value Proposition to capture what makes them special in one sentence. Here are some examples that helped to attract millions of customers:

- “Empowering the world to design” (Canva)
- “Payments infrastructure for the internet” (Stripe)
- “The platform commerce is built on.” (Shopify)

In Canva’s case, for instance, the Unique Value Proposition implies that you don’t need to be a designer to design with Canva. Rather than putting it that way, their UVP triggers curiosity and opens a conversation during which they can reveal specific attributes and the value they create. When crafting your own, keep in mind that the U stands for “unique”. Generic UVPs don’t work.

To elaborate further, explicitly answer the three fundamental questions any potential customer has on their minds in a single perfect paragraph:

1. What problem do you solve?
2. What’s your solution?
3. What’s the upside for me?

Plenty of businesses, and not just startups by the way, focus on the second question in their messaging and all but ignore the all-important first and third. If you skip the problem and offer your solution right away, your prospects lack context and probably don’t consider your offer to be relevant to them. They absolutely need to be reminded of the problem to consider your solution. The same is true for investors who will always ask what specific pain point your product addresses.

The answer to the last question tells the customer what result or transformation they can expect. Without spelling out the positive change they will see as a result of using your product or service, they may not give your offer a second thought. The transformation can help them overcome either their external or their internal problems. If it empowers them to overcome both, you are off to the races.

You may want to check if your current messaging addresses these points as convincingly as possible. Stating the problem, the solution and the positive outcome makes your offer relevant to your prospects. That's why this is the text you want to use on your website, in conversations and in your marketing. The whole team should know it by heart.

Create Your MUST-Have Offer

Once customers are curious and understand what you do, they will wonder how you do it. That's where your offer comes in. Weak offers are vague and interchangeable. A great offer is a MUST-have, meaning it is **M**easurable, **U**nique, **S**pecific and **T**rue, a concept developed by Mike Shreeves of Peaceful Profits. Show your prospects that their dream outcome is highly likely with your offer. Then address their concerns. Everyone worries that it will take a long time to get to that dream outcome, and that it will require a lot of time and effort on their part. Even if the promised outcome is appealing, few people are looking for another big project to take on. Delivering your offer shouldn't feel like a sales pitch but like a memorable conversation. Ideally it is prompted by the other person.

Great messaging takes your audience on a journey. Your UVP piques their curiosity, your perfect paragraph draws them in, and your MUST-have offer explains how your product works and what specific result they can expect. On top of that, you have your brand story which we discussed in the previous chapter.

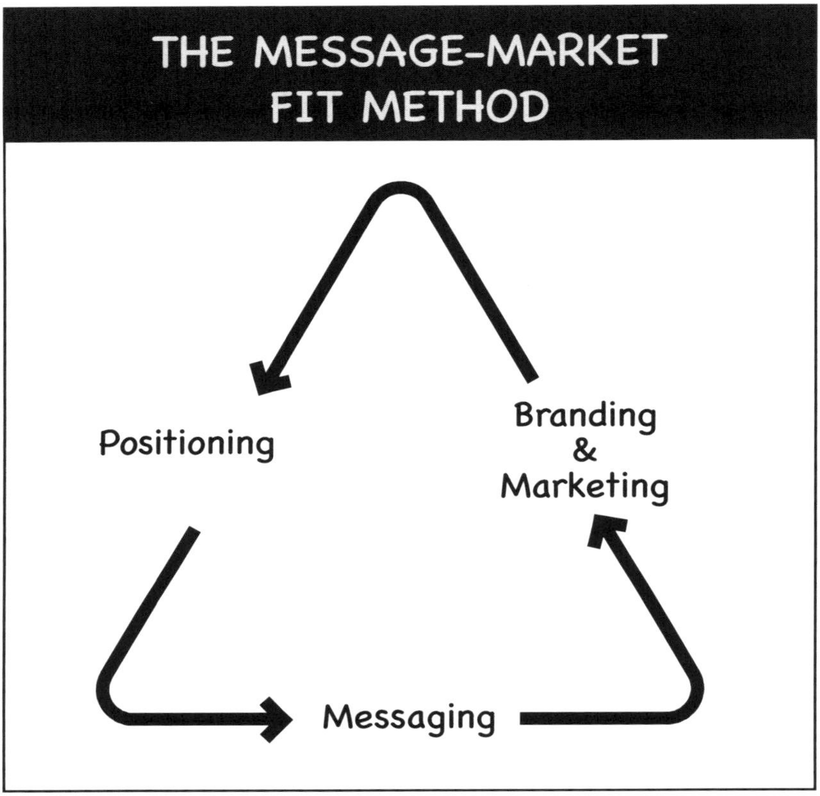

Your story makes your startup memorable and remarkable. Together, these elements form the backbone of your messaging. Everything else can, no *should,* be derived from them.

The Message-Market Fit Method brings these elements together. Your positioning gives you the right answers to these questions:

- What is unique?
- What value do we unlock?
- Who cares most?
- What's our category?

- Why now?

Your messaging provides the right words to bring your positioning to life:

- Unique Value Proposition
- Perfect Paragraph
- MUST-have offer
- Brand story

Your positioning and messaging feed into your branding and marketing, which in turn tell you if your positioning and messaging (still) work. This is how you get to message-market fit.

But: Many startups skip some of the steps, tackle them in the wrong order, or believe their marketing is not working when in fact the problem lies with the positioning or the messaging. All of this results in poor sales, often without understanding why.

If It Hurts, It Helps

Whether you're selling a can of tuna on a shelf in a retail environment, or you're having a conversation with a private equity investor looking to invest in your growth-stage company, or even if you're trying to poach a talented executive from a competitor to join your team, the same principles generally apply over the lifetime of the company and its products.

The message-market fit method is one of those principles. Message-market fit means that what you are creating is something that a certain segment of the market will crave, will pay good money for and will tell others about. Go out and test it.

Apply the same process you would apply to your product-market fit. Hypothesize, test and pivot. No one gets this right the first time. Having experience simply means that you may start with a better hypothesis. Start with friends, family, peers, co-founders. See what candid feedback you can elicit. If it hurts, it's probably useful. (We are not advocating violent communication here; just honest feedback, delivered with kindness.)

You can test your hypotheses by A/B-testing your website as well as social media ads. Then you move to split testing and applying the messaging in focus groups and real customer conversations. Throw a hypothesis into the room and let others discuss it without interacting with you directly. You will get more brutal and honest answers this way than from people that want to be nice to you or don't want to hurt your feelings when addressing you personally. This combination will tell you a lot about how to communicate your product, service or company so that it is perceived as "hot" or solving the problem best. **Identify what is working and double down on it.** Fortunately, beyond the seed stage you can increasingly rely on real-life data you have collected from your customers.

Stick to Your Message, Always

Once you are on the path to achieving message-market fit, you want to ensure that your whole organization executes it and becomes a fast-growing Message Machine. Your messaging should be codified in a single messaging document to ensure consistency. Message discipline is the ability to stick to your message, even when you're tired or frustrated. And it's one of the most important skills for founders—and for anyone else who wants to be heard in today's world.

When companies grow, many leaders struggle with maintaining message discipline across the organization. The key contributors to the company may be well informed, but as you work toward the edges of the organization and the end-nodes, they begin to realize how the bullet points from the all-hands meeting presentation aren't really having the desired effect. A good test is to have lunch with various employees who don't work in marketing and ask them what the company actually stands for. You might be surprised about the answers you get. This can usually be fixed by improving the messaging, and then repeating the message over and over until it sticks. And of course, keeping your ear to the ground.

It's therefore vital that founders spend time with all parts of the organization. We've seen some founders at growth- and late-stage companies take small groups of executives who don't directly report to them out for dinners each week. We've seen CEOs invite their direct reports for weekly breakfast meetings at their homes. Brian Chesky at Airbnb has been known to spend several evenings each week taking small groups of employees, including those that don't report to him directly, out for casual dinner. This way, the leaders keep their ears to the ground, and the rank and file get to hear the message and story directly from the decision-makers.

The most effective way to maintain message alignment is to have a single communications plan and a regular touchpoint to update it. These meetings provide the perfect trigger to discuss messaging. The following visual shows you what a one-page communications plan – often called a grid – can look like. Both of us first experienced the effects of the grid when working in political communications. Alastair Campbell, who was British Prime Minister Tony Blair's communications chief, famously used them to coordinate announcements across various government departments. He told us of how "[they] thought of communications in the context of supply and demand." His job was to regulate who was saying what, to who, and when. The 'grid' was invaluable in helping the government communications team to first easily visualize, and then maintain a stranglehold on the supply of high-quality information that news organizations demanded from dozens of government departments and hundreds of communicators.

Today, many organizations use simple one-pagers like this to ensure everyone is aligned on strategy, content and timing when speaking to internal, external and financial audiences. It also grants the chief communicator a birds-eye view of everything that's going out at any time. You can use weeks or months as your timeline, and use it as a basis for discussion in your regular all-hands and editorial meetings. For early-stage companies, a monthly grid makes sense as there is less to announce. More mature businesses are better served by weekly plans like this one.

Message alignment and discipline are probably the most important factors in achieving success within a fundraising context. In our experience, far too many founders fail to recognize how their messaging is interconnected, or worse, isn't actually aligned across the different faces and functions of the company. The most compelling fundraising narratives are the relationships between different data points, and not the presentation of specific data points themselves. Take a

COMMUNICATIONS GRID

	Monday	Tuesday	Wednesday	Thursday	Friday
All-hands	Topic: Q2 results				
Slack		Share team offside info			Announce new partnership
PR			CEO interview with Sifted		
LinkedIn		Employer branding post			Announce new partnership
Investor	CFO investor calls re Q2			Leadership dinner with investors	

company that positions itself as a provider to large enterprises, with complex decision-making structures and likely long sales cycles. If the pricing page on its website shows its products sold at a price-point that's more suited to individuals, then it's likely a potential buyer sitting in a swanky corporate office will pass on your offer. They may easily come to the conclusion that your company is new to selling to enterprise customers, and as such could be pushed for discounts. You probably need them more than they need you.

It's even clearer for an investor to see the lack of alignment within the organization. This may be acceptable for a very early pre-seed company, but tolerance will wear thin for a company that has already raised money and has an executive leadership team in place.

ASSESSING MESSAGE-MARKET FIT

We are often asked whether it is possible to measure message-market fit. Unfortunately we can't offer you a single MMF Score, mostly because your messaging needs to work with your internal, external and financial audiences, and what they expect is constantly shifting. However, there are a number of proxies and metrics that tell you if you have message-market fit at the various stages of your company. These become more qualitative as your company grows.

It's no coincidence that trust is the emotion that is most highly correlated with evidence of message-market fit. Both are easiest to track via a series of qualitative signals and proxies familiar to most metrics-driven organizations. Similar to trust, as you build a track record of validating the hypotheses your business is built on, you'll find MMF increasing.

The Early Stages: Exposing Passion

The important work you do as a communicator in the early days of your startup's existence will give shape to the organization in years to come. If you ensure that the organization is already striving for message-market fit in the earliest stage, it'll be imprinted within the company's DNA and noticeable later on.

In the earlier stages of a company's existence, you could even think of it as more like 'Vision-Market Fit.' Early stage companies start with a spark of passion, like the founders of SumUp who went from door to door to promote their card reader. Passion – or the absence of it – comes across in the words you use and the demeanor of each and every person who works at the company. In the early stages, startups rely heavily on passion as they have yet to build proficiency. You want to hold on to that passion while you are becoming more competent as a business rather than exchanging it for competence. Highly successful, mature ventures are both competent and passionate.

Without exception, it's always the CEO and leader of the organization who sets the tone and acts as the lead driver of the company in its search for message-market fit. Simply put, no one else has the authority. This is not about being a great speaker or a natural communicator. It is about the CEO compelling the entire organization to take the search for MMF seriously. The future of the business depends on it, so the CEO needs to own it.

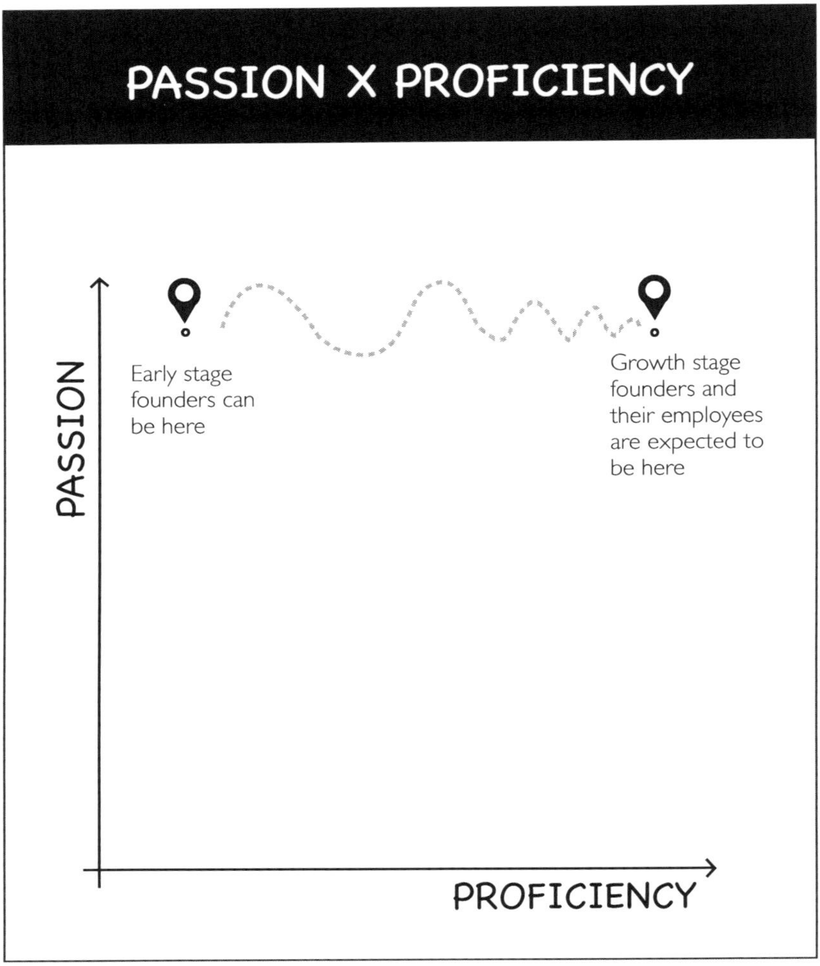

This is most obvious when it comes to investor interest. It is a strong indicator for whether or not a startup gets its messaging right. After all, investors have not got much more to go on, apart from the track record of the team.

Audience engagement metrics that essentially focus on when and how your team and your customers are engaging with your messaging are most crucial. The two we recommend tracking are message reach and message adoption rate. If your key messages actually reach your intended internal, external and financial audiences, and if a significant chunk of those audiences can either repeat those messages back to you or take timely actions, then you're on your way to message-market fit.

Engagement and pulse surveys, one-on-one meetings and interviews are the primary ways of measuring message-market fit for early stage companies. Our rule of thumb: if you think you're not doing a good job of striving for MMF, then you probably really should spend a bit more time on it.

In the early days, this is usually not all that scientific. Sabrina Kelly, the Chief Talent Officer at WhoCo once told us "you can usually see if your co-founders or the few employees you have interact with the content you put out, or if they're just skimming past it. You always want to track interaction and engagement rates. When you have fifteen employees, you can usually just look at people's faces to figure this out – you don't need fancy analytics software."

The Growth and Late Stages

As the organization grows, the metrics used to signal MMF become more quantitative in nature, and you'll also likely have more financially-grounded metrics that indicate message-market fit. In organizations that are only just beginning to scale, the CEO must still own this function, even if they likely have a dedicated person on the team who can further drive change. The plethora of metrics, and the tools used to track them all, can be overwhelming. It's also at this point that agencies and

MESSAGE-MARKET FIT METRICS

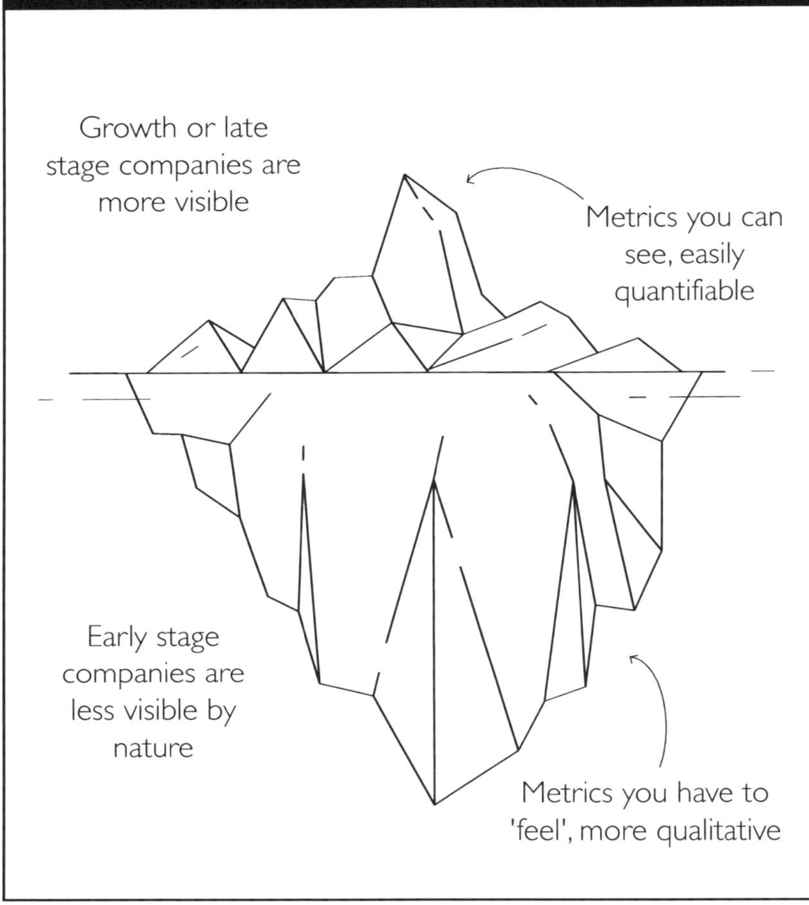

external advisors really begin to deliver value, though we still can't recommend entirely outsourcing this process.

Measures of narrative alignment, engagement rates, employee feedback and cohort retention (i.e. the percentage of users who have been retained until a certain day) also start to become easier to track at this stage. You'll want to start looking at how specific messages cascade through departments, or in new markets as you launch them. External validation also becomes more pronounced. You know there's cut-through when investors and specialist trade publications start repeating the new (sub-)category you've created.

Roles like SVP of Communications or VP of Marketing will take a lot more ownership of improving your MMF in growth and later-stage companies. They'll be coordinating across teams, and will find that the other business units like Finance and People will contribute to their efforts to maintain message-market fit.

They'll also be able to measure how behaviors and attitudes shift. Metrics like Net Promoter Score, employee turnover and financial performance are the indicators of message-market fit. If you continue to improve it, you will notice increasing inbound approaches from media, talent, investors and customers as a result.

Everything needs to line up for a startup to be successful. The perfect positioning executed with clumsy messaging won't allow you to scale. Nor will the wrong positioning combined with great messaging do the trick. But with the right positioning AND the right words to bring it to life, you can unlock growth. This unlocking is what we will turn to now. The following three chapters will give you all the principles you need for your branding, for your marketing and for gaining visibility through PR and other channels.

MESSAGE-MARKET FIT SIGNALS

	Internal	External	Financial
Early Stage	- People other than the CEO can tell the story and pitch the product.	- Word of mouth referral rates increase seemingly on their own. - You start to understand where you stand in the "different vs better" debate (category building).	- Investors start to ask about you. It means they can explain what you do to other investors.
Growth Stage	- Improving employee feedback - You are able to attract 'mercenaries' instead of mostly 'missionaries.' - HR metrics like employee turnover become measurable. It's not a bad thing to have to terminate the employment if there isn't a both-way fit.	- Customer feedback and NPS improvement - Cohort retention - Category evangelization efforts start to pay off. - Early stage startups begin to include your logo in their decks, painting you as the 'enemy.'	- Meaningful revenue growth, which also translates into increased investor interest with pre-emptive offers to invest.
Late Stage	- High audience engagement	- Positive reputation metrics - Category domination	- Investor & analyst interest

Chapter 4

BUILDING YOUR BRANDS

"People underestimate the power of brands. It's a lie we tell ourselves," according to entrepreneur and NYU Marketing Professor Scott Galloway. "Branded beer tastes better than non-branded beer. Allergy medication is more effective after you watch branded advertisements. Labradoodle vs. Labrador, Star Wars vs. Dragon Ball, iOS vs. Android, NYU vs. Columbia — we are a tribal species, and we sort ourselves with logos."

Brands are such a constant presence in our lives, we seldom marvel at the mystery of it. Like gravity, a brand is always there. You cannot touch or see it but you definitely can feel it. And you can approximate its impact. Perhaps unsurprisingly, 2021 saw Amazon top the list of the world's most valuable brands with an estimated brand value of $684 billion, followed closely by Apple ($612 billion). It is not an exact science but the enormous value of a brand for a business is undeniable.

This chapter focuses on growing your brands - company, product and personal. Consistency builds brands, and once you have built and earned them, they are incredibly valuable. If you have a strong brand, you can charge more for your product or service and generate higher margins. You attract top talent, sell more and find it easier to grow your company. Your product may be a t-shirt that you sell for $10. If you brand the t-shirt well, you might be able to sell it for 2x or 3x, maybe even 20x the original price. **People don't buy the product, they buy what it stands for. The brand. The values. The status.**

Brands radiate towards customers, but also to investors, employees, the media and talent – in fact, all of your internal, external and financial stakeholders. A strong brand helps you to win them over and then retain them, as being associated with your company brings status, opportunities and emotional gains. The bottom line is: you build brands for your bottom line. You build them every day as you build your company, and you want to do it with great intentionality.

What is a Brand?

"A logo and a misspelled word do not make a brand", writes British entrepreneur Tom Hodgkinson. Instead, a brand is what others think about you. There are dozens of definitions of *brand,* but we prefer this one: **your brand is the personality of your business**. As with your own personality, you can shape it but you can't control it.

Your brand is partly created by how you present your company to the world, and partly earned through consistent action. You control the first part. The second part is harder to control, because what matters is the perception others have of you. You may think that you offer great customer service, but if your customers disagree, bad customer service becomes part of your brand. Everything impacts the perception of your brand, from how your employees behave to the way pricing information is displayed on your website to your marketing. Let's say we have a person in business attire selling the product versus a teenager on a skateboard. That has an impact on how a customer thinks about the price and ultimately the brand.

Brands work because they make people feel a certain way. To coin Maya Angelou's phrase, **no one remembers what you told them, but everyone remembers how you made them feel**. If your brand focuses only on the product or service, people will not see a reason to engage. So whenever people come across your company, product or service, your brand should trigger certain emotions and intangible associations by design. It also works in the other direction. Customers come for the product, like it and then stay faithful to the brand. Many people bought the first iPhone for its design and functionality and have since remained loyal customers willing to pay a premium for the brand.

Whilst brands are not rational, they are being rationalized by their fans who are able to give rational-sounding arguments for their emotional choices. Therefore, a smart brand both elicits emotions and provides rational arguments, winning hearts and brains. Even if we can rationally explain why we choose certain brands over others, we simply justify our emotions. A central question for any brand is therefore: What emotions should it trigger? Do you want your customers to feel safe and secure, because your car scores high on safety? Do you want to convey status? Do you want it to make someone feel special or maverick-like?

If you do not have a strong brand, you have to compete on something else. That could be the price. That's a difficult game to win, as you then have to compete with larger businesses with lower unit costs. You could also compete on product and build something superior to anything on the market. But how would customers even discover it? It is possible, but it definitely makes your life harder. The graveyard of failed companies is full of startups that built superior products. What you want to do is build a great product and a great brand at the same time and get it all into the hands of customers. “Businesses survive. Brands thrive. A brand is the best defense to commoditization,” notes entrepreneur and author M.J. Demarco.

Belief Brands vs Promise Brands

There are three types of brands: company brands, product brands and personal brands. There are advantages to building your brand around your company rather than your product, because your products are likely to change over time. Most early-stage startups build one product anyway, so the company and product brands are identical. As a founder, your personal brand matters as well. In a world oversaturated by products and services, consumers want to support the individuals whose values or ideals they share. That’s a huge opportunity that we discuss later in this chapter.

Let’s focus on company and product brands first. These brands fall into one of two categories: belief brands and promise brands. Promise brands make promises in order to sell products. For example, *this shampoo will give you shiny hair.* Belief brands, on the other hand, ask their customers to buy into a belief system before introducing the products. Disruptor brands like Oatly have gained a dedicated following by articulating their beliefs, stating that “our sole purpose as a company is to make it easy for people to turn what they eat and drink into personal moments of healthy joy without recklessly taxing the planet's resources in the process." And the oat milk manufacturer does it in a quirky way via packaging and messaging. This has won them many customers and celebrity investors such as Oprah and Jay-Z. Meanwhile, many of the traditional brands are losing support as a result of their failure or unwillingness to transition to more purpose-driven practices.

Belief brands like Patagonia follow their purpose. They make reconciling the textiles industry with environmental protection their North Star. Recently, Patagonia founder Yves Chouinard even handed over the whole company to a trust to promote conservation. This dedication triggers strong emotions and makes them different. Those kinds of brands work extremely well, because they stand out and attract loyal fans and customers.

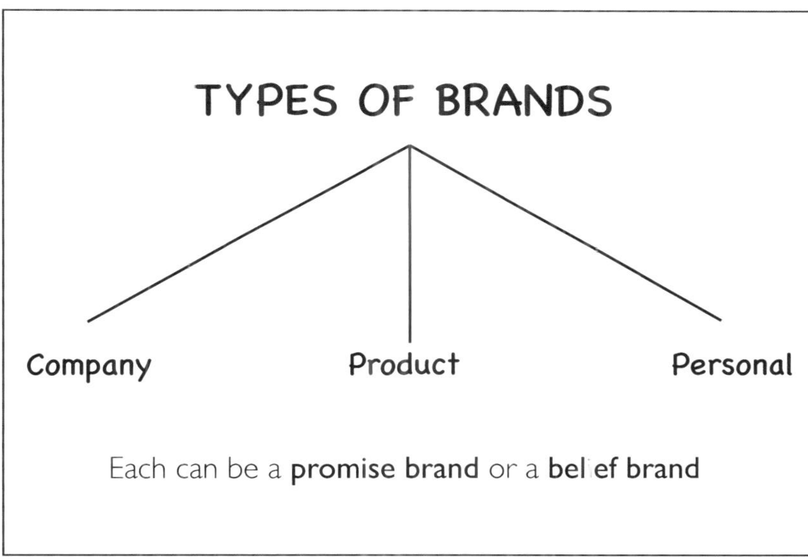

There's nothing wrong with building a business that promises to deliver the goods. But belief brands are stronger than promise brands – if their purpose is genuine. Don't be tempted to invent a purpose. Do Snapchat filters really make the world a better place because they make someone smile for a second each day? Your audience will see through any self-serving BS.

Branding Means Differentiation

The goal of branding is to occupy a category in your customers' minds. Hence **branding means differentiation**. If you want to be remarked upon, be remarkable. If you want stories to be told about you, be worthy of a story. In a sea of me-too brands, we sometimes forget that. In any market, the tendency is for brands to converge or to emulate the leader. But if a brand is just like the others in the space, it's weak and forgettable. Big incumbents can sometimes get away with that, but only because they have market power and because they spent millions to get their brand in front of customers (aka advertising).

As a startup, you do not have the luxury of a bland brand. Homogeneity is your enemy. "All human beings ignore what is average, and discuss what is different. Competency doesn't create conversation," write Stan Phelps and David Rendall in *P!nk Goldfish 2.0*. As a startup, you want to cultivate what makes you different.

How important your brand is depends on the stage and type of your business. Investors don't see branding as crucial in the first few years for B2B companies. For direct-to-consumer businesses, branding can be a difference-maker from the get-go. "Liquid Death is killing it," writes The Hustle. "It's a business idea so silly you might just laugh at it: canned water with punk-rock branding. Oh yeah, and it's called Liquid Death. But that silly little brand is laughing all the way to the bank: Three years after launch, the company just raised $70m at a valuation of $700m."

Gymshark is another scale-up that's killing it in a crowded space thanks to its branding. Its humble origins lie in a garage in Birmingham, UK. In 2012, 19-year-old founder Ben Francis set out to conquer the crowded sports apparel market, armed with only a sewing machine and screen-printer. He spotted a niche that balanced style with functionality. Unlike other athletic apparel companies, the brand's sole focus is on the gym crowd. "Today," says Ben Francis, "we create the tools that help everyone become their personal best: the clothing you'll sweat in, the content you'll find inspiration in and the community you'll become your best in." He is now the head of a global billion-dollar brand with a huge social media following. This could never have happened with an accidental brand. Let's be clear: undifferentiated brands are over. If you don't stand out, you won't stand a chance.

FROM ACCIDENTAL TO INTENTIONAL BRAND

Branding becomes more relevant over time, in particular for B2B companies. As you build your company every day, you also build your brand every day. The two are inseparable. Every step your company takes (backward, forward, sideways), your brand needs to follow in lock step. The Uber of today is not the

Ubercab that started in 2009; Meta rebranded nearly 10 years after Facebook's IPO; Google – now Alphabet (XYZ) – rebranded for primarily financial and corporate reasons; FreightHub became Forto; AirBednBreakfast became Airbnb. Chances are that beyond Series A or B, you may also have to rebrand or at least pivot your brand.

The main reason is that many founders start out with more or less accidental brands due to a lack of time, funds or knowledge of branding. This is completely understandable, especially if you target enterprise customers. At some point, however, you realize that you need to build a strong, differentiated brand to unlock further growth, whether you keep the name or not. But how?

The process of creating a Minimum Viable Product follows this formula:

Product = product hypothesis + customer feedback

Similarly, you may still use a Minimum Viable Brand (MVB) that was created at the very beginning in a similar fashion. Now you want your brand to become the vessel that carries your message and ensures it is present even when you are not in the room. You want it to be memorable (by being different) and thus encourage recognition and word of mouth. You want to make it matter. Enterprise companies like Twilio, Hubspot and Dropbox are brands that have been through this process and have therefore become more intentional and relevant over time.

Twilio launched in 2008 as a product that enabled developers to build applications that could make and receive phone calls with web services. They called it the Web Service API for building Voice Applications. Today, Twilio is a publicly listed company worth tens of billions of dollars. That first product is now called Twilio Voice, and is just one part of a suite that includes 70 others trusted by more than ten million developers worldwide. The company used its brand to market itself to both business buyers and developers, tying everything from the name of their annual conference ('Signal') to their 'State of Customer Engagement' report – where they survey both customers and non-customers about what's relevant to them – to their vision of offering a product or service that makes developers' lives better.

To create an intentional brand, apply the following formula:

Brand = organizing idea + customer feedback

Your organizing idea is a big idea that captures the essence of what you stand for and that you can rally your company around. The first question you need to answer to find your organizing idea is why do we exist? Ask people outside of the company how they would feel if you didn't exist. And now that you do exist, how does that make them feel? And once you've delivered your product or your service, how does that make them feel? You want more answers: What does your brand stand for? Which emotions do you want to trigger? What aspirations do you want to convey? What do you want to be associated with your brand? Is it serious? Is it youthful? Is it premium? How is it different? Phil Rumbol, a CEO with 30 years experience in branding and marketing sums it up perfectly: "**Find the organizing idea of your brand and make it matter.**" Twilio's organizing idea is to help developers make voice applications as easy to set up and maintain as web applications.

Keep in mind that the brand is defined by the whole customer experience, so your brand identity should be reflected by your name, logo, website, color palette, visual identity, PR, customer service and so on. Don't assume you know. Keep asking your customers for feedback. You will at first have a bunch of sentences that might not make sense. But if you aggregate that, you're going to find that your brand already exists in your customers' minds. Your job is to build on what's working, to strengthen and to improve the brand.

You want to follow an approach that captures both qualitative and quantitative feedback. You can get quantitative data by running split tests or questions in a multiple-choice style with clear answers or yes/no options. And you want qualitative analyses from talking to customers. This combination can give you not just data, but knowledge. Customers can tell you why they do or don't like something, data can't.

Brands are Constantly in Motion

Communications are the opposite of one-and-done: you iterate, iterate, iterate. You may start with ten potential customers, ask for their input, then iterate, come up with a better hypothesis of what your brand should look like and ask another ten to twenty. And you keep going until you've received enough data to have confidence in getting started and going to market with that brand before the cycle repeats. Start with the less relevant prospects before you approach your dream customers, as it will take a while before your brand is as appealing as possible.

Brands evolve, and sometimes decisions even need to be reversed. Stay flexible and design your brand to be malleable enough to adapt to a new market when you spot the opportunity or if your initial market isn't the right one. Market here can be a completely different demographic, segment of the population, country, geography or even a consumer group with different price sensitivity.

Nugget makes modular sofas. It was originally marketed to young people going off to college who needed a small couch in their dorm rooms. Essentially, they sold pieces of foam. Whilst they were marketing it to young adults as their first couch, the market that really picked this up was parents who wanted a play area for their younger kids. The modular aspect of these sofas meant that kids could build forts and slides out of them. So, all that was required was a slight softening of the brand – changing some of the colors and using a few new words to describe how this product could be used for the company to make 100 times more revenue. This happened in the span of nine months. Don't be so tied to your initial idea that you lose sight of opportunities on the periphery that may just seem so marginal to begin with, but could end up completely reshaping your business. Keep an open mind about who your customer actually is.

Adapting Your Brand As You Grow

Repositioning a brand is one thing, rebranding is quite another. Rebranding a company or introducing a new product brand is a major pain point for many startups. The bigger you are, the more is at stake. It's not unusual though. Larry Page and Sergey Brin intended to call their search engine BackRub as a reference to "back links". The name lasted less than a year, and "Google" was trademarked on September 15, 1997. Caleb Davis Bradham invented an overnight sensation which he called Brad's Drink. Five years later, he rebranded because he believed it was a health drink that helped with indigestion, also known as dyspepsia. And so Pepsi-Cola was born in 1898. Amazon was originally named Cadabra by Jeff Bezos, a shortened version of 'abracadabra'. The name lost its shine when a lawyer mistook it for 'cadaver'. Bezos also briefly toyed with the name Relentless, but was told it had a sinister ring to it (it does). The Swedish alcohol brand Absolut Vodka was originally known as 'Absolute Pure Vodka.' Since common adjectives aren't suited for trademarks, the word Absolute changed to Absolut, also as an homage to its Swedish background. The word "pure" was left out for the same reason.

You get the point: lots of companies rebrand. Unfortunately naming your company or product is not straightforward. Most good names have been taken. You may have an idea but the URL costs a fortune, or you may not be able to trademark the name. The pressure is on to come up with something really clever. Where do you even start?

Firstly, put yourself in the right mindset. Creating a brand should be fun. At this stage, you are merely experimenting. Secondly, don't do it in isolation. Brainstorm with your co-founders, colleagues or external branding experts. Keep the input circle large but the decision circle small. A brand is not a democracy, and big groups tend to agree on bland brands.

Thirdly, take a look at what the competition and companies in other sectors are doing. Not to copy them, as you want to be different, but for words or phrases that trigger your creativity.

Start by coming up with words and phrases that you think best encompass your brand as well as feelings you want to elicit. The broader the better. This way you will also identify what kind of name is not on the table because it elicits the wrong associations. Adjectives in particular are excellent triggers. These help you establish the direction you want to take. Over time, you narrow it down to a few words or phrases that sound right. You need to trust your gut, because brands are centered on emotions, not facts. If it feels wrong, it probably is. Given the importance of search engines, you want your brand name to be remembered and spelled easily. You also want to avoid a name that makes it impossible to find you when people search for you online, which can happen if you use common words.

Should a Brand Be Obvious?

When it comes to naming your company or product, there are two schools of thought. One argues that your brand name has to imply what your product or service does. Salesforce, Shopify, Facebook, Instagram - all use existing words in their brand names. The advantage is that you don't have to fill words with meaning but tap into associations we already have. It's a short leap from "Shopify" to e-commerce software.

The second approach is to fill unrelated words with meaning to create an emotional connection between company and audience. The founders of Apple managed to link their products with the idea of being and thinking differently. Now check out the competition at the time: HP, IBM, Dell, Microsoft – these either refer to the names of the founders or describe the company in technical words. It was immediately obvious that Apple was different. The same goes for Tesla, Google, Alibaba and Amazon. These words or names existed, but the companies filled them with new meaning. Taken to its logical conclusion, you can also create words that do not exist and try to own that phonological space.

In the summer of 2003, a Swede, a Dane and four Estonians launched their telecommunications product that reduced the cost of voice calls to virtually nothing, by using a P2P protocol that had previously been used for file-sharing. This product would go on to revolutionize the telecoms industry, and was initially launched as Sky Peer to Peer. Unfortunately, it felt rather long, and was then abbreviated to Skyper. Janus Friiz, one of the founders (the Dane), explains it like this: "But as happens in the Internet world, some of the domain names associated with *skyper* were already taken, so they thought what the heck, let's just drop the *r* and make it *Skype*. It sounded good and the domains were available. Initially the name didn't make sense to many people. Probably still doesn't."

There is no right or wrong here as these examples show. However, there is a clear advantage for a startup to go for a pretty self-explanatory name. If it is immediately obvious what you do, you don't have to spend time, money and energy explaining this to customers. Big brands spend millions to get themselves in front of customers. You do not have that luxury. Dollar Shave Club became a billion dollar company partly because the name is the message.

Before you decide to move forward, you want to carry out a number of checks. Make sure that your brand name isn't taken, and that it is not copyright protected or trademarked in any relevant market. You don't want to receive a cease-and-desist letter from a bigger company after launch that forces you to rebrand. Ensure that the URLs and social media handles are available, partly because you want to have them, and partly because you want to avoid confusion. You may not find that easy anymore. This is why many companies go for artificial words or known words with weird spelling.

Connotations are key for brands, so you want to avoid a brand name that triggers the wrong emotions or associations. Words mean different things to different people though, so ensure that you include a diverse group of people with regard to gender, age, background and mother tongue. Check on social media, the Urban Dictionary (for slang), in different languages and on Google. A friend of Oliver's once inadvertently created a brand name that means "small p*nis" in Dutch. Spoiler: The company failed.

Ask customers what connotations they think of. Not just whether they like your brand or not, but what kind of ideas they would naturally associate with the brand name. Is it confusing? Does it remind them of an existing brand? Do they have the same connotations as you? If you believe your brand stands for being different but your customers give you the feedback that it sounds conformist, you're on the wrong path and need to rethink.

Your customers will not think consciously about your brand. They will not spend precious cognitive energy to understand what you're trying to tell and sell them. **It needs to be**

immediately obvious. That's why emotions are so important in the branding game – because of the time people give a brand. If you are lucky, your target audience gives you enough time to elicit emotions. They won't spend their precious time thinking about you consciously.

When Everyone Has an Opinion, Show Leadership

You have developed a brand hypothesis and tested it with your target audience. Chances are you have gained some valuable data, clarity and understanding of your brand, but there is still uncertainty – just like your MVP. In that case, it is up to the founders to take a decision, commit to it, and move forward. When you enter the market, a brand is better than no brand. You need to give the company direction when it comes to product, and it's the same for your brand.

In many startups, the founders are focused on the product, the technology or sales. Someone else on the team is tasked with all things relating to branding. This person needs to have a clear brief from the leadership team. It's fine to delegate it to someone to come up with ideas, but of course, the CEO and all the C-levels need to be involved in the process. If it is your company, the brand is too important to leave it up to someone else.

The situation often arises where three people have different ideas and views about the direction of the brand. None of them can rationally show why their ideas are better than the other ones. You need data. At the same time, you should not follow customer feedback like a slave. No one understands better what the company is about and what your values are than the founders. Not your team, not your customers. Gain their input and insights, and then make a decision.

GROWING YOUR BRAND

Every startup wants to grow its brand to win more customers. There are many things you could do, but there are only a handful that are truly effective. These are:

- Consistently delivering a great product or service that goes beyond what is expected
- Delivering a consistent message and that matters to your audience
- Having a clearly positioned and differentiated brand

We've already said this, but it is worth repeating: Any successful business needs to be different from its competitors. Creating a meaningful distinction between you and the competition is the objective of branding.

In her book *Different*, Harvard professor Youngme Moon highlights three strategies startups can employ to differentiate their business and brand:

1. Reversal: do the opposite of what everyone else does
2. Breakaway: do something completely different
3. Hostility: be a rebel

VEJA Sneakers reversed the apparel industry playbook by creating sustainable, vegan, ethically-produced sneakers and selling them without the industry's most important traction channel: paid ads. They don't do ads because 70% of the cost of a normal big sneaker brand is related to advertising. A pair of VEJA costs five to seven times as much to produce, but since there are no advertising costs, they can be sold for the same price. The VEJA founders believe transparency is more effective than advertising. The France-based footwear brand now has a presence in over fifty countries and has sold two million pairs of their sleek sneakers since their inception in 2004 — all without advertising, and by focusing on the brand story.

While VEJA's no-ad sustainable strategy is based on doing the opposite of other brands, Netflix is a textbook example of a breakaway company that chose to do something entirely different. As a result, they upended the entire movie and TV industry. Their breakaway idea was to mail DVDs to customers at a time when film lovers were expected to go to a rental store if they wanted to watch a movie. They then added another breakaway idea. Netflix moved away from familiar movie rental methods and gave customers access to a streaming platform where they could watch movies and TV shows from their computers (and later TVs). Today, Netflix dominates the streaming sector and most people will consider a Netflix account a must, not to mention the emergence of the term "Netflix and Chill".

Rebels take it a step further. They are deliberately obnoxious, controversial or aggressive. If done right, the public starts rooting for the underdog, which is a great story. If done wrong, you alienate your audience. Positioning yourself as a rebel, challenger or underdog means being in the firing line of the incumbents. This can work in your favor, if the consumer realizes you are the David to the market's Goliath. Richard Branson perfected this approach, taking on the dinosaurs in the music, airline and insurance industries. Europe's two largest low-cost airlines, Ryanair and easyJet, also followed this approach, albeit in different styles.

Both aggressively positioned themselves as challengers, strategically picking fights with incumbent airlines. For easyJet, where Oliver headed communications during the scale-up phase, that meant fighting the consumers' corner against the former monopolist flag carriers. For Ryanair, the only thing that mattered was the lowest price possible, even if that meant treating their customers like an afterthought. The two airlines evolved at the same time. Both picked fights with the big incumbents. Both targeted similar markets but had very different communications strategies and message-market fits. One airline tried to put a smile on passengers' faces. The other announced its intention to charge customers for using the lavatories, because it drove home their core message: "We are the cheapest." It was infuriating, even to their own customers. It was infuriating by design.

Being controversial can be a smart choice to make a name for yourself, if it is genuine, intentional and follows a strategy. You must fight for a cause or your customers, not for yourself, and the target of the aggression must be a big, unpopular company that rips people off – a classic bully. Alternatively, it can be a problem like climate change that is attacked as a villain. That's a brand story that resonates. But: If you are building a luxury brand or business that conveys status, this is not the right strategy for you. Playing the underdog or rebel creates connectedness. It does not signal status.

Risky Business

A brand is a living, breathing creature. As a founder, you are its guardian. As Warren Buffett said: “It takes 20 years to build a reputation and five minutes to ruin it. If you think about that, you’ll do things differently.”

You need to monitor and observe it over the entire lifetime of your company as your customers and the market matures. How does your brand also need to mature? Think about Google’s logo when it came out, it was literally a squiggly cartoon. But as they started selling to larger enterprises, they changed the logo. The font experts we asked suggested that Google’s approach of simplifying colors and designs as the company grew older was in part to offer a fresh-faced and welcoming feel when the web had become more stand-offish. Google’s brand changed how they could speak about the company, and its place in the world. They not only changed how they projected their visual identity, but also how they used all the assets or all the components that comprised the brand.

For your brand to thrive, your acts must match your values and your story. If they don’t, you’ll lose control over your own brand. **In branding, perception is reality.** If your customers believe your brand is boring, then it is. It doesn’t matter what you think. For instance, bad customer service is a liability in itself, but if you make the customer the hero or heroine of your story, your customer service better treat them with respect. Similarly, accusations of whitewashing, greenwashing and pinkwashing can arise if your actions don't match your brand story. Patagonia collaborating with a company that is chopping down the Amazon? A pride campaign going hand-in-hand with discrimination suits? In today's ultra-transparent world, you better walk the talk.

Like many companies, Oatly found this out the hard way. When the cuddly oat milk manufacturer announced an investment by controversial US fund BlackRock, Oatly's fans considered it to be treason to the cause. While Oatly survived the blow to its image, in the eyes of their customers they had lost their innocence.

Situations like these can develop into a fully-fledged reputational crisis that makes or breaks a company. We'll dive deeper into the fun topic of how to manage a crisis (which will eventually hit you too) in Chapter 9. For now, just remember that the easiest brands to build are the ones that are truthful. The same applies to personal brands. As a founder, do you believe you should have a high profile?

PERSONAL BRANDING

Founders often ask us if they should build a personal brand. As Oliver has argued in his previous book *Unignorable*, there are a lot of advantages to it – as long as it is done to help the company, and not for one's own ego. If it supports the business, as it often does, it is perfectly legitimate to invest time and resources into this area – provided the CEO or founder has the skills, bandwidth and infrastructure to do it.

"Personal brand" is an emotional term for some. It elicits all kinds of images. Actually, it is nothing but a reputation that is being taken care of. Since we all have a reputation, it does make sense to take control of it. If you don't, a vacuum exists that other people will fill for you. And that may not be the story you want to tell.

There are good reasons to take charge of your reputation and build a personal brand. There's a battle raging for our attention which makes it very hard for any company to stand out. We all get bombarded by 10,000+ ads and messages from companies on any given day, almost all of which we ignore. In this environment, having an authentic, credible messenger who stands out is an asset for any startup.

The CEO's reputation now accounts for 58% of a company's overall reputation. **People want to hear from people, and they trust people more than companies or brands**. This is particularly true on social media, which thrives on human-to-human (H2H) communication. It explains the rise of influencers and "social CEOs", i.e. business leaders who are very active on social media. Spanx's Sara Blakely, serial fintech entrepreneur Miriam Wohlfahrt and investor Kevin Rose are winning on social media. Look at any startup and you see that CEOs who are active have more followers than the company. Startups are in a great position to capitalize on our desire for personal connection. They often have inspirational leaders and are less constrained in their tone and messaging than listed companies. In our experience, it's precisely the founders who are most interesting offline who are also the most interesting online.

Money follows attention. If you are visible as a founder, you attract more investors, customers and talent. Even your company's valuation is likely to benefit. Studies have shown that a significant share of a company's market value is attributable to the reputation of its leadership, in particular the CEO. And for the CEO personally, there are advantages to being harder to replace, for instance in a negotiation or during a merger.

There is a flip side though. Investors have a love-hate relationship with inflated egos, which are often part of strong brands. This is because it becomes a challenge of succession planning and management on the one hand, and a corporate profitability issue on the other. If a very strong founder can threaten to leave, thereby taking a big chunk of the business with them, investors would lose out. Investors want to exercise control, not all the time, but when the time comes. Thus, an uncontrollable founder represents the difference between an investment that can be saved and one that cannot, as in the case of WeWork. To save Uber, Travis Kalanick had to be replaced. So, what is the right answer? As a founder, you want to take the self out of self-promotion. **If you build a personal brand, do it in the service of the company and your own reputation will flourish.**

The life of a startup is divided into different phases, which does have an impact on the founders' approach to personal branding and thought leadership. This is merely a framework on how to think about your own visibility. There are no hard and fast rules, and your approach is inextricably linked to your business as well as your own personal plans, preferences and ambitions. Let's look at each phase in turn.

Phase 1: Building a Personal Brand

In the first, initial phase it does make a lot of sense for at least one of the founders to be visible because the company is not known yet. The founder of Berlin-based fintech unicorn Raisin, Tamaz Georgadze, had the choice between a product-centered or a person-centered approach to communication when he launched the company. Tamaz explained how the company would seem to an outsider without any knowledge of the product or the team: "There is this strange Georgian guy, a company which exists since a month – it sounds super fishy. Like, why would I trust my money to you. It smells like fraud." To shift the perception, Tamaz focused on telling his story: a chess child prodigy who had received two PhDs by the time most of us would start thinking about our careers. He didn't want to be in the limelight, but he realized it was the best way to build trust and raise awareness. Once Raisin matured, they changed their story and focused more on the business and the product. Now, Raisin is a leading finance company in Europe with multiple sub-brands attached to its name. Not so fishy after all.

Before you start, you need clarity about your objective, strategy, audience, brand positioning and narrative. Most importantly: What is the one thing you want to be known for? Do you have an original point of view on a topic that you want to own? Madeline Lawrence, an investor at Peak, often reminds founders that "standing out isn't strategy, it's survival - especially in VC-backed industries defined by outliers." **To build a personal brand, you have to stand for something.** What would you write on the t-shirt? In other words, what is the short, bold slogan or the one word that describes what you stand for? Your reputation can't be a vanity project though, it needs to be authentic and in the service of others.

To gain trust, you want to include personal elements in your narrative, and not just your professional life. Be someone who cares, have a clear purpose and make it part of your personal narrative. Unlike twenty years ago, when showing personality was still largely frowned upon in the business world, today authenticity helps us get noticed. Being true to ourselves makes us unique, and uniqueness stands out.

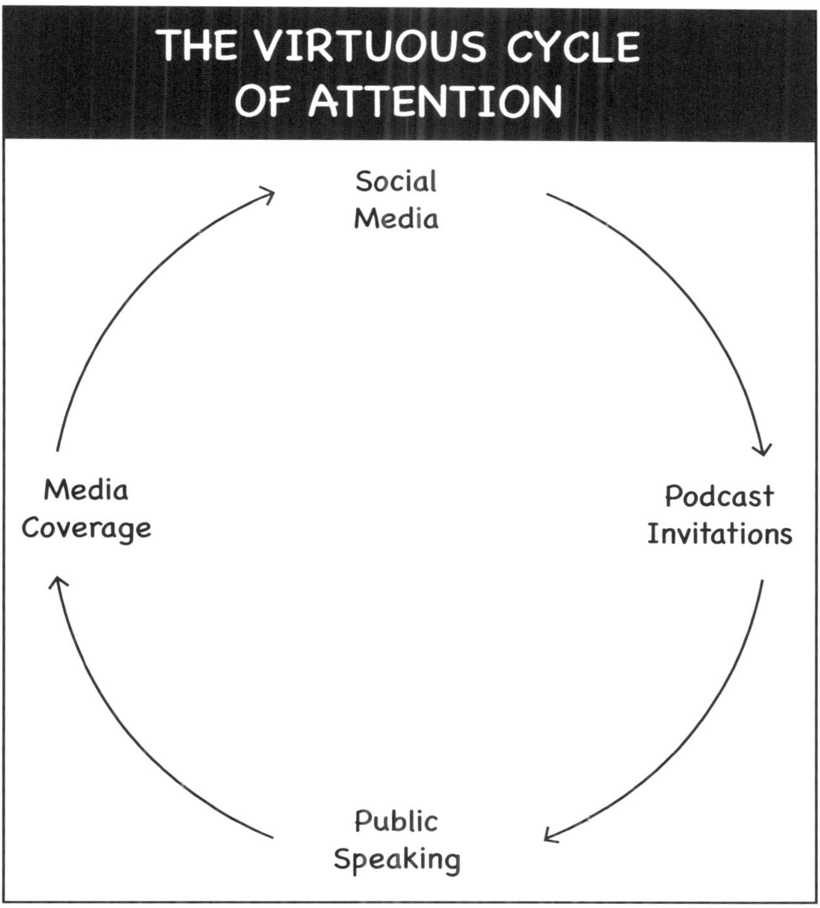

Start with a quick digital makeover. Then increase your visibility. Social media is like gravity. It is non-negotiable. Choose your main platform to publish content that adds value. If your audience is on LinkedIn, you want to be big on LinkedIn. Of course, there is a lot of pseudo-deep and cringe-worthy content on LinkedIn and elsewhere. That's an opportunity to do it better, not a reason not to do it.

You also want to ensure that the media feature you, that you are a guest on podcasts and speak at events. We are strong believers in the virtuous cycle of attention, where one interview will lead to more coverage, more podcast invitations, more social media mentions, and so on. This is how you create momentum. And once you reach that kind of visibility, you can branch out into other topics.

Many CEOs have a dedicated team member or an agency to manage their social media profiles and help them build their presence. This is certainly an option, however, for CEO communications to be effective and to build trust, it needs to be the CEO's voice. That doesn't mean founders should write every word or click on *publish* themselves, but they need to be involved. Your team or agency needs to have access to you and internalize your ideas, insights and values. Once you have an established workflow and great people around you, you get strong content without spending a lot of time on it. Be mindful that a founder's voice often gets lost when they delegate and be done with it. This is why so much content on LinkedIn and elsewhere is so bland and forgettable. A strong personal brand requires personal involvement.

Phase 2: The More the Merrier

The second phase comes when the startup grows and becomes more professional in its communications. Often, the founders pull back as the company becomes more widely known. At this stage, there is a team in place and the company has achieved some brand recognition on its own, so that others can talk about the company as well.

As the company grows, there are good reasons to increase the visibility of different key executives. Firstly, this is important for the valuation, as investors want to ensure a startup does not depend on one person or just a few people. Secondly, it increases the agility and resilience of the company. If one executive leaves, which inevitably happens at some point, other people with strong personalities and brands are ready to take over.

Similarly, different executives can share the workload by focusing on different stakeholders, audiences or markets. For example, the CEO may be the person who represents the company to the outside world, the media and the public in the event of a crisis. The CFO may have a strong brand and recognition in the investment and financial communities, and so on.

Finally, bringing in or promoting big names can send a message that the company has changed, and that broadens its appeal from the perspective of employer branding. When Sheryl Sandberg joined Facebook, it was to communicate that there was a safe pair of hands surrounding Mark Zuckerberg at all times. Sheryl herself already had a brand, which made her even more visible. Similarly, the brand of Marissa Mayer, one of the first employees at Google, blossomed because the Google team decided it would be good for the company and put a plan in motion. Therefore, having a number of people in the executive team with a strong personal brand can be an advantage when your business grows.

As a founder, it can be tempting to speak about many issues and also to be politically active. Does that make sense? It can do, especially if it is linked to what your startup does. Showing your purpose can attract the right kind of investors, conscious consumers and top talent. Purpose can lead to brand differentiation. For instance, Whitney Wolfe Herd is the founder and CEO of the dating app Bumble and the former VP of marketing at Tinder. Wolfe Herd regularly uses her social platforms for campaigning and promoting social justice-related issues. For instance, she's a big advocate of laws against unsolicited lewd images. This seems heartfelt, and also helps Bumble to differentiate itself from other dating apps, in particular with women. It shows that a CEO can be a powerful cheerleader-in-chief, if they believe in a certain cause or purpose. But it has to be genuine. Not everything should be politicized.

Phase 3: The Next Big Thing

In the third phase, as founders are about to prepare for life after a particular venture, they often become more active again. Having an eye on the future, they want to be perceived as success stories or thought leaders to move on to potentially bigger and better things.

As Oliver outlined in his e-book *From Business Leader to Thought-Leader*, there is an elite group of founders who truly stand out. This tends to happen in Phase 2 or 3 when the company and the founder are already on the map. A thought-leader is a business leader who is perceived as a leading voice on a relevant topic or in an industry. Often they are famous for the few, not the many. In fact, thought-leaders are often relevant for a small audience because they are experts in that particular field or niche. They're future-oriented and think long-term. They make meaningful contributions to current debates and anticipate issues and trends that will occur years down the line. This is why people listen to what they have to say. And that puts their companies on the radar of investors, talent and customers.

If you aim to become a thought-leader, you want to be so good and so visible that your target group can't ignore you. This means you really need to differentiate yourself. That's why many thought-leaders – the big hitters – have written books, host podcasts or appear in content series on YouTube or elsewhere. *Speak Like a CEO* has been a game-changer for Oliver. His weekly podcast interviews with inspiring CEOs and founders have helped to build his brand and it paved the way for several books on leadership communications.

Now, can any founder become a thought-leader? In principle, yes. The playing field is really level these days. We all have access to the same tools, and most of them cost little or nothing. Everyone can leverage technology and social media. It follows that anyone can become a thought-leader – but not everyone. By definition, there can only be a few in each sector.

The most likely person in a startup to become a thought-leader is the CEO. They usually have the story, the infrastructure and the resources. Successful CEO communications can lead to thought-leadership. It can even be the prime objective of CEO communications, if it fits the company's strategy. Of course, the CEO's communications should always be part of the overall strategy and support the business objectives. At the same time, the CEO needs to have a distinct and authentic voice. That's the balancing act.

And it's one that Melanie Perkins manages exceptionally well. Together with her now-husband Cliff Obrecht, she founded design software Canva and turned it into a global brand. Her persistence and communication skills played a big part in it. As a student, she noticed how complex design software could be and how long it took to learn to use these software suites. She decided to democratize design with a software that was much easier to use. After hearing "no" from more than 100 investors, her pitching became more determined – and risky. She decided to learn to kitesurf to get a foot in the door with a group of kitesurfing venture capitalists in her native Perth in Australia. Her daring approach worked and gave her the opportunity to turn her idea into reality. In the process, she became one of the youngest female CEOs of a tech unicorn and one of Australia's richest women. She is a leading voice for democratizing access to technology and design as well as a voice for philanthropic causes through Canva for Nonprofits and the Giving Pledge.

Bringing Company, Product and Personal Brands Together

Whether you want to increase revenue, have a positive impact on the world or get your message across on an issue you care deeply about, building a personal brand is key. Visible founders help their companies because customers, talent and investors want to know who the people behind the brand are and if they share their goals and values.

Especially in the early days, a founder with a strong brand can attract customers, investors and employees. Over time, the company and product brands increase in significance. At that stage, all brands of a startup – personal, company, products – should reinforce each other, as in the case of Whitney Wolfe Herd at Bumble.

The process of building and growing your company, product and personal brand is a combination of listening to customer feedback and the leadership element of having a deep understanding of what your company stands for. Successful brands never stop asking themselves many questions. Who is our customer? What experience do they have when they interact with us and our product? How do they feel when using it? What upsets them? The answers keep them on track of building a strong brand.

The most important ways to grow your brands are to consistently tell your story, and to let people experience the product. What you now need is a system that systematically attracts more and more customers. That's where we turn next.

Chapter 5

ATTRACTING CUSTOMERS

You have a great product, kick-a** messaging and an enticing brand. Now what? How does your product get into the hands or onto the screens of your customers? That's not a minor question, of course. The most common reason why companies fail is that they don't have enough customers. A great product is nothing without distribution. Naval Ravikant sums it up best: "Learn to sell. Learn to build. If you can do both, you'll be unstoppable." But there is a big paradox in sales, as we will see shortly.

Although it has become easier to build, launch and scale new software and physical products, finding enough customers has become more difficult. That's precisely because there are more offers to choose from. In this chapter, we dissect what makes marketing and sales work, and what many startups get wrong. Libraries have been filled with marketing books, so our goal is not to give you a crash course in marketing that you don't need, but a fresh way to think about marketing at a deeper level.

If you have an awesome product, do you still have to do marketing? Yes, because customers will only discover that your product is awesome when they try it. “A good product or service is a customer retention tool,” says marketing expert Allan Dib. How do you get them to try it? In one word, marketing.

Give or Take?

The principles of marketing and sales are simple, as blogger Tim Denning pointed out:

- Give more than you take
- Develop an understanding of human psychology (such as: people need to trust you before they buy from you)
- Focus on your customers, not yourself
- Communicate your value simply
- Understand that people buy from people, not companies
- Provide evidence of why someone should buy your service or product

The underlying theme is: be a giver rather than a taker. “Marketing is the generous act of helping someone solve a problem. Their problem,” writes marketing Yoda Seth Godin. And that’s the paradox of sales and marketing: You sell by not selling, at least as it is commonly understood. *Buy my stuff!* does not work anymore. You sell by helping people so they become long-term customers. Because **everyone wants to be helped, but no one wants to be sold to.** And if you want people to believe you can help them, help them.

What do people want help with most? In two words, surviving (food, shelter, health) and thriving (wealth, love and human connection, saving time). These desires are the driving forces behind most big industries. As always, Maslow's hierarchy of needs provides a good starting point for the study of human desires.

Hold on, you may think, *that's great but why would people allow us to help them? They know we are selling something.* Ah, good point. You need to take them on a journey. *Know me, like me, trust me, pay me* is a business cliché for a reason. Trying to sell without creating trust first is a mistake. **The aim of marketing is to ensure that you build trust and an emotional connection with your ideal customers. You want to attract, not chase.**

Who Am I Talking To and How?

Ramping up sales in a startup is always a race against time. Keep a laser-like focus on a narrow target market. Target everyone and you target no one. If you serve a very specific customer, you can convert more leads into customers, because your product serves their particular problem. Your messaging will be much sharper and your marketing more targeted. If you offer the best possible solution to their specific problem, why wouldn't they buy from you? Lead generation is expensive, so targeting high-probability customers keeps your customer acquisition costs low. **To improve your marketing, always come back to the question: *what is working, and why?* Then double down.**

In addition, you can charge your perfect customer more. Pricing matters less if you offer the best possible solution, not the second best. The fastest way to double revenue may be to double your prices - not haphazardly but based on pricing surveys to gauge if the market would support such an increase. You gain this kind of market power thanks to your clear positioning and the frame of reference your messaging triggers. In the process, you develop ever-deeper expertise in your field. Ideally, you become oversubscribed and become the buyer instead of the seller. This ultimate reversal in market power means you pick who you want to work with, rather than being picked. This works particularly well for business models that have a limited capacity, or those that can induce artificial scarcity.

In direct-to-consumer businesses, you want to identify and describe your ideal customer. If you are running a B2B business, you want to identify not only the company but also the owner of the problem that you solve within that company, and speak to that person in their language. It's crucial to talk to your ideal customers and to understand their motivations and internal and external challenges.

Instead of conversing like a sales-bot, the premise is to build an emotional relationship with your customer or audience. So, at every juncture, at every potential interaction, you need to know who your audience is. You may also deliberately offend audiences that are not your target audience, or disregard their views.

If the first rule of marketing is 'no one cares' and the second is 'know your customer', the third surely is 'don't be boring'. You can't bore people into buying. By god, it has been tried. Boring marketing tends to focus on the company and the product (*Look at us!*), captivating marketing focuses on the customers and their problems (*We feel you!*). Your customers want to be entertained, or at least educated in an engaging way.

The fourth rule would be 'the money is in the follow up.' You want to **take your prospects on an emotional journey at the end of which they would feel stupid not to buy from you**. The number of touchpoints you have to create to move someone from conversation to conversion is significant. Trying to sell too fast, or even in a single conversation, is doomed to fail in most markets.

There are many different models, but we believe the classic AIDA model captures the essence of the customer journey. To turn a stranger into a customer requires:

- Attention
- Interest
- Desire
- Action

If you are running campaigns, each of them should be designed to bring your target audience one step closer to a buying decision. You therefore need at least three different types of campaign: one to build awareness and trust; a second to convert those who know and trust you into customers; and a third to nurture existing customers so they come back.

GAINING TRACTION

Different tactics work in different phases of your company. In the beginning, as Y Combinator co-founder Paul Graham put it in a well-known essay, "do things that don't scale". Gaining traction often means winning people over one by one. "The most common unscalable thing founders have to do at the start is to recruit users manually. Nearly all startups have to. You can't wait for users to come to you. You have to go out and get them."

Today Amboss is a unicorn with hundreds of staff and a market leader in medical education. In the early days, the founders, medical students themselves, struggled to gain traction. To overcome the cold start problem, they went to every single medical school in Germany, organizing meet-ups and talked to students. The result of this tactic: a 90% market share.

Your network as a founder can be essential for your go-to-market strategy, especially if your product is large or expensive. It can provide you with your first customers since you already have a level of trust with them that you would have to build from scratch with new customers. These connections can also help you to create network-based content. For example, a podcast, a YouTube content series or Linkedin Live conversations where you invite dream customers from your network to have a conversation about your topic. Creating content together tends to forge an emotional bond and directs the conversation to how you could help them.

Of course, these approaches are not scalable. But they can lead to first customers and provide priceless feedback to achieve both product-market fit and message-market fit.

The Right Channel for the Right Audience

There are around 20 channels and tactics at your disposal. You know them already: different social media and digital channels, as well as PR, SEO, advertising, affiliates and influencers. They are often categorized into paid, earned, shared and owned (aka PESO). So how do you know which ones you should prioritize?

Many companies build a product based on an idea and some early feedback. Once they are ready, they launch, but struggle to attract more customers. They experiment with different channels, which is a race against time before they hit the end of the runway. Many hit the wall before they manage to sell at scale. To avoid this problem, you want to build your product or service while testing different traction channels in parallel.

The second mistake to avoid is to assume that there are a number of equally good distribution channels. Some startups try lots of them without a strategy or framework. "That is a really bad idea. It is very likely that one channel is optimal," notes Peter Thiel. "Most businesses actually get zero distribution channels to work. Poor distribution – not product – is the number one cause of failure. If you can get even a single distribution channel to work, you have a great business. If you try for several but don't nail one, you're finished. So it's worth thinking really hard about finding the single best distribution channel."

Wunderflats lets furnished apartments on a temporary basis. The platform is primarily aimed at young professionals and expats and supports them in finding accommodation on a short- to mid-term basis. When they started out, they tried multiple channels. They organized events and tested performance marketing, content marketing with a focus on blog posts, and also affiliate marketing – nothing worked. Except for Google AdWords. And what worked in 2017 is still their main traction channel today.

Your ideal channels depend on your business and your target audience. Marketing in startups is primarily growth or performance marketing today. It is analytically driven and focuses on return on investment. It encompasses SEO, digital advertising and often content marketing. This is especially true for B2B and software companies, whereas direct-to-consumer businesses rely more on product marketing. This may change in the coming years, and we may have seen peak performance marketing already. Consumer behavior adapts, and it gets ever-harder and more expensive to stand out with performance marketing. In the future, the authors believe the most successful marketers will be the ones who combine technology, creativity and psychology to reach the right customers at the right time with a message that stands out and appeals on an emotional level.

In *Traction*, Gabriel Weinberg and Justin Mares offer a three-step framework called Bullseye that any startup can apply. The first step is to brainstorm every single traction channel that's *possible*. That's the outer ring. The second step is to find out what's *probable* by running cheap traction tests in the channels that seem most promising – the middle ring. The aim is to quickly gather data on acquisition costs as well as the number and profile of potential customers on the channel.

As Naval Ravikant puts it, "Traction is basically quantitative evidence of customer demand." The inner ring, the bullseye, stands for *what's working*. Based on the evidence, you can now direct the majority of your attention and budget toward your core channel. "The way this step gets most messed up by founders is by keeping around distracting marketing efforts in other traction channels," write Weinberg and Mares. **Successful businesses tend to scale thanks to one core channel.**

Only once your bullseye channel is well established, it is wise to reinvest some of that free cash into other channels to reach new audiences and to reduce risk. For instance, startups that relied heavily on gaming Amazon or Google search results found themselves bereft of their main channel after algorithm changes. With one eye to the future, you therefore want to dedicate a small part of your budget to continuously experimenting with other channels. This will help you to grow your brand visibility, create additional touchpoints and understand what other channels could work well for you once your main channel is saturated.

When your marketing gets more sophisticated and you run different campaigns for awareness, conversion and nurturing existing customers, you are likely to use different channels as well. For instance, awareness may come through SEO, conversion through targeted ads and nurturing through email newsletters.

Your brand should start to pull its weight too during the scaleup phase. This should give you "free" sales through brand conversations. You can even reinvest the revenue into sales channels that have a negative return on investment but create high visibility and brand recognition.

The key insight: Figure out what the bullseye traction channel is, and only then move to establish other channels. Trying to get several channels to work at the same time is usually a dead end for startups. Once you have traction and reliably produce leads, your business will scale – provided that your team closes.

The Snowball Principle

Your customers don't buy because they understand you. Rather, they buy because you understand them.

Acquiring customers is expensive, and it tends to get even more expensive as you scale. To keep customer acquisition affordable, it's necessary to provide evidence of why someone should buy your service or product.

Marketing used to rely heavily on advertising, and it still does in the form of performance marketing. While paid ads can play an important role in your overall strategy, be careful not to rely too heavily on them. If your marketing strategy is to "run ads", ask yourself when the last time you made a buying decision purely based on advertising was. A strong paid campaign may make us aware of a product. But we are much more likely to base our actual buying decision on personal recommendations, social media and peer reviews. We check the reviews on Google, Amazon or Yelp because we want to know whether users were happy with the experience.

Word-of-mouth is the most powerful marketing tool there is. 90% of people are much more likely to trust a recommended brand (even from strangers), and it is more effective than paid ads. That's why endorsements by "people like me" are crucial to seal the deal.

Unfortunately you don't have the time to sit around and wait until people start to talk about how great your product is. You need to kickstart word-of-mouth. Most marketers use word-of-mouth marketing because it has the potential to increase both brand awareness and sales. For instance, you can entice customers to share their experiences by creating memorable stories that they feel compelled to share. Or you can simply ask them to share their experiences, so you can share feedback for them on social media or your website. You can also ask them for referrals ("if you know anyone who is in a similar situation to yourself, here is a voucher").

Product launches use the term "drop" to attract attention and get people to talk about the hot new release. This buzzy format combines countdown clocks, limited editions of customized goods, launch events, collaborations between brands and influencers and an addictive cycle of continuous new releases. People want to own and sometimes resell the product, which leads to increased brand awareness, which leads to an exponential increase in the amount of buzz generated with each drop.

It is also possible to bake virality into your product and your offer. Clubhouse, a voice-powered social network, managed to get a lot of celebrities involved. By having those people on the platform, others showed interest in it immediately, which made it easier to create buzz and PR. Secondly, they gave every user the possibility to invite only two others so that access to the platform felt exclusive. This brought the cost of acquiring new users down to almost zero. Within months, the platform was worth billions. It then stalled for a variety of reasons, but the launch strategy worked a treat.

KEEPING CUSTOMERS

Fast-growing businesses have to be excellent at keeping customers. It is not only easier and way cheaper to keep customers instead of winning new ones, your existing customers can also help you attract the next batch. If you provide value and exceed expectations, some of your customers will become evangelists. The goal is therefore for your customers to be emotionally attached. The emotional attachment that you create in them around your product, brand and people should result in them continuing to buy, use and share your product.

Pulling this off requires a clear strategy involving marketing, sales and customer service to nurture customers throughout their lifetime, from first contact to last order to winning them back if necessary. Responsibilities and metrics need to be clear, and everyone needs to pull in the same direction. (The Message-Market Fit Signals table at the end of Chapter 3 provides the most important metrics for each stage of a startup.) Silo thinking achieves the opposite. If each team is only focused on their own metrics, no one will own the whole customer experience.

A former colleague of Jag's, Jonathan Fentzke, is a rocket-scientist-turned-entrepreneur who's now General Partner at Far Out Ventures. He often reminds later stage deep-tech startups that "customer centricity when you're a series B startup means something very different than when you're a seed-stage startup. You need to have the social proof mechanisms in place to show customers and investors that you're not just selling a widget, but that you're selling a proven solution to a real problem." He argues the easiest way to show this is by demonstrating how exactly you're helping your customers "get made, or get paid." If the buyer of your product gets promoted, or if their company makes additional revenues because your product has delivered the value you originally promised, then communicate this to all your stakeholders, including other customers.

What frustrates customers most is perceived indifference on the part of the company. *Now that they have my money they don't care anymore.* That's why your customer communications need to send the signal: We care, you matter to us, you made the right decision to go with us. When a customer has an issue that needs resolving, go out of your way to make that experience smooth. Turn a negative experience into a positive one. Too few companies do this. The surprise effect of *oh, that was easy* breeds customer loyalty and word-of-mouth. And it can go beyond admitting a mistake and apologizing, for instance by giving them a voucher or a surprise apology gift. However, people are much more likely to share stories about bad experiences, including on social media. You want your social media managers to work closely with the customer team to be able to react quickly and turn things around in plain sight.

Like all other forms of communications, the way you communicate with your customers needs to evolve. Jag was one of the first investors in neobank Eversend. They were aiming for a very young demographic, and they needed that demographic to be their champions. With that audience in mind, they were using a ton of emojis in their communications. This rubbed a large number of people the wrong way. They could have smoothed out their communications but they didn't. Those people weren't their target audience.

It played into their business model, into their plan to start off with younger people and then evolve. As the company, the processes and the banking systems matured, the plan was to make some headway into older demographics. In recent years, there's been a marked decline in the use of emojis as they grew market share. They needed to be more tried and tested and eventually needed to appear to be more boring in some ways. Their message-market fit matured with them as a company.

Firing Customers

Oliver's company was recently fired by the phone company that provided the landlines in their offices. The company sent a termination letter without any explanation and requested they send the phones back to them. Then they called and requested written confirmation that Oliver's company had received the letter. Why did you fire us, Oliver asked? The company rep explained that they wanted to focus on a different kind of customer.

Fair enough. Not all customers are a good fit. Some can be a real pain in the neck and are never satisfied. Others are easy to work with but need a different partner to get results. Fire them. Fire them for your own sanity and for the reputation of your startup. Unhappy customers or those that are not a good fit bind a lot of resources that are better spent on customers with long-term potential. They also have a nasty habit of telling others that they are dissatisfied. The question is, how?

There's no magic formula for dealing with humans. You simply can't guarantee that taking a rational approach will always lead to a reasonable response. Learning to discern the subtle cues of a difficult customer's verbal and body language, and then formulating an appropriate response requires time, practice, and tact – just like we talked about in Message Mastery 2: Listening to Understand! The simple answer is to keep it human. Fire a customer in the way that you would want to be fired yourself. The real challenge is in how you articulate it to your audiences. Investors seek confidence that you've fired the customer for a specific purpose, and that you understand the ramifications. Your employees will have their own questions, and other customers will want certainty that you've got their best interests at heart.

If Your Marketing Doesn't Work ...

There are plenty of traps that we can all fall into when it comes to marketing. A common mistake in early-stage startups is not talking to customers enough. Some founders want to stay in their comfort zone and tinker with the product instead of talking to the people who decide whether their startup will succeed. *We are not ready yet!* The underlying issue tends to be subconscious: Once we share our idea with customers, they may reject it and this dream of ours comes crashing down. Just like Mike Tyson pointed out, everyone has a plan until they get punched in the mouth; and no product strategy survives contact with the customer. Startups grow by talking to potential customers, not by avoiding them.

Many founders also vastly underestimate how many people they have to get their offer in front of to generate a sale. How many people need to see an offer for someone to convert? The precise answer depends, but the general one for a consumer-focused company is *an awful lot,* especially when you are new and have not yet built social capital. To put things in perspective, the average click-through-rate for an ad on Google is 3%, which means that out of every 100 people searching for a specific phrase that you've bid on, 97 people will likely not find your offer compelling. And that's just the top end of your funnel.

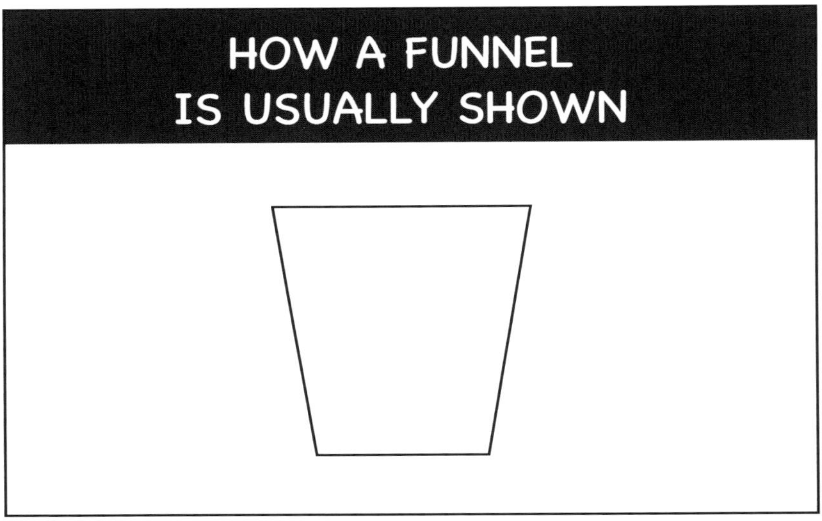

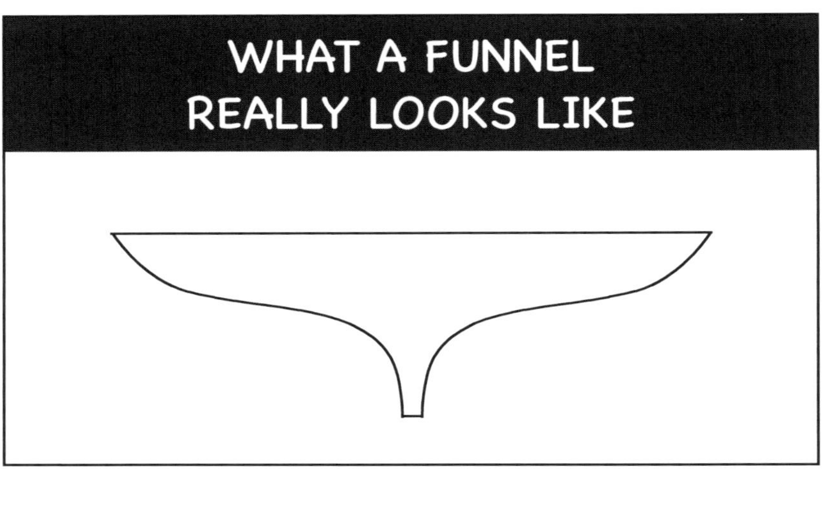

There's more. Scott Galloway argues that "the biggest mistake we make in marketing is believing choice is a benefit. No, it's a tax. Consumers don't want more choices, they want more confidence in the choices presented." Buyers suffer from information overload. To help them make a buying decision, provide simple information and make straightforward recommendations to them.

More unexpectedly, even experienced entrepreneurs tend to set a marketing budget. This implies that their marketing is not effective, or they don't know if it is effective. This can and must be corrected to avoid bleeding money, by either fixing the marketing or by introducing clear KPIs. As marketing expert Allan Dib argued, you want to "have an unlimited budget for marketing that works." Because if you spend x to acquire a customer, and the value of that customer is 2x, why would you not spend more to profitably win customers? True, it has become more challenging to pin down why a customer converted, but strong marketing can use testing to identify the winning formula.

Stop Chasing and Start Attracting

Effective marketing is the result of long-term thinking and excellence in execution. It gives your business more leverage than anything else. Improve it by 1% every day and you will see the results in your bottom line. What's more: if you get sales and marketing right, it is a very effective way for startups to build their brand, even without the advertising budget of a large corporation. You turn prospects into customers and customers into raving fans who tell your story for you. And that's what it's all about.

The goal of marketing is to stop chasing and start attracting. Fortunately, marketing is only one tool in your communications tool kit that helps you attract customers, investors and top talent. There are several others, including PR, social media and building a community, that are equally important. But should a startup actually aim for high visibility, or rather stay under the radar?

Chapter 6

GROWING YOUR VISIBILITY

We like to ask founders two questions. First, how visible do you think your company is on a scale from one to ten, where one means invisible and ten means omnipresent like Hubspot or Salesforce. Second, how visible do you think you need to be to reach your goals (such as winning over a market or becoming a unicorn)? The answer to the first question tends to be three or four for projected visibility, while to reach their goals founders usually aim for an eight or nine.

As a scaleup, you want to be top of mind. As we noted in Chapter 1, visibility is fundamental to building trust. Take Wunderflats, who we met in the previous chapter. Search Engine Advertising is their main traction channel to find tenants for their short-term lets. But they also need to win over landlords, investors, employees and regulators, which they won't be able to do via Google Ads. That's why a broader visibility strategy made sense for them, as it does for many other startups.

A key difference between a run-of-the-mill startup that's not going anywhere and a (future) unicorn is perception. Because perception can become reality, and if a startup is seen as the next great thing, customers, funding and talent will come more easily. You don't need to be top of mind among the general public, but with your target audiences. A stakeholder map, like the example shown below, can help you visualize your audiences and their importance.

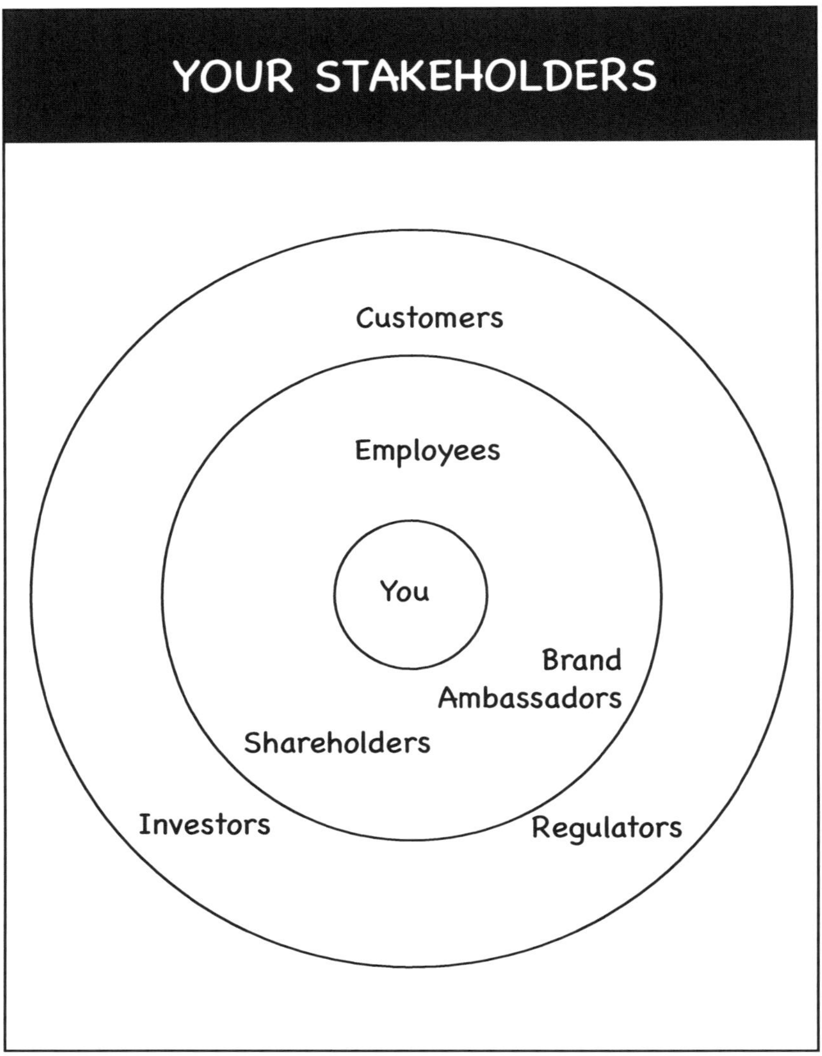

What Are You Waiting For?

One of the most common mistakes is to start communicating with the outside world too late. Many founders think they can switch on visibility when everything is finally ready. Worse, many wait for specific milestones – like closing a round, or closing their fifth enterprise customer – before even thinking about what to communicate. Unfortunately, this doesn't work because **communications take time to build and can't be turned on and off at will**. It's all about people and your startup's relationships with them. Therefore, if you are building a business, you need to consider growing your visibility as a strategic and integral part of your mission.

There is another side to this though. One of the mistakes that many founders make is over-communicating. Over-communicating occurs when you are communicating to the wrong people in the wrong way on the wrong channels.

When Jag built his first company in 2006, it was a different world. Twitter and TikTok didn't exist and our grandmothers weren't on Facebook yet. Instead of communicating directly with the thousands of existing users to build up engagement numbers, he spent vast amounts of time and energy trying to cultivate a media presence, in the hopes that this would attract investors. What precious few resources that existed were directed toward sponsoring booths and afterparties at conferences, lunches with print journalists and guerilla marketing stunts aimed at appealing to bloggers. A cheaper and simpler plan might have involved running a drip-email campaign directly to users from his email address. Investors often worry about premature scaling, and Jag's experience was a clear-cut example of prematurely scaled communications and marketing. He did eventually run that cheaper, simpler, effective plan a few months later. And… achieved his objectives within a week.

We see the same patterns these days when companies decide to 'do' TikTok. The platform is fashionable, so some companies throw money at it although their audience is not there. Other companies give their CEO unfettered access to Twitter, especially if they are the kind of CEO who raises eyebrows. Or there is undue emphasis on getting media coverage, without a strategy for how that helps the company achieve its goals.

Omnipresence or Stealth Mode?

There are also times when you may not want to be visible to your competitors. This is especially true in the earlier stages of a company's lifecycle. Companies in the pre-seed phase used to tell investors that they don't want to tell the world what they were really doing. This stealth mode added a layer of intrigue and became a common practice among companies to attract investors. We now encounter companies that have already raised three or four rounds and that still claim to be in stealth mode.

Being in stealth mode can be a way to reduce pressure from the outside world. Siri, the now ubiquitous voice assistant began as a startup that was only later acquired by Apple. Adam Cheyer, the co-founder of the company argued that "as a startup, we were potentially competing with large companies with lots of resources (e.g. Google, Microsoft), and we needed a good running head start before anyone knew precisely what we were trying to accomplish." But don't make the mistake of thinking that spending a long time in stealth mode is more convenient than communicating. Low visibility creates other challenges.

Stealth mode can also be a deliberate communications strategy to generate interest. Zillow is an American tech real-estate marketplace company. It found tremendous success by launching only after they had unveiled data that showed a value estimate of every single house in the US. Had news of this feature leaked earlier, their competitors could have stolen a march. This example shows that it is just as important for companies in stealth mode to have a clear message about what they're doing and why it matters – both for themselves and for their audiences. It's just the timing that differs.

Stealth mode is often associated with startups that want to retain control over their product roadmap and keep competitors from stealing their ideas. But there are plenty of other ways to do this without hiding from customers and potential employees. The biggest reason you should avoid being in stealth mode is because it doesn't work well for attracting investors, customers or new hires. The best way to build interest in your company is by communicating what you're doing and why people should care about your product or service.

So, how can we reconcile these two views? Is omnipresence or stealth mode the way forward? We believe that startups and scaleups should not communicate for the sake of it. Rather, all communications should support the overall business objectives. That's the ultimate test – is visibility crucial to the success of the business? And if so, what kind of visibility, and with whom? The default position should be to maximize awareness because it will help attract investors, talent and customers – unless there are good reasons not to. Whether you aim for high visibility or keep a low profile, it should be the result of a strategic business decision, not personal ambition or someone's comfort zone.

If you aim to be visible, how do you show up? Future unicorns are convinced from the start that they will be very successful, without succumbing to hubris. They manage to build the reputation of a team and a product that is bound for success. They communicate with confidence, regularity and clarity. They know why they exist and what kind of impact they want to have in the world. They follow a clear strategy concerning their competition, whether that's to attack or ignore. And once they reach unicorn status, they reassure their audiences and shareholders that they are losing neither their mojo nor their head, despite the inevitable bumps in the road. It doesn't end there, since these unicorns still need to provide their investors the chance to exit or liquidate their holdings, and return money to *their* investors (called Limited Partners).

Developing a Communications Strategy

So far this chapter has provided a framework to think about your startup's visibility. Let's now get practical. How do you devise the right strategy? And how do you execute it?

A communications plan like the grid we showed you in Chapter 3 ensures you are always aligned on strategy, messages and timing. It is based on your communications strategy which is a masterplan for how to get from the place you are now to the place you want to be in the fastest and most effective way. Without a strategy, you risk ending up with a series of unconnected and confused actions that will have little impact on your goals. To quickly define your communications strategy, we recommend you apply the Objective-Strategy-Tactics approach. It's the fastest and simplest way to get clarity on your direction. It's a Swiss-army kind of mental model that you can apply to many areas of communications.

This is how it works: First, define one clear objective. Second, summarize your communications strategy in one catchy sentence everyone on the team can remember. Third, decide on a small number of tactics that you believe have the biggest impact. Imagine a startup that developed an innovative way to use AI to produce audiobooks that sound natural:

OBJECTIVE - STRATEGY TACTICS

Objective	Become the market leader in audio-book production automated by AI
Strategy	Ensure every self-published business author understands that we are the fastest and cheapest way to create their audiobooks
Tactics	1) Speak at events aimed at authors 2) Launch a podcast (video and audio) aimed at authors 3) Build the founders' personal brand on LinkedIn and engage with business book authors on the platform

The O-S-T approach forces you to keep things short and simple. Everything fits nicely on one slide and can be remembered easily. This approach also makes it harder to mistake tactics for strategy. Buy-in is fast – you can get the team in a room and hammer it out in one session. Of course, you will need more precise plans to execute the strategy, but this is straightforward once the direction of travel is agreed upon.

For your O-S-T to work its magic, avoid listing more than one objective. Your strategy needs to be short and memorable. And given the plethora of potential tactics, resist the temptation to list every possible avenue to reach your audience. Sure, you can't rely on a single channel for visibility. But don't give in to shiny object syndrome either and list ten different tactics.

Let's look at some of the key tactics to gain visibility: PR, social media, events and podcasts.

WHY PR?

PR's role is to establish the company's narrative and to build and protect the brand. Far from being old school, creating positive media coverage is essential for the long-term success of a startup for a number of reasons.

Establish your narrative: Getting your story out through PR creates a "public record" and aligns your internal, external and financial audiences, according to Techcrunch editor-in-chief Matthew Panzarino.

Raise your profile: Media coverage puts you in a virtuous cycle, because coverage begets more coverage. Articles provide perfect material for your social feeds and lead to new opportunities, including partnerships, invitations to events and podcasts. They also boost your SEO, as media outlets are ranked highly by search engines.

Fundraising: The right kind of PR helps build a strong equity story. Highlighting how you solve a real problem for a big market tells investors that your equity will be valuable. This is also true for later rounds, as media coverage gives your company credibility and history.

Recruiting: PR allows you to highlight your purpose as well as the unique and challenging problem you are solving. Interesting problems attract the best people.

Sales: Getting press humanizes your company. It builds your brand as well as trust and credibility through independent endorsements. Whilst PR is not part of marketing nor is it a quick fix to a sales problem, media attention can support sales if it is part of a wider strategy.

Protecting your reputation: At some point, someone will publish something negative about your company. This is inevitable. However, if you have created a public record of your startup, it will survive a few negative articles or reviews, or even a crisis. Without that public record, the negative content stands unchallenged and will severely harm your company's reputation. PR is therefore an insurance policy against the inevitable.

At the beginning, your only chance of getting coverage is through building relationships and storytelling. PR is a people business. Research relevant journalists, respect their time and provide them with a compelling story. They are under enormous pressure to produce several stories a day that prove popular with their audience. If you address this need, your chances of getting published increase considerably. Some founders do their own PR in the earliest phases. That can be incredibly powerful and effective, but can also become a distraction or go completely wrong if they are not aware of the rules of engagement.

Existing Is Not News

Regardless of the phase you are in, PR can be time-intensive and risky and therefore requires someone with experience on the team or externally to facilitate the process. It's therefore advisable to have a communicator as an intermediary between the founders and the media, certainly after Series A.

Working with the media means giving up control about what appears about your business. Reporters are under no obligation to discuss their story with you, take your suggestions on board or write positively about your startup. That's what makes it valuable as an independent source in the first place. Getting free publicity and not being in control are two sides of the same coin. You can't have one without the other. This is the key difference between your own channels and earned coverage.

As a founder speaking for the company, you need to be ready and willing to give interviews. This requires regular media training by an expert (meaning someone who has actually given plenty of interviews themselves) and setting aside enough time to prepare for each interview. **In an interview, be a *spokesperson*, not an *answerperson*.** Tell your story and shape the conversation rather than answering questions.

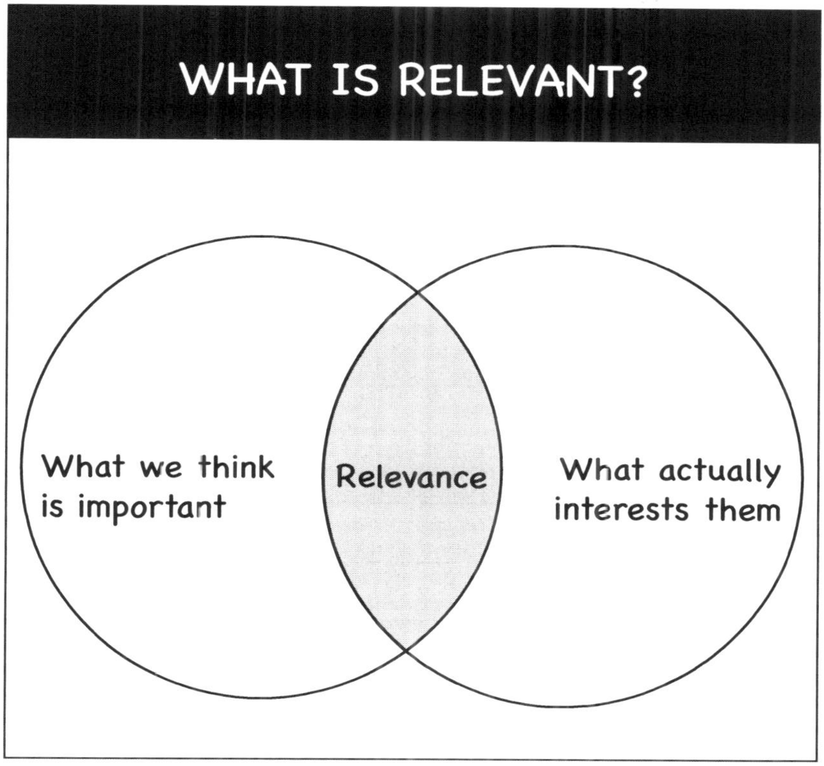

Never go into a meeting with a reporter unprepared. Whenever your team pitches a story or sends out a press release, you want to have time blocked for media requests. Teasing journalists and then denying interview requests is a huge red flag. In fact, when the team approaches journalists, they want to highlight that a founder or CEO is available for interviews to reduce the perceived risk for the journalist.

The most common mistake startups make is to assume that they are the story. "Existing is not news," as Edelman GM Margot Edelman puts it bluntly. When pitching a story, it is not about what matters to you but about what matters to the audience. That's why reporters will always ask themselves:

- Is this new?
- Is it exclusive?
- Why cover this now?
- Does this affect a large chunk of the audience I am writing for (such as a new trend)?

How PR Kicks A** For You

In 2017, Shilpika Gautam became the first person ever to paddle the river Ganges in India from source to sea. The inspiration and motivation for this expedition was to tell the story of climate change from a human perspective – across caste, class, gender, faith and political alignment and to highlight the need for equitable climate solutions. This expedition entered the Guinness Book of World Records for the longest ever stand-up paddle journey in history. It attracted significant media coverage and was turned into a 100m viewership documentary for the Discovery Channel. The journey also helped to inspire the origin story of SALT, the climate fintech Shilpika founded in 2022.

PR is successful when it builds a narrative arc instead of one-off stories, as in Shilpika's case. That arc ideally builds towards a strategic milestone like a funding round or an IPO. Announcing a funding round can be a great opportunity to tell your story and build your brand, although interest has waned due to the sheer number of rounds in recent years. You can send the signal that well-known investors with a strong reputation believe in you. Details make such announcements interesting: Who is investing? What is the valuation? What will the funds be used for?

Often startups use press releases to communicate with journalists. Unfortunately, many press releases have no news value, especially if you consider that a well-known reporter may receive hundreds a day and only has time to consider a few. Only use this tool if you have hard news to announce. Otherwise all your press releases will be ignored in the future. The times when companies using “spray and pray”, i.e. sending their press releases to as many outlets as possible, worked in PR are over. And that’s a good thing. A more promising way is to go exclusive and pitch a story directly to a journalist. Here are a few steps you can follow to get coverage this way:

Step one is to nail down your story – a story that audiences can relate to. Media coverage often creates a first touchpoint, an opportunity for people to understand what you stand for.

Step two is to identify publications, blogs and podcasts that already attract your audience. Start with your dream ten to twenty outlets that you would love to be featured in. Be ambitious but realistic. Identify the right person at each outlet, i.e. the reporter who writes about stories like yours.

Step Three is pitching. Pitching is the process of convincing a reporter to publish your story. You should have a pitch ready both verbally and in writing so that you can quickly and confidently send something to a journalist when the opportunity arises. Keep it short and sweet. If your story can be boiled down to a single, intriguing sentence, you’re onto a winner. Normally they will have to pitch your story to their editor, and a catchy headline is easier to convey for them internally. Reporters think in headlines, so it pays to do the same.

Step Four is to follow up with more information. As soon as a reporter expresses interest, you want to send them a press release with more information so they can base their article on the information and quotes you provided. The press release comes after the conversation, not before, unless you have hard news to announce.

Another way to gain the trust of journalists and get your company's name out there is to enter an existing conversation by providing statements. The minute an event relevant to your industry occurs – be it the merger of two companies or the bankruptcy of an industry stalwart – your team can reach out to trusted reporters with a few quotable sentences reflecting your opinion on the subject. Your aim is not to be self-promotional. You want to provide relevant insights quickly. Let them know what you think the future of your industry will look like because of that event. Over time reporters will see you as a source of quality information or interesting insights and come to you for comments. You start to pull rather than push.

The key to "getting press" is to understand the media and to think like a journalist. If you put yourself in their shoes, you can create a good news pipeline with stories that get picked up.

Making an Announcement

An announcement is a formal public statement that usually takes the form of a press release, social media content and an accompanying internal memo or video. We will tackle announcing negative news in Chapter 9 on crisis communications. The point here is usually to produce PR and buzz around a positive event or occurrence. It is a useful tool to publicize a significant event such as a major funding round, a merger or an acquisition. Unfortunately, some founders try to elevate the importance of something that does not justify a formal statement. The reasoning is usually "let's try it, there is no downside". Except, there is a reputational cost to it. An investor once responded to an announcement of a 200k funding round by saying that with the effort it took to put the news out the team could have raised another 100k. Ouch.

Every announcement is loaded with risks and opportunities. If an organization communicates them well, its reputation grows and the initiative is more likely to succeed. If it fumbles, it might not get buy-in from its key stakeholders and the project fails. Regardless of what is announced, it is paramount to have one clear communications plan in place that everyone works from. It needs to include the communications objective, roles and responsibilities, key messages, a Q&A and a plan for execution. Your communications are already aligned as you are working from a grid (see Chapter 3). A communications plan for an announcement allows you to zoom in on a particular event. It helps to think of the execution plan as a simple matrix that clarifies who will communicate in what way to your stakeholders.

Here is an example of a high-level plan for the announcement of an acquisition.

PLAN FOR AN ANNOUNCEMENT

	Before	On the Day	After
Internal	Prepare announcement and lines to take in case of questions or leak	Townhall at 9am by CEO, followed by memo to be sent by communications	Weekly updates on integration in all-hands meetings
External	Prepare press release and reactive statement in case of questions or leak	Press release to be sent by comms at 10am, followed by social media posts	Marketing to run campaign on improved offer thanks to acquisition
Financial	Formal discussion with Board (CEO); informal conversations with all investors (CFO)	Email to investors at 8.55am by CFO	Update at next board meeting followed by email to all investors afterwards

SOCIAL MEDIA

Algorithms change daily, human psychology never. That's why we focus on evergreen principles in this section (and this book) instead of tactics that change with the rise and fall of platforms, news cycles and popular trends. Social media can be your most effective traction channel, build your brand or help you become a thought leader. Social media can also be an utter waste of time. There are legions of businesses that are well-intentioned and put in the effort but don't get anywhere on their platform of choice. So what makes the difference?

Zero effort equals zero results. No one grows an audience by (almost) never posting. That much is obvious. However, inconsistent effort or quality also gets you nowhere. If your company's social media presence is irregular, or lacks strategy and systems, you won't get traction. Two engaging posts a week for one month and then nothing or mediocre content the next month will greatly limit your outcome. The biggest pitfall is to underestimate social media – both its importance in reaching your audiences, and the effort it takes to be successful.

Results come in when we approach social media strategically. Early on, you want to define your brand strategy for social media, your channel strategy and your content strategy. This includes utter clarity about your primary audience for each channel as well as the tone and manner you want to consistently use.

Select your channels carefully. It is better to master one channel than to be mediocre on several. Learn from the best on each channel, then make it your own. What works right now tends to be in plain sight. Expand only once you have achieved mastery of one platform. Put the right people in charge of the channels and define clear objectives together. Develop a workflow and an editorial calendar that can be updated in a monthly editorial meeting. Reusing and repurposing content can help feed multiple channels. In that case, you want to optimize your content for your primary channel and then adapt it to your secondary ones.

Whatever your channel of choice, consider your PACES:

Profile: Optimize your profile, including images, description and tonality.

Audience: Don't just rely on your content, actively grow your audience if the platform allows it, e.g. by sending direct messages or invites on LinkedIn.

Content: Follow your editorial plan and add spontaneous posts to react to topical conversations. Avoid adding to the noise. You want to follow a value-driven, people-first content strategy. Tell stories, and make your content personal and engaging.

Engagement: Interact with the community and other content creators. The more you do that, the more they will engage with your content. Ignore them and they will ignore you.

Sales: Do you use social media for brand building and awareness? Or also for sales and lead generation? Whatever the decision, be intentional about it and be careful about mixing brand building with sales. Too much sales content is a turn-off on social media.

Who should post for the company? Naturally, you want engaging company accounts that build the brand and don't rely on individuals. However, people want to engage with other people on social media. A founder who is also a thought-leader can add panache to a company's social media presence.

Another avenue to explore is employee-generated content. Many startups empower certain team members to post about the company, often called brand ambassadors or evangelists. These can be ordinary employees who are interested in representing the company, or members of the leadership team. For example, there may be an engineer in your company who has the potential to be an interesting voice in that particular community. This would strengthen your employer brand. Another team member may be an enthusiastic user of your product. She would be more credible than a paid influencer. Companies can use this approach to their advantage by identifying the right employees, giving them the tools and knowledge to make the most of it and increasing the company's visibility in certain communities or audiences.

One mistake we see over and over again is that companies think about the internet in isolation. As digital marketing heavyweight Sabri Suby put it, "on the internet you compete with half-naked supermodels and Joe Rogan smoking pot with Elon"; not to mention everyone's favorite influencers, podcasts and commentators as well as their friends' and families' latest whereabouts. Even on LinkedIn, the most professional of channels, you compete with the world's most inspiring business leaders.

Content is a meritocracy – consisting of credibility, interestingness and value. People tend to apply three filters to establish whether someone is worthy of their attention. The first is credibility: *Why should I listen to you?* You may post fantastic content, but if you lack the social capital or it is unclear why someone should pay attention, it won't work. Explain why people should listen to you first. The second filter is whether the content piques their interest. So before you hit the "post" button, ask yourself: will anyone speak about this? If the answer is 'yes', go ahead. If the answer is 'unlikely', you may want to go back to the drawing board. Start with a killer sentence, use stories and emotions and dare to be unconventional. Most importantly, interrupt patterns so that your content stands out. The third filter is whether the content adds value to people's lives or businesses. If you consistently post credible, interesting and value-adding content, in our experience people will take note.

The good thing is that we don't have to guess what works, but can test, track and reassess what your audience finds interesting and helpful. Your team can systematically test your content, tonality and the timing of the posts, as long as they are on brand. For example, one month you might test different headline formulas. Next, you might test the colors that you use or different types of images. There are some great headline testing tools that predict their appeal. Certain tools also offer split testing, where two or more variants of your content are shown to your audience. Statistical analysis is then used to determine which variation performs better amongst your audience. These tools can cut out a lot of the work of collecting and analyzing your own data.

While testing one aspect, keep the other elements largely the same. Over time, the team will build a deep understanding of what content works best for your audience, and this ensures that you can continually produce content that your audience finds valuable. This is an ongoing process. Trends change. Your audience will change. Over time, creating, testing and pivoting becomes an organizational habit.

To succeed on social media today requires both quality and quantity. There is no trade-off: the more the team posts, the better they get at it. Over time, they become real channel experts, if they approach it systematically. More effort does not automatically yield better results. Strategy and systems – that's what gets results.

COMMUNITY-BUILDING

Networks of like-minded people are an invaluable resource in any aspect of your life. Building a community as a startup takes conscious effort but the return on investment can be very high.

A lot of companies approach community building from the outside-in, as tech community builder Fabian Pfortmüller pointed out. They build a funnel and try to get their content in front of as many people as possible, often by paying for the visibility. Many people will have to be made aware for a single person to convert. This can work of course, but it is not the only way.

The alternative is to build a community from the inside-out, starting with your "1,000 true fans". The concept was coined by Kevin Kelly, founding executive editor of Wired magazine. The idea is to build a hard core of fans who spread the word for you, lending your company their social capital and providing social proof as well as social capital and status. The key to building such a committed cohort is to have a direct relationship with your fans. Small wins lead to big wins, and there are many steps that you can take to speed up the process. Approach people in your industry or network, and engage with their content. Join groups. Participate in conversations. Be an active member of your chosen platforms and throw yourself into the community. Then you will start to attract others.

When building a community, relying on someone else's platform is dangerous. It means you are one algorithm change away from irrelevance. Social media is great to get noticed, but you want to communicate with the members of your community via a channel that you control such as an email newsletter or a Discord group.

London-based scale-up Finimize prides itself on being the world's best finance community. Their mission is to empower users to become their own financial advisers, and give them the tools and information to do so. Within four years of its inception, Finimize had built a newsletter subscription list of one million users, despite spending next to nothing on marketing. The first few thousand subscribers they got from features in blog posts and from recommendations. After that their referral program led to a big influx of new followers. That scale allowed them to partner up with the likes of Wired, where they agreed to mutually recommend each other in their newsletters. From the community that was built around the newsletter, they began to host events and meet-ups, and eventually launched an app with a monthly subscription fee. Rather than trying to sell a subscription too early, they did the smart thing: building a community with a newsletter at its core – all without relying on external platforms.

If your audience feels that you are solving their problems and taking their needs into consideration, they will spread the word to others in a similar situation. Your audience will grow itself and trust you more deeply. They will become much more inclined to invest in future products and services, even bringing you business, because you have already been proven to have their interests at heart. If that community is online, behave as if that community were interacting with you in real life. They are real people, not numbers.

In your organization, it is important not to interact with your community in silos. You want to ensure, for instance, that your community management works closely with customer service, and that customer service understands the value of the community to the business.

PODCASTS

Podcasting offers intimacy and immediacy like few other formats. It is estimated that the spoken word is two to three times more effective than the written word. They are also almost always positive, unlike media coverage. If you want to position yourself or your startups as trusted advisors, podcasts are an excellent place to demonstrate your expertise, build trust and raise awareness.

Who listens to podcasts? Your own people and all the top talent in the world. The intimate nature of podcasts makes them a particularly appropriate channel for internal communications. Employees can actually hear the CEO speak as if they were having a face-to-face conversation, which is infinitely preferable to a dry one-way email or memo. On top of that, candidates researching your company as well as your dream applicants may come across your podcast and will appreciate the unfiltered expertise you offer.

There are two ways to use podcasts to increase your visibility. The first is to be a guest on podcasts. The advantages here are that you can reach and build trust with an entirely new audience and take advantage of the listener base that someone else has built without spending the time or money to launch your own. There are plenty of great startup shows out there such as *How I Built This*, *Pivot* or *Masters of Scale*. More realistic than the blockbusters of the genre are industry- or country-specific podcasts. To be invited as a guest, you pitch them the same way you pitch to the media: Offer the right people a compelling story.

The second way is to create your own. Hosting your own podcast has many advantages. The most important is that it allows you to have insightful conversations with people in your industry and build relationships with them. Podcasts are the ultimate networking tool. In addition, podcasts give you plenty of opportunities for content, from social media posts, to blog posts, to books.

Developing a podcast isn't right for every founder or company, but if done right the ROI can be very high: growing your network, gaining your listeners' trust and proving your expertise are the keys to enhancing your brand, after all. If your business success depends on strong bonds with a small number of dream clients, you can target them as guests and build relationships with them. Creating content together creates a bond. Podcasts can be the ultimate networking tool.

And not only can you meet them, you have half an hour to have a meaningful discussion and talk about what your company is good at. Obviously, it's important not to take the spotlight away from your guests, but a two-way conversation about your field of expertise helps to cement your reputation, both with your guest and your audience. If you have a podcast on the subject, your expertise in the field appears much more legitimate, as you have the content to prove it.

Given the plethora of podcasts out there, you need a strong concept, a catchy title and a subject matter that is attractive to your target audience. After that, the keys to a strong podcast are the three P's: people, production and promotion. You need hosts and guests who can carry a conversation and tell a story. The production value should be high: cheap mics and choppy editing are a real turn-off. The real winner is promotion. A large community of podcast listeners exists out there, many possibly sharing an affinity with your topic. The challenge lies in making your podcast stand out and drawing the community to you.

A good rule of thumb is to spend 50 per cent of the time and energy you invest in a podcast into promoting it, regardless of whether you are a guest or the host. Many more people will learn about your podcast on social channels than on podcast platforms. Ultimately, the key to growing your audience is to create as much content as possible on the back of it and share it on social media.

EVENTS

Whenever you attend events or conferences, try to be on stage. Speakers usually attend for free. More importantly, public speaking can be a powerful tool to raise awareness and connect with others. It is part of human nature. We have the desire to listen to great ideas and stories. And speaking in public is as simple as that. You share your ideas, stories and messages with an audience.

There are some fantastic events such as SXSW, Slush or Web Summit. Paddy Cosgrave, the founder of Web Summit, often speaks to the importance of personalizing and professionalizing communications with all audiences. It's how Web Summit grew in three years from a 500-person event focused on nurturing the Irish local tech community, into the largest startup tech conference in the world. However, most talks at startup conferences are boring. Really boring. They consist of a founder on stage, showing slides and talking about the company. That is good news for you – because it means that you can stand out if you apply the principles of this book to your talk and understand what organizers are looking for. Mikko Mäntylä, the president of Slush, told us that they are "looking for founders who can give radically honest advice for (future) startup founders and operators. The program is ruthlessly focused on timeless and practical company-building lessons."

Panel discussions are a great way to get started. The next step is securing your own speaking slots. The pitching process is similar to pitching stories to the media: identify the right person, get in early and present them with an irresistible proposal for a talk or panel. Irresistible means it fits the theme of the event, is original and tackles a problem that is central to the audience. Keep sales and marketing out of your talk.

As always, **proper preparation prevents poor performance – the five Ps**. You may only be on stage a few times per year, so ensure that what you say and how you say it are spot on. Ideally practice with a coach (that's what every TED speaker does). Record your practice runs and watch them. This will allow you to look back and see what worked and what didn't, and most importantly, whether it was interesting. The camera is your friend. As always, make it about the audience, not your company. Provide so much value that you get invited back.

You can still be strategic and find success at events, even if you aren't on stage. Our award-winning investor friend Chris Adelsbach reminded us of a founder who approached him shortly after he gave a presentation highlighting neurodiversity. The founder's cleverly targeted and timely elevator pitch was simple, yet resonated with the subject of Adelsbach's presentation.

Making it Rain

Why did Coinbase run a hugely expensive and hilariously retro Super Bowl ad in 2022? Why did Tim Ferriss advertise the 500th episode of his podcast on a single billboard in the middle of nowhere? They understand how powerful the right combination of online and offline channels can be. Nowadays, the purpose of a TV ad is to entice the audience to go online and check out the product, because that's where the purchase occurs. This is exactly what happened to Coinbase. Their Super Bowl ad was so successful that their website crashed due to the sudden influx of traffic. In Tim Ferriss's case, a number of people posted pictures of the billboard online, and the content went viral. One cheap billboard created awareness and organic traffic for his podcast.

Piecemeal communications are wasteful. You want to tie everything together and create numerous touchpoints with your audiences. That includes your website, marketing, PR, social media and offline events. Together, they create the virtuous cycle everyone craves. The question is how.

The answer is pretty straightforward. The founders and the whole organization take communications in all its forms seriously, put the right people in charge and agree on an overarching strategy, messaging and workflow. It's the Message Machine in action. Startups are able to do this because they are pragmatic by nature. That's a big advantage. In large companies, pragmatism is often a distant memory. You want to encourage creativity and experimentation, but crack down on silos, vanity projects and disjointed initiatives. These things happen a lot in large companies, because of a need to justify headcount and budgets. Keep your communications simple, even as your startup scales and complexity increases. Stay lean, stay focused.

As with all communications initiatives, you want to know if your investments pay off. There are many great tools but no perfect ones. To find the right one for your tracking and reporting, define your parameters such as views, reach, engagement rate and follower count and test a number of options. Again, keep it simple, and avoid wasting precious resources on overengineered reporting.

All of the above is only possible with the right team and culture in place. How do you actually build a Message Machine?

Chapter 7

THE HUMANS POWERING YOUR MESSAGE MACHINE

This chapter as well as the next one focus on what is perhaps your most important group of stakeholders: employees. As a fast-growing company, you need to continuously hire people who are motivated, skilled and a strong cultural fit, and then keep them engaged. These are the people who will power your Message Machine.

You will also need to create a culture, an internal communications system and an employer brand to attract and retain the best and the brightest. And you have to do all of that in a highly-competitive labor market where there is little loyalty between employers and employees. We are about to show you how, starting with the people you want to hire.

As you know, a Message Machine is an organization that has mastered communications and uses these skills strategically to achieve its overall business objectives. Building it starts at the top. As with any key strategic decision, it needs the initiative and sustained commitment from the leadership team. While ownership stays with the founders, and in particular the CEO, their role undergoes a transition.

BUILDING AN ALL-STAR TEAM

In the early stages, founders do it themselves. Right from the beginning, one of the founders needs to truly own communications. That chief evangelist is the CEO. The founders do pretty much all the communications themselves in the early stages, talking to investors, the media and the team. Of course, it doesn't stay that way.

In a high-growth company, a marketing person is hired at some point and a communicator or PR person as well. Which role is more important depends on your customers, business model and growth strategy. Enterprise and sales-heavy companies often prioritize a quantitative growth marketing approach and do little PR. Other businesses like Twitter or Tesla were built on stirring debates to attract talent, investors and customers. When you start hiring for these roles, be mindful that there are significant differences between a numbers-driven growth marketing role and a story-driven communications role. Someone who is brilliant at one isn't necessarily good at the other, so the first hires are crucial.

Once you delegate communications, marketing and sales, things can really go off the rails. Jag recalls a successful serial founder who had outsourced to their CFO the initial outreach to investors. This was a founder who'd successfully exited two companies, and had returned a great amount of profits to the investors, and so it stood to reason that investors would fall over themselves to speak to them again. The CFO's job was to arrange the initial introductions, get the meetings booked, and then bring in the founder to lead the conversation from there. The kink in the plan came when the vast majority of investors passed on the startup without even asking for a meeting. They realized a couple of weeks in that the CFO had forgotten to mention the CEO's name in the initial email!

As a founder, you don't need to understand the intricacies of performance marketing or media management, but you do need to have a proper grasp of the principles in this book and commit to improving your personal communication skills. This will ensure that you hire the right people who can execute your vision. Your first hires should already bring in additional expertise in communications, marketing or sales. Hiring interns, for instance to build your social media channels, is usually ineffective. Bring people in who have done it before so your startup benefits from their knowledge.

Growth Stage: Putting Teams into Place

Throughout all stages, the CEO remains the Chief Communicator. By the growth phase, they should have acquired all Message Mastery skills discussed in Chapter 2 to ensure they don't hold the business back but rather unlock its growth. During the growth phase, the CEO and the other founders still represent the business to its key audiences. But they do take a step back from the day-to-day running and instead provide direction from a 30,000-foot view. The CEO is now also responsible for ensuring that the right people work within the right structure, and that the strategic role of communications is fully understood within the organization. She needs to reign in complexity wherever it creeps up and keep communications simple. But what is the right structure?

There is no single right structure, just a structure that is right for you. There are a few commonalities though. After Series B, startups tend to hire VPs to build and lead a number of teams that are involved in communications to varying degrees. There are variations, but typically, these are:

- Communications: folks who tell the story inside and outside
- Marketing: folks who generate leads
- Sales: folks who close leads
- Customers Success: folks who make customers happy and upsell
- Product: folks who send plenty of signals to customers
- UX/UI/Design: folks who decide what the product looks like
- Finance, Legal, HR Admin: folks who speak to stakeholders on behalf of the company
- Recruiting: folks who help find the right people (this is not HR, although many startups still treat it as such; HR is an admin function)

While there are advantages to having specialized teams, the traditional separation of marketing, PR and internal communications makes little sense today. The main reason is social media. Advertising, influencer marketing, media coverage, employer branding and your internal communications are all shared on the same platforms. Everything feeds into the reputation of the company. On the other hand, the required skills are much more diverse and specialized now, from data analysis to copywriting, from design to code, from human psychology to insights into how journalists work. So how do you solve this dilemma?

Finding Your Perfect CMO

As you grow, the most effective approach is to combine marketing, PR, branding and internal communications into one function led by a VP of Communications or Chief Marketing Officer. Your strategy will determine who the right CMO is. If you are a SaaS company and user acquisition is your sole focus, you want someone with experience in growth marketing. If your approach is more consumer- or brand-led, your CMO needs to excel in these areas. Whatever the focus, just like the CEO, the CMO will need to have or develop a thorough understanding of all areas of communications. It's the fundamental requirement of the job. Otherwise your company will not become a Message Machine.

All major communications functions – internal, PR, marketing, employer branding – should report to this one person to prevent friction and duplication. The right person is an agile leader who is excellent in decision-making and in building a cohesive team that consists of experts in various fields. He or she will ensure that the right people are on the bus and on the right seats, and that they work together for the greater goal instead of getting in each other's way. Everyone works from one communications plan to avoid constant coordination about who posts what on your company's LinkedIn channel or the CEO's personal accounts. You share services like scheduling and monitoring tools. Most importantly, the company speaks with one voice.

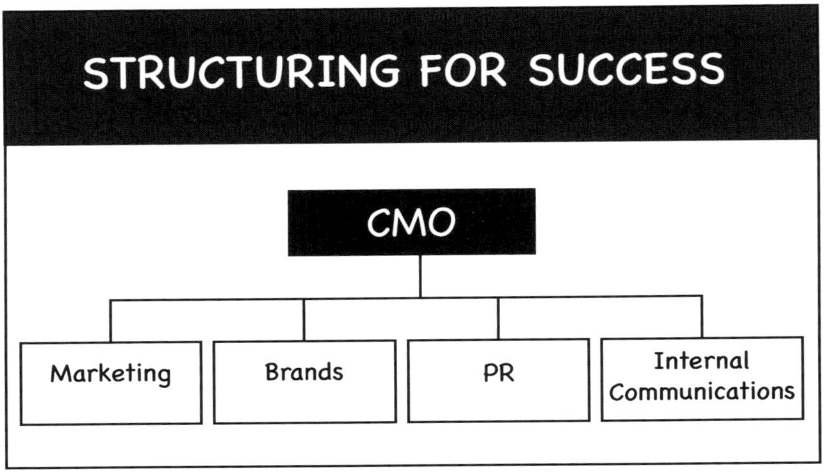

"The lines between PR and marketing were so unbelievably clear. PR people talked to reporters and marketing people bought ads," says LinkedIn CMO Shannon Stubo Brayton. "It's so different now, and (...) the CMO has to be such an agile, versatile player. You have to be good at a hundred different things." She adds: "The number one thing you need in a CMO is somebody who is an excellent leader. Because you are never going to be an expert in the hundred things you now need to be good at."

The role of the marketing department is to deliver leads to the sales department. The sales department's role is to execute those leads, in order to turn them into paying customers. It is vital to create a feedback cycle between the two departments and to clearly define their roles within the organization. The sooner this happens, the faster you can continue to build your business and scale. Unfortunately reality isn't always this neat, and marketing and sales instead point at each other for not doing their job properly. That's where the leadership needs to have visibility and step in when necessary, whether it's a founder or the CEO.

It is often between Series A and Series B that startups build their communications or PR team, regardless of the business model. Not having a professional communicator onboard at that stage is a mistake, especially if you want to become a category leader. Over time, your PR team will grow, and the question arises of where it sits in the organization. Having the PR team report to marketing is risky because of the functions' different key objectives. Marketing focuses on the product to grow revenue, PR's role is to establish the company's narrative and to build and protect the brand. If PR is forced to focus on product and revenue, it can't fulfill its most important functions: to build trust, shape positive opinions about the company and mitigate any reputational damage. Companies that treat PR as an extension of marketing therefore struggle to establish their narrative and to hire and retain top PR professionals. In essence, marketing promotes the product, PR promotes the business. Both are strategic functions that should stand tall next to each other, not one bowing to the other.

As mentioned above, you want your internal communications as well as marketing and PR to be in one team reporting to the same person, not separated into different functions. This ensures you speak with one voice. You may not need a full-time person for internal communications for some time, but you definitely need someone who is responsible for it. Internal communications used to sit under HR when it amounted to little more than email updates and a clunky intranet. Today you approach employee communications in the same way you approach marketing. Your "customers" are different groups of employees who you want to reach with specific messages on particular channels – think riders and coders in a fast commerce startup. One group works at a desk, the other on the street.

Late Stage: Professionalizing

While the CEO continues to own communications, several high- and mid-level leaders are also highly visible to share the workload and to signal that the business is not dependent on a single person.

The role of leaders shifts from building their own skills (which they have acquired by now) to building the communications capacity of others. Founders should hold the bar high, for themselves and everyone else in the organization. A high-growth enterprise is not a playground for amateurish communications but a hotbed of skills where every presentation, memo, performance review, sales demo and media interview makes an impact. This kind of upskilling doesn't happen by accident but requires targeted coaching and training.

At this stage, often a new "professional" CEO or CFO is brought in to manage rather than build and to prepare the company for an exit or IPO. In the beginning, the investor relations team is almost always just the CEO. As you grow, the founders want more than one person to deal with investors. Someone who speaks the language, understands the nuances and how to package a story for investors. This is where investor relations (IR) starts. You wouldn't expect an early-stage company to have an investor relations team full of Wall Street professionals, but it's something you would expect from a company about to go public. Financial communications and investor relations tend to be part of finance and report to the CFO.

By now, we would expect every startup to be fully prepared to manage any crisis. In certain high-stakes situations like a crisis or an important announcement, the leadership team may decide that not the CEO but a different person speaks to internal and external audiences. Rather than Mark Zuckerberg, the more empathetic Sheryl Sandberg led Meta's response to the myriad of public controversies the company faced. In general, the board often speaks when there are far-reaching management changes to announce. If your company is the victim of a cyber attack, the CTO may be your first choice. An important financial decision? The CFO. If you have a case of injury, loss of life, or job losses, the responsibility falls upon the CEO. But in all cases, the leadership of the organization needs to step up and understand that they can't delegate the responsibility for communications in challenging situations to someone in the team.

Managing Friction

As we outlined in Chapter 2, friction is a necessary evil and competitive advantage for startups compared to corporates who avoid open friction, strive for consensus and move slowly as a result. But there's healthy friction and unhealthy friction – or friction you can manage later versus friction that you need to manage now.

A challenge that most high-growth companies face is aligning the communications, marketing, sales, legal and investor relations teams. You need them to tell one story, even if it is told from different angles and with different voices. You want the angles to reinforce each other and make sure that the hooks are big enough for their respective different audiences. This process will inevitably lead to some friction.

The investor relations team are professionals who have extensive backgrounds working with financial institutions. They tend to be cautious and want to say less. The media relations and marketing folks have a different mindset. They don't seek the same level of control, and they are comfortable with this. Instead, they enter into calculated risks and try to manage these as well as they can. Their job is to get the company noticed and build trust so the business thrives. They need to work with stories and opinions rather than providing facts about the company, which the media and social media users find inherently boring. So there's inherent friction there too.

Shortly after its IPO, the easyJet media team did a stunt where they distributed a mock newspaper called the "Flynancial Times" on the London Underground. The stunt raised eyebrows and generated lots of attention, including from the Financial Times, which called the CFO and threatened legal action. A shouting match and an official apology later, the issue was resolved, but IR and communications didn't become best friends that day.

Legal and compliance teams tend to be as cautious as IR. Some even hold the radical view that nothing of substance should be communicated in critical situations. They come from a risk perspective. The equation is: no communication equals no risk. What they often fail to see is that not communicating meaningfully is actually the bigger risk when a company's reputation is at stake.

Especially at companies such as Airbnb, Uber and Coinbase, communications need to work hand in hand with legal and compliance. These businesses operate in highly-regulated industries. Their growth depends on keeping markets open, and public backlashes are common. Uber lost its license to carry paying passengers in London over passenger safety and security concerns in 2017 and 2019, and Airbnb was curtailed in Barcelona where residents were up in arms about being priced out of the market and having tourists partying next door. When that happens, politicians will react, usually with more regulation. In these situations, a company's response needs to entail a communications campaign as well as a regulatory charm offensive. Of course, there can be friction between legal and communications when the company is under pressure. What must be avoided though is finger pointing and silo thinking. An external threat can be a great rallying cry for a company. The experts in the court of law and the court of public opinion must collaborate to avoid punitive measures.

When Your Teams Speak Different Love Languages

You get the point. Investor relations, legal and communications inherently have different views and operate in completely disparate mindsets. It's like a throuple where every person speaks a different love language. So how do you deal with this inherent friction?

Always make sure that there is close contact and alignment between these functions. Most importantly, they should establish the ground rules once and then trust their colleagues to do their jobs. And they shouldn't surprise each other. If the CEO is to give an interview, investor relations should know about it. This doesn't mean they have a veto or that they can dictate the messages, but they should be able to raise any concerns before the interview. A founder or CEO is often in the position of the arbiter. You will hear different, even conflicting positions from three departments and have to decide what's best for the good of the company, which isn't always easy. Always try to bring it back to ground rules and principles – for instance, what numbers are confidential, and which ones do we communicate publicly? How do we communicate strategic decisions?

Who owns what channel is often a cause for friction as well. Should LinkedIn be run by the HR team or communications? Twitter by PR or customer service? Instagram by marketing or the employer branding team? Sure, many teams can make justified claims. But it is the wrong question to ask. It's not about which team you put in charge, but what your objectives are. Take a step back and define your brand strategy for social media: What are your objectives, and who are your audiences? All teams will then have to follow the strategy, and the channels become more active and engaged as a result. This also prevents social media channels from being abused for job ads, press releases or salesy marketing speak. None of these will help build a brand on social media. The teams need to communicate with each other, for instance in a monthly editorial meeting. The social media managers need to be empowered to say no to requests that are off-brand or don't fit the strategy, regardless of rank.

Working with Agencies and External Teams

To scale your startup you want to build a dream team that consists of effective communicators in-house complemented by selected external advisors. Ideally your internal team is great at ongoing internal, external and financial communications – the things that happen regularly. In marketing, your team should truly master your main traction channel.

However, there are certain areas and situations where external expertise can be extremely helpful, including messaging, media training, CEO coaching, crisis communications, IPOs and upskilling the leadership and the communications team. These areas require deep expertise and seniority that you may not have in-house until you reach a certain size. Some areas like crisis communications are only relevant from time to time so you don't need specialists in-house to run an annual crisis simulation. Outside advisors worth their money also bring a level of depth and structure to communications. They are sparring partners who help to professionalize your organization.

What we would caution against is offloading standard tasks like writing social media posts to an agency, because the results will probably be mediocre. That's not necessarily the agency's fault. If their task is to write content for the CEO's LinkedIn channel, but they do not have regular access to them, how could they write engaging, personal posts?

When it comes to agencies and external advisors, the key is to be 100% clear about the outcome you expect from the partnership. Then select people who have actually done that particular thing successfully. There are too many ex-journalist media trainers who have never given an interview, crisis experts who haven't steered a company through major upheaval, and social media experts who never built an audience.

Like in any industry, there are good and bad marketing and communications agencies. But there can also be unrealistic expectations on the startup's side. Both sides should be upfront about their expectations, define a workflow and set clear targets together. For instance, if you want ongoing media coverage, you need to develop a stream of stories together. Stories are what the media need, and existing is not a story, as we have seen.

The key to making your relationship with external advisers a success is to treat them as partners, not service providers. If you develop strategies and tactics together, and have regular exchanges among equals, your external partners will have the knowledge and motivation to crush it for you. If you don't value your partners, they won't go the extra mile for you. They need to be embedded in your Message Machine.

Measuring Success

As with all strategic functions, you want to set up a system to measure success. Your metrics will look different for marketing, internal communications, PR and investor communications. You want a good mix of qualitative and quantitative information. In PR for instance, that would include the number of articles and reach in terms of quantity. On the qualitative side, you want to know whether the tonality of the articles was positive, neutral, or negative, and whether your key messages came across.

Before you decide on the right tools, test them properly, and consider the ease of use as well as the return on investment. There are too many tools and options available to discuss them here, and they continue to evolve. Ideally you will have a single source of truth like a dashboard that tells you whether you are making progress towards your goals. What's important is that you do measure your results, because what is measured usually gets improved. It is also an opportunity for marketers and communicators to show the contribution they make to the success of the company.

In a high-growth company, reorganizations are a fact of life. The humans powering your Message Machine need to be comfortable with chaos. What ties them together is not the organizational chart, but something more meaningful: culture.

COMPANY CULTURE

"How people are with each other is the primary driver of the outcomes they get," notes Ray Dalio. In other words, **culture is destiny.**

Culture is the driving force behind your Employee Experience (EX) – the reality of working at your company. We cover culture in this chapter and internal communications and employer branding in the next chapter on becoming an employer of choice. Together these three levers make up the "Employer of Choice" virtuous cycle. If you pull them and become a company everyone wants to work for, you prevail even in a highly competitive labor market where everyone is fishing in the same small talent pool. This is a mission-critical

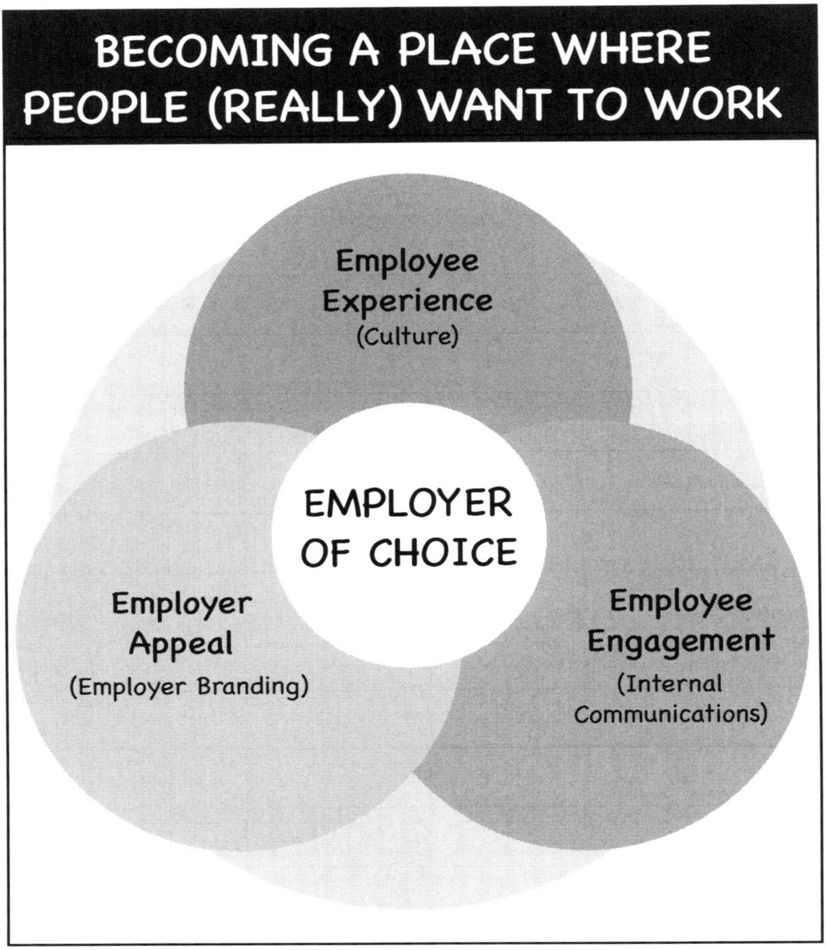

part of building your Message Machine as your success depends on the people you attract and retain.

To enter this virtuous cycle, start with culture. Improving your internal communications and employer branding will always make an impact. But if working at your company is pedestrian at best, any improvements in your communications and branding won't translate into long-term business results because people won't stick around long enough.

Creating a Magnetic Culture

Continuity equals speed. High turnover puts the brakes on a business, and is usually a signal that something is off. Like culture. Culture is what your team experiences every day. Culture is what happens when the boss is not around. It is not sushi lunches or open-space offices. **Culture is about creating shared beliefs, values and behaviors that lead to extraordinary results.** It is also your best insurance policy against burnout and mental health issues at work. If you get culture right, you supercharge your team. But if you get culture wrong, it will be death by I-have-no-energy-left-to-deal-with-this-sh*t.

Culture is not a nice-to-have. It's how you get results. Because **as a founder, you can't enforce results**. You can't even enforce behaviors that produce results. But what you can do is create alignment on beliefs and values. If that culture is alive and your team behaves in alignment with it, it will produce the results you set out to achieve. This is crucial to understand, because some founders try to enforce results by setting OKRs or KPIs without creating a high-performance environment in which teams can achieve them. This command-and-control approach does not work. It leads to frustration and poor performance. Instead, getting results starts with the right communication.

Culture is especially important in a fast-growing startup. At this stage, you likely have a high degree of message-market fit and a sizable team, and don't know everyone personally anymore. You may have just received a big round of funding and feel that there is no time to work on improving your culture. That's a terrible idea. If you as a founder don't steer the ship, you may not like the destination. Very quickly you find yourself in an environment where people may have great skills, but there is no alignment of beliefs and behaviors. Everyone does pretty much whatever they want.

Without alignment, and mixed with the madness of the day-to-day running of the startup, you will bring out the worst in people. Quickly, you will find that there is competition between team members, and they won't work well as a collective. With no alignment, there is no proper execution and therefore no results. Things start to fall apart. If you think culture is fluffy,

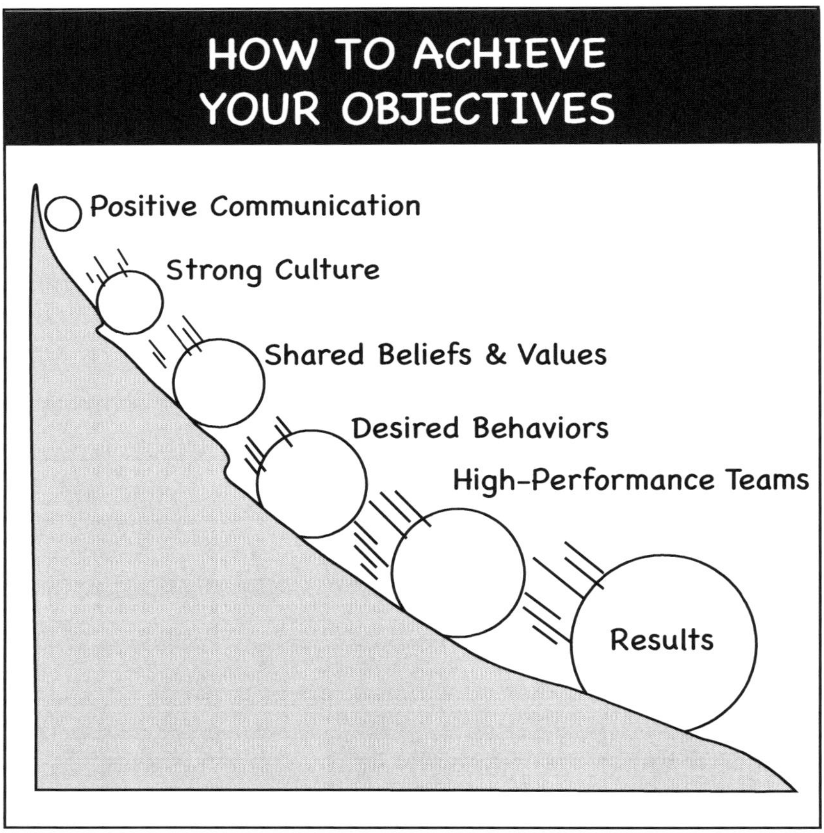

consider this: a strong culture increases net income by 765 percent over ten years, according to a Harvard study of more than two hundred companies. A great culture impacts the bottom line in multiple ways. It leads to higher retention, faster and better hiring and increased productivity overall.

Sometimes, to maintain a high-performing company, things need to fall apart. We've seen quite a few later stage startups, including a few that have gone public, reorganize large cross-sections of their managerial positions and reassign hundreds or thousands of roles, as the company changes to respond to market changes. Snowflake, a cloud computing 'data-as-a-service' company, led several rounds of multiple 'reorgs' as they're called in the industry, shortly before it went public. The company articulated these changes as absolutely necessary to ensure its long-term viability, even though it introduced a little bit of chaos in the short term. These reorgs were ultimately successful because the Snowflake leaders articulated how they fit into the plan to become a high-performing company, and that ultimately the short-term pains were a necessity for the long-term investment gains everyone was aligned to achieve. Let's be clear, a reorganization can mean people lose their livelihoods, projects get canceled, and employees and investors see a depreciation in the value of their holdings. But the way you communicate this to your audiences is where culture becomes part of the answer.

Improve Your Communication to Improve Your Culture

You influence culture directly by the way you communicate. As retired US submarine commander and leadership expert L. David Marquet said: "What is leadership but language? Changing the way we communicated, changed the culture." He inherited a dysfunctional environment when he took over the command of a submarine, and turned it around to become the best performing sub in the whole navy.

You foster strong communication by putting the principles of this book into action. Be the leader everyone always wanted to have. Promote a culture of appreciation. That's not just saying "thanks buddy" or "you guys are all the best", according to company culture thought leader Kristen Mashburn. Instead, appreciation needs to be both sincere and specific to cultivate gratitude. In a startup context, appreciation is particularly crucial because it is stressful and painful to build something meaningful. If you ask your team to enjoy the pain, make sure you acknowledge them when they do so. A focus on appreciation and catching people doing things well can make startup culture better than traditional corporate culture which often focuses on weakness. Mistakes are frowned upon, and feedback tends to be about catching people doing something wrong. This often leads to mediocrity, risk aversion or worse. Toxic work environments are characterized by:

1. Bullying and putting people down verbally
2. Cliquey and exclusionary behavior within the team
3. Controlling, disengaged or aggressive leadership

4. Unmotivated teams
5. Stifled growth
6. Rapid employee turnover
7. Absence of work-life balance
8. Absence of forward momentum

Poor or negative communication is central to all of these criteria. It can happen between the leadership and employees and between team members. Leaders need to keep an eye on how people communicate amongst themselves. If someone is putting a team member down just for the sake of it, it is the duty of the leadership to put a stop to it, in one way or another. Wherever you spot signs of toxicity, you have to take action quickly because it will spread throughout the organization. If the leadership team tolerates toxicity, it can rapidly bring down the company. It's the rotten apple theory in action. The upshot: Positive, intentional communication is the basis for a strong culture.

Be a Believer! Purpose, Vision and Mission

Group culture is one of the most powerful forces on the planet. We feel its presence inside successful businesses, championship teams and thriving families, and we sense when it's absent or toxic. It happens in companies when everyone in the organization connects with a galvanizing idea. The work has *meaning,* it is relational instead of transactional. This is easy when it's only a small team that knows each other well, but harder to sustain post-seed. That's why high-performing, fast-growing ventures tend to have some version of a Culture Code, a term popularized by Daniel Coyle's book with the same title. A Culture Code is usually composed of a company's vision, mission and shared values and how these translate into behaviors.

Startups tend to go through this process several times, usually when the company hits a certain milestone. This is completely normal, as the beliefs and behaviors of a five-person seed stage company tend to differ from the culture of a 200-person unicorn. Sometimes the values and beliefs already exist in the heads of the team, and it is just a matter of putting them on paper. In other cases, it requires the leadership team and ideally a cross-section of the company to define them together. **Culture is never done. It's always a work in progress.**

To ensure that the Culture Code message will be understood and shared within the team, your mission, vision and values need to be memorable. They can't be generic but should be unique and specific to your company. You want your employees to understand the deeper meaning of each aspect and keep this in their minds while working.

Start with your vision and mission statements. They clarify why your company exists and how it contributes to a better future. These two elements are part of your North Star which we discussed in Chapter 2. Together, they form your beliefs. Both should be short, simple and specific to your business. At first sight, they seem similar, and in fact they are often confused. So what's the difference?

A vision statement provides the future state you would like to see. It answers the question: Why do we exist? It's your purpose.

Your mission statement is derived from your purpose and states how you intend to build, achieve and maintain it.

It answers the question: How do we make our vision a reality? Let's take LinkedIn as an example:

Vision: *Create economic opportunity for every member of the global workforce.*

Mission: *Connect the world's professionals to make them more productive and successful.*

LinkedIn exists to create economic opportunity for everyone – its vision or purpose. How? By connecting the world's professionals. That's the mission. Together, these two statements provide guidance and alignment for everyone, from the CEO to the most junior person.

You can also decide to separate purpose and vision, as European fitness scale-up Urban Sports Club has done:

- Purpose: *We inspire people to live an active and healthy life.*
- Vision: *A world where everyone enjoys doing sports.*
- Mission: *We enable people to continuously discover all sports they love through the power of technology.*

You can treat your purpose and vision as one or not, there is no right or wrong here. The aim is to clarify why you exist. Here's another:

Our company exists to design, create and deliver purposeful innovations to people across the globe so they transform the way they discover, share and connect with the world around them.

Can you guess which company this is? Probably not, because it is so generic. This also makes it harder to remember. The statement belongs to Motorola, but it could be any tech company really. Random and forgettable is not what you want. Can you guess the next one?

Making humanity multiplanetary.

Correct, it's SpaceX. It's short, specific and unique. That's what you want in a mission statement.

A compelling "why" won't solve all your team problems, but it will help you to hire and to retain great people. A mission that is related to, for instance, sustainability, health, mental health, inclusion and community can be a massive motivator for employees.

Daniel Coyle in his book "The Culture Code" offers guidance on how to determine your company's vision and mission statements:

1. *Write them down.* You may need to revise them several times, try out different phrasing, or come up with multiple options to pick your favorites.
2. *Collect feedback.* Treat them like a theory. Ask your team and colleagues to test the theory, improve it and build on it. It's crucial to invite your employees to engage with your vision and mission rather than ordering them by decree. However, that does not mean you are putting your purpose up for a vote. Before you enter this process, be clear about what is a given and what is up for debate.

3. *Support your vision and mission with values.* You want your purpose to shape every decision in the company. That is done via a set of core values that connect your why with real-world priorities and actions in your company's everyday hustle.

Think of the vision as your fertile soil out of which a tree grows. Your mission is the trunk of this tree, with your products forming the branches that grow out of that mission. No tree can grow without sunlight and rain. Those environmental factors are your values and behaviors.

What Do You Value?

How should a company determine its values? Usually this is done by a group of people in a room debating what values best represent them. That common approach is wrong. Brainstorming a list of generic terms is unlikely to lead to strong cultural foundations for your startup.

As US entrepreneur and CEO coach Eric Partaker points out, a better way is to think of two groups of people. The first group consists of all the people you've loved working with. Establish what the individuals in this first group did that made you feel this way. These reasons represent behaviors that you truly value in others. "The second group consists of all the people you couldn't stand working with. Perhaps they required an incredible amount of effort to improve their performance or attitudes. Or perhaps they were ultimately fired or asked to leave," according to Partaker. "Similarly, now list out all the things these individuals did that made you feel this way. The antithesis or opposite of the reasons you didn't get on with these people are also great candidates for behaviors that you really value in others." These two collections of behaviors will reveal what is truly important to you and your team, and will even help you hire and fire right.

Some startups are guided by one core ethos, like Uber's *Always be hustlin'.* Alternatively, you can define what drives your business with three or four values. If you have too many, no one will remember them. If they are too generic and could apply to any company, they lose their power. Values like *integrity* or *respect* should be a given. They are not unique features that define your company unless you fill them with specific meaning. Once agreed upon and written down in your culture document, your values need to be lived – not once but all day every day. Sure, put them on posters if you like, but way more important is that they are repeated like mantras and displayed by the leaders every single day. The energy in your place should mirror the culture.

Since values on their own are often too abstract to guide our daily actions, a final step is necessary: to specify behaviors for each of your values. Behaviors should also be clearly defined and known to everyone. For example, if "total transparency" is one of your values, there may be a related behavior where team leaders share relevant numbers monthly and every team member has a weekly one-to-one meeting. Every employee can then hold their team leader accountable if these meetings don't happen or relevant information isn't shared.

Zenjob co-founder and CEO Fritz Trott provided an excellent example of values and behaviors on Oliver's *Speak Like a CEO* podcast. "At Zenjob, culture means to behave according to four values: Hungry, Honest, Helpful and Humble. They are our standard and how we make decisions." Each of the four values comes with two or three behaviors. For example, honesty has three defining actions: act with integrity, give honest feedback immediately and don't talk behind your colleagues' back.

They decided to take this approach because as soon as the company started to grow, the values that had been interpreted in the same way by a small team were now given divergent meanings by a diverse and international staff. Fritz attests that "you can have an office with the values written on every wall,

YOUR CULTURE CODE	
VISION	Why do we exist?
MISSION	How do we make our vision a reality?
VALUES	Hungry Honest Helpful Humble
BEHAVIORS	Honesty: - Act with integrity - Give honest feedback immediately - Don't talk behind your colleagues' back

but they will be meaningless unless you have behavior attached to them." That's the power of a strong company culture. Culture can make thousands of employees act as one.

Please Behave

The behavior of the founders has a huge impact on culture. Recently, we asked the leadership team of a successful startup how new hires learned about their culture. They joked: "by attending a meeting with our founder", an intense and driven CEO. It's funny because it's accurate: employees look up to see what the founders and other leaders are doing and what is important to them.

It is incredible how fast culture can change under a new CEO. Oliver worked closely with the first three CEOs of easyJet, and once a handover occurred, it took only a few weeks for the culture to change. This was by design. The Board wanted a leadership team and a culture that fitted the different growth stages of the company from startup to scaleup to post-IPO. The airline had a real startup vibe in the early days, and the mission was to fight the consumers' corner against expensive incumbents. The brand was built on irreverent, in-your-face PR and advertising. There were none of the usual C-suite perks under the first two CEOs. The third CEO, however, came from a legacy business and immediately injected a more corporate way of working, and the place felt different from one day to the next.

Founders need to be hyper-aware that they shape culture through their actions. When words and deeds match, they reinforce the culture. However, if leaders' behavior differs from what is officially defined as the culture, people will follow their actions and not their words. For instance, if "honesty" is a value but leaders don't give honest feedback, the result is a culture where honesty is not truly valued. It is only a short step to "toxic culture" from there.

High-performance teams send strong belonging cues which make employees feel part of the team and perform better because they have a sense of ownership. Belonging cues like high-fives are very visible in successful sports teams. In the office, these cues are smiles, friendly greetings in the morning, or rituals at the beginning of a meeting like asking everyone on Monday morning to share one fun thing they did that weekend. Because actions speak louder than words, a ritual that is backed up by a story to explain its significance is a great way to remind us of our culture and the bond we have with our co-workers. Kudos shoutouts on Wednesdays, "coffee with a colleague" on Thursdays, or Friday afternoon BBQs – great teams have rituals where they connect.

Companies like Nike actively foster rituals embedded in a storytelling culture to preserve their heritage and foster an emotional bond between employees. New starters experience many of the origin stories (as recounted by founder Phil Knight in *Shoe Dog*) during corporate campfires, the week-long "Rookie Camp" and trips to places of significance. While it may be too early for you to write books about the early days, start documenting your own history: your first sale, first financing, first lost customer, lessons learned. They are all part of your story and should be passed on to new joiners. Create a document, a wall of fame, a shrine in the office. Your organizational memory is valuable, and rituals keep it alive.

Culture Creates Crazy Productive Teams

We have seen how culture drives behaviors and therefore performance. Company culture expert Kristen Mashburn even holds that the right culture makes teams "crazy productive". Which founder doesn't want crazy productive teams? To sustain such a high-performance culture, you also need the right approach to hiring, motivation, training and your reward system.

Let's briefly touch upon hiring, which we dissect in the next chapter. While you want diversity of backgrounds and other attributes in your company, you want cohesion in values and baseline culture. Put strong filters in place to **hire people with common values. You can train for skills, but you can't train for culture**. Founders who compromise on values always regret it. Constantly remind the team of your values in words and deeds every day, until you get sick and tired of them. That's usually when the message starts to stick.

Once you've hired motivated people, you now need them to stay motivated, both at the individual and at the group level. In *Drive*, Daniel Pink outlines what motivates us:

1. Autonomy: doing the work on your own terms without being constantly controlled. Control leads to compliance whilst autonomy leads to engagement. (Every leader needs to find that sweet spot between autonomy and control. Employees don't want their boss to micromanage them, nor do they want to be left to struggle alone.)

2. Mastery: the desire to constantly grow and improve. If managed well, people are stretched but they can do the job if they put their minds to it. It's the sweet spot between boredom and overwhelm.
3. Purpose: working in line with my beliefs.

If autonomy, mastery and purpose motivate us as individuals, what about teams? Google performed an internal study to attempt to answer the question: What makes a team effective? They assumed it would be a particular combination of talents and skills. The results surprised them. Using data and rigorous analysis, they discovered that *who* is in the team matters less than *how* the team interacts and communicates, structures their work and views their contributions. Google summarized its findings by putting forward five key dynamics that set successful, high-performance teams apart:

1. Psychological safety: Do I feel safe to take a risk without feeling insecure or embarrassed?
2. Dependability: Can we count on each other as a group to deliver high-quality work on time?
3. Structure and clarity: Are the roles, goals and plans in the team clear?
4. Purpose: Are we working on projects that are important personally to us?
5. Impact of the work: Do we believe that our work as a team matters?

Given the importance of psychological safety, how should employers deal with the comfort and discomfort of their employees? In an ideal culture, team members feel secure, respected and comfortable about being part of their company. They should never be made to feel uncomfortable about their personality. However, they should feel a degree of discomfort about their work. They should, to a certain extent, feel stretched and challenged so that they grow and achieve mastery. This is an important distinction.

Training Employees to Succeed, as Part of Your Culture

Setting each team member up for success should be part of your culture. This requires training for their role, of course, but also to become better communicators. How many companies actually train their employees to be better presenters, writers, leaders? Not enough. **A high-achieving work environment is the result of strong technical skills AND strong communication skills,** because what is true for you as a leader is also true for everyone else. The better each team member communicates, the more successful the company.

In a high-achieving culture, there is a constant feedback loop for quick learning and improvement in all directions. High performance is coached on a day-to-day basis. Leaders give feedback all the time rather than waiting for an arbitrary date in the calendar set aside for the next annual or quarterly review. Leaders actively seek feedback, as they want to improve as well. New joiners immediately gather that they will be working in a high-performance culture, as part of a high-performance team. This will encourage them to focus and deliver immediately.

Adapt Your Reward System

It is sometimes said that half of the compensation of a job is social. Indeed, the social rewards we all get from working in a team toward a shared goal or purpose can hardly be overestimated. Other EX themes such as recognition, wellbeing, Environmental, Social, and Corporate Governance (ESG), as well as Diversity, Equity, and Inclusion (DE&I) also gain importance. On the flip side, a lack of positive social interaction, for instance due to remote work or a toxic culture, can lead to depression and disengagement.

That still leaves the other half of the compensation to be accounted for. In addition to money, the question is how to incentivize a team in the right way. Companies, nowadays, revert to perks for their employees – football tables, free food, discounted gym memberships, and many more fun things. More than the nature of perks and freebies themselves, these sorts of incentives are important because employees feel engaged and valued. For them to be effective, it's crucial to understand what your employees really want or need.

Kartik Varma, one of the co-founders of PropTiger, India's leading online real estate platform, reminded us about the early days of the startup boom in India. In 2010, startup founders didn't have the brand appeal or fancy offices to compete with the more established and prestigious multinational tech companies. In some cultures, the prestige that comes with working in a specific industry, or company, is all the perk you need to offer to an employee.

In the so-called emerging markets like Asia and Latin America, where long-term stability matters more than anything else, your culture will need to adapt. Varma told of how he'd extend offers of employment to very excited potential employees, and "things would go smoothly until they got home to their parents, where the responses would range from 'why can't you get a job at a real company like Microsoft or IBM' to 'How will you get married? Who would want a son-in-law who works in a small company?' and so at the time, the only way we could really compete was by focusing on the cash compensation component."

We spoke to several companies based in India that had adapted their hiring processes to include the option of bringing spouses and parents along before signing employment contracts, to ensure buy-in from *all* key stakeholders in the decision making process. The key point is that while there are cultural differences, we are all individuals and value different perks. Again, ask your teams what they would really appreciate and save money on offers that don't move the dial.

Also be careful when taking a perk away, even if few people use it, because people hate to lose anything. One founder recently told us how they asked employees to contribute 10 bucks toward the free public transport pass the company provided them with at great cost. What happened subsequently surprised the founder: employees were upset, and even team members who never used mass transit protested. It just shows: if you take anything away, make sure you explain it properly and expect questions.

Appreciation is not only about bonuses or money, but they are important. If your teams are heavily incentivized by profit share, stock options or growth targets, they will optimize their focus and behavior accordingly, potentially at the expense of something else.

Fixing a Toxic Culture

Sometimes a culture is simply broken, and everyone knows it. Fixing it requires an honest analysis of the root causes by the leadership team or the board. The problem may be a few toxic people who make work hell for anyone else. Or it may be that the leaders are terrible managers. Ultimately, the buck stops with the CEO. They need to either fix the problem or step aside to let someone else fix it, as a toxic culture jeopardizes the entire business.

Whether a change process succeeds ultimately rests on a single factor: Can the leadership team improve the emotional state of the company? Can they turn negative emotions like pessimism, fear and anger into positive emotions such as optimism, excitement and togetherness?

When developing a change strategy, contrast the prevailing emotions of today with your desired emotions, then come up with a plan to bridge that gap. Your messages, tonality and channels will be informed by this analysis. It's best not to beat around the bush when you have to change or reorganize things. Make it tangible for the team. Explain clearly what is happening and why.

In any change process, there are three camps: those endorsing the new direction, those against it and the undecided, often the largest group. An in-person meeting can be the igniting event, followed by an ongoing effort to get as many people on board as possible. Since you can't succeed on your own, you need to encourage your supporters to convince the wait-and-see faction. Those who do not feel at home in the new environment will leave anyway if they see that the new direction is permanent. But if you fail to convince the silent majority, the change process will run out of steam and the company will be caught in limbo.

Culture Gets You Results

Culture is not just about feeling confident and excited at work, even though that should be an outcome. It's much more than that. Culture is how you get results. That is the reason why startups with a strong culture leave those with a weak one in the dust.

There is certainly a trend at companies to codify their culture, often pointing to Amazon's setup. Years ago, Amazon banned Powerpoint presentations and instead created a new way to hold meetings. Meetings start with each attendee sitting and silently reading a memo for the first 30 minutes or so of the meeting. Jeff Bezos called it "probably the smartest thing we ever did". Startups codifying their way of working, including their meeting culture, is a positive development. If you haven't done it yet, make it a priority. If you have a culture document, here is an easy exercise for you: Which of your values or behaviors are different from your competitors? If there is no meaningful difference, then you haven't done it right yet. It's probably too generic, as in "we strive for brutal honesty, delivered kindly". Consider this: What do you need to change for your culture to give you an edge over the competition?

What culture would entice their top people and most lucrative customers to switch to you?

Culture is the foundation. It's one thing to codify it, but completely different to put it in place. In the example of Amazon promoting memos over presentations, the company also dedicates a significant amount of time training employees to write better. In the next chapter, we discuss how to put a system in place to ensure your Employee Experience translates into you becoming an employer everyone wants to work for. Another unfair advantage that your Message Machine gives you, if you get it right.

Chapter 8

BEING AN EMPLOYER OF CHOICE

With a strong culture in place, you now want to increase Employee Engagement. It is the second step in our "Employer of Choice" virtuous cycle (p. 200), a crucial part of building a Message Machine.

In order to grow fast, you need your people to be engaged. And engagement is driven by internal communications. Internal communications have gained in importance in recent years, in particular since the pandemic. For good reasons. Research reveals that up to 95% of a company's employees are unaware of or do not understand its strategy. The gap between strategy and execution is one of the most consistent frustrations for founders as their companies grow. Leaders believe that strategy and priorities have been clearly communicated. But their teams quietly disagree and disengage. How is this possible? And what can be done about it so that the team is not just well-informed but fully engaged, regardless of where they are?

These are the questions we seek to answer in this chapter which covers internal communications and employer branding. We have combined them because they serve the same objective:

to be seen as an employer of choice by those already working for you and by those you want to hire in the future.

For founders, it often comes as a surprise to see how challenging it is to maintain employee engagement as you grow. They may think that 'communicating up' to the Board or investors is the hardest part. Sure, that can be intimidating, but in a way it is also straightforward: work hard on the key message and prepare convincing answers to the big questions. Then, be bold, be brief and be gone. 'Communicating down' is more complex, messy and multi-layered.

INTERNAL COMMUNICATIONS

As a leader, you can devise an excellent strategy, but without consistent execution, results will be poor. What's more, you need to instill purpose in your organization, over and over again. This becomes even more mission-critical if your workforce is remote or decentralized. That is where internal communications come in.

Traditionally, internal communications were used to cascade information. Again, this is telling people what to do, and it doesn't work anymore. You want a system to set the team up for success which provides information and inspiration (push), gathers feedback (pull) and exchanges views with the team. The more you grow, the more crucial a state-of-the-art internal communications system becomes. It's how you bridge the "frustration gap" between strategy and execution. With a hat tip to Simon Sinek, your strategy and system are the 'how' and your content is the 'what.' But first, let's look at the 'why.'

Internal communications have three central goals: promote alignment and focus, reinforce culture and keep motivation high. If you get all three right, the result is sky-high employee engagement.

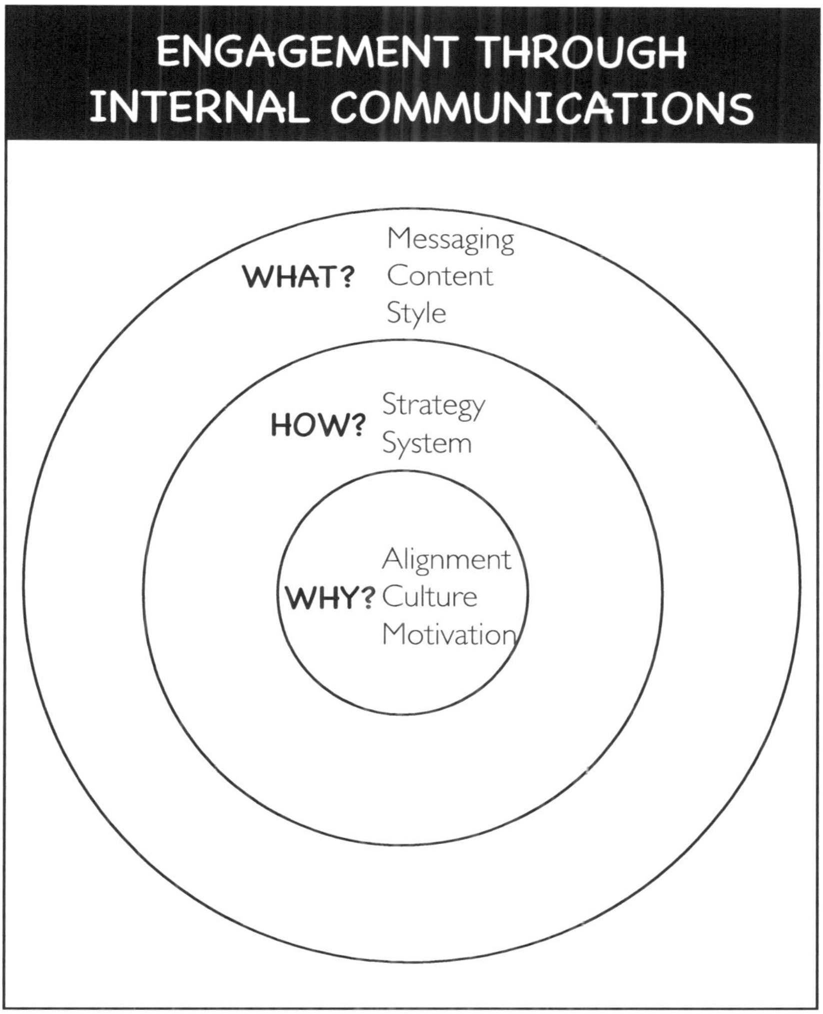

The First Why: Create Alignment and Focus

Internal communications promote alignment and focus on the common goal. Businesses are way more productive when employees have a clear understanding of the purpose and strategy of the company and how their own work is helping the company achieve its business goals. This may sound obvious, but it never fails to surprise us how little information filters down through businesses. As mentioned above, as little as one in 20 employees have internalized their company's strategy.

However, things are getting better following the wake-up calls of the COVID-pandemic and the Great Resignation. In a recent study, internal communications professionals who said they have an 'overarching internal communication strategy' reported much higher levels of employee understanding: 72% for purpose and vision, and 55% for business strategy. In other words: startups that turn pro in internal communications fare way better. It is precisely for this reason that high-growth companies have by and large stopped treating internal communications like an HR sideshow and are taking it seriously.

The Second Why: Reinforce Culture

Strong internal communications establish and maintain a strong, positive culture marked by trust. Management guru Peter Drucker was completely right when he remarked that "culture eats strategy for breakfast." Genuine and effective internal communications lead to a well-rounded company culture, which in turn results in more satisfied employees and ultimately a more successful company. As a founder, you – and your communication – are the reference point for culture and values. There is no one else in the organization with the ability to steer culture quite like its leaders. If you show that they are open and accessible, willing to listen to employees and give honest feedback, then a culture of trust and positivity emerges and eventually filters throughout the entire organization.

However, company culture is constantly in flux. And once the company has grown to a certain size, there will not be one singular company culture. This is exacerbated by the fact that most companies now work in a hybrid fashion where not everyone is in the office all the time, which may contribute to higher employee turnover. Companies are increasingly recruiting in a borderless fashion, anywhere in the world, which also has repercussions on culture. For all of these reasons, it is now harder to develop and maintain a strong culture. Internal communications are key to overcoming this challenge.

The Third Why: Keeping Motivation High

Lastly, internal communications help keep motivation high. True, founders should aim to hire individuals who have strong intrinsic motivation and who believe in the mission of the organization, but this motivation will inevitably diminish if employees do not feel valued in their work or feel that they do not have a voice. One of the key drivers of motivation is empowerment. By empowering team members, you establish the feeling of belonging and ownership, which boosts engagement and improves retention as well.

Empowerment is closely interlinked with employee engagement. The low-cost US airline Allegiant Air has found an original way to engage with its employees. Every month, they organize a pet contest, where employees use the company app to submit photos of their pets. Everyone is always eager to enter the contest every month and the submissions fill up quickly. What this does is direct people to the internal company app. We can even think of it as a form of gamification. Whilst it may seem odd to use a game to engage with employees, employers have to recognize that employees don't turn into robots the moment they walk through the company doors. Gamification and fun opportunities like this make people feel welcome, giving them a sense of belonging while also allowing them to express their individuality.

Creating alignment, reinforcing culture, keeping motivation high – all of that is easier said than done. In fact, employee disengagement is now seen as one of the biggest challenges for businesses. Quiet quitting is just the tip of the iceberg. Fortunately, as an exciting, high-growth company, you are in a strong position to avoid the myriad of problems that come with low morale.

Once again, solving this issue starts with a mental shift. Instead of an HR topic, **think of internal communications as you think of marketing.** You need to **deliver the right message to the right person, at the right time, on the right channel.** If successful, this approach drives understanding of the direction of the company, and the outcome is a motivated and focused team. By fostering a positive atmosphere in which employees are regularly reminded of the integral part they play in the success of the business, internal communications can drive engagement, enhance well-being and safeguard mental health in the workplace. The result: you can retain your best people.

How #1: Your Internal Communications Strategy

We have seen that internal communications can promote alignment and focus, reinforce culture and keep motivation high. Get all three right, and the result is an engaged team. To ensure this is happening in the hectic day-to-day of scaling a business, you need an internal communications strategy and a system for execution – the 'how'.

Your internal communications strategy needs to identify the various audiences and understand their needs and wants. You can then build your system for execution accordingly. If you employ 20 people who sit together in one office, that's relatively straightforward. If you employ thousands at multiple locations, it gets trickier, but the same principles apply. DoorDash is a publicly-listed scale-up technology company that started out by facilitating door-to-door deliveries between people and local businesses. For fast-growing platforms and marketplaces like DoorDash, drivers (or riders) and engineers have very different expectations, but both are crucial for the success of the business. One group can sit at a computer in the comfort of their own home, the other is on the road. One is highly paid, the other is not. One works in teams with hierarchies, the other is likely to be classed as a self-employed contractor. Naturally, the contrasts in messaging and channels need to be tailored to address their wants, needs and interests.

Because high-growth companies now generally understand these challenges, we have seen a drastic change in the channels used for internal communications. Reaching the right people with the right message at the right time can't rely on email and an intranet. These tools are outdated, because internal communications thrive on personal contact. Sure, a state-of-the-art social intranet and well-written emails can be part of the mix, but only if complemented by other formats. So, what does an optimized system for internal communications look like?

How #2: Your System For "Push, Pull, Exchange"

Your internal communications system to maximize engagement needs to **get information and inspiration across (push), gather feedback (pull) and exchange views with the team.**

While it is necessary to adapt your channel strategy to hybrid working, we believe that the objective should be to foster more personal interactions, virtually or in-person. Personal contact is your most important tool. Employees want to see and hear the leadership team, in real time, with opportunities to interact and ask questions. So your job as a leader is to inspire internally and to create a system of recurring formats that makes this not just possible but easy.

Speak to the team about what they need and value, similar to how you speak to your customers – internal communications equal internal marketing, after all. Then come up with some bespoke solutions, for instance "Five Minutes of Fame" presentations by different teams or "drumbers" (drinks and numbers) to share business results on a Friday afternoon. Make your work environments a fun place to work with a mixture of formal and informal fixtures. There are plenty of great formats for personal interactions: 'Ask Me Anything' or 'Deep Talks' sessions, coffee meetings with the founders, in-person or virtual town halls. If you worry about emotional exchanges during Q&A sessions, or if the cultural norms differ across all the countries you operate in, you can ask for questions to be submitted in advance. This allows you to answer the burning questions without any drama. There is no shortage of experts who can help you design these experiences. Julia Singh, Jag's wife, is one such expert. Her company pioneered the 'Deep Talks' guided conversation format to help companies transition their employees from being mere co-workers to a community of people that really understand, support and value each other.

Employees also appreciate opportunities for personal growth. We know of fintech and proptech startups that help their employees create personal wealth. Others invite external speakers, like fintech startup lemon.markets and their lemon. chats on Fridays after work (with pizza to sweeten the deal). Oliver's company once ran a series of Poolside Chats (summer's answer to fireside chats) with inspirational yet relatable contributors. You don't need much to test or launch formats like that. The pool was simply a paddling pool for children, filled with just enough water to cool drinks on a warm summer evening.

In addition to synchronous communications, you can ensure that the team encounters the founders as much as possible through asynchronous communications (i.e. not happening at the same time). This is particularly important for companies like DoorDash where the majority of people are not in the office. You can use videos, audio messages, messaging apps and internal podcasts – all great ways to communicate to a large, dispersed audience. If you choose to have an intranet, make sure the return on investment is high enough to justify the time and resources spent on maintaining it. It should be a knowledge hub, which means you have to figure out what matters to the team and meet that demand. See it as a service to the team, not a way to cascade information.

With all of these formats, consistency is key. Grant yourself permission to experiment with innovative formats, but once a channel or format is established, keep going. Stop-and-go sends a terrible message to your people, namely that they are not important and that they don't need to bother with new formats or initiatives because they won't last long.

Find Out How People Really Feel

Half the battle is to ensure that people understand why things are happening. They want to know that even if they can't change the outcome, they can at least shape the process. If you want to know how people really feel about working at your company, take stock and establish some benchmarks with regular employee surveys – the pull. It's the right thing to do, but it has to be done in the right way. You want to find out how many people have internalized your values and strategy, how aligned the company is, how motivated your people are and how likely they are to recommend you as an employer (your Net Promoter Score). You want to keep your questionnaire short to get a high response rate.

While surveys fulfill certain objectives, you should not rely on them exclusively. If you really want to feel the pulse of the organization, initiate annual leadership focus groups and team focus groups. This qualitative approach goes deeper with fewer people, to complement the quantitative approach of employee surveys.

When analyzing the results, be aware that how people feel about work is not solely an inward-facing affair. The external perception of the company is tightly interwoven with the way the internal stakeholders view and feel about the company. Take the 2008 financial crisis. Employees at hedge funds and financial institutions were markedly unhappier as the perception of their employers was brought into disrepute. Not long ago, tech giants were highly sought after. They are still attractive employers, of course, but recruiters tell us that "ad tech" companies such as social media platforms and search engines are losing their shine. Top talent is now more attracted to companies with a purpose, and some to the frontier of Web3. The point is: The higher the status of your company, the better people will feel about you as an employer.

It goes without saying that you want to take your survey and focus group results seriously. It is typical in toxic work cultures that leaders don't listen to employees and stakeholders when they express their discontent. In fact, any concern raised is an opportunity. If you show that you listen and address them, this will reinforce a positive culture of trust. If you can't address them right now, explain why.

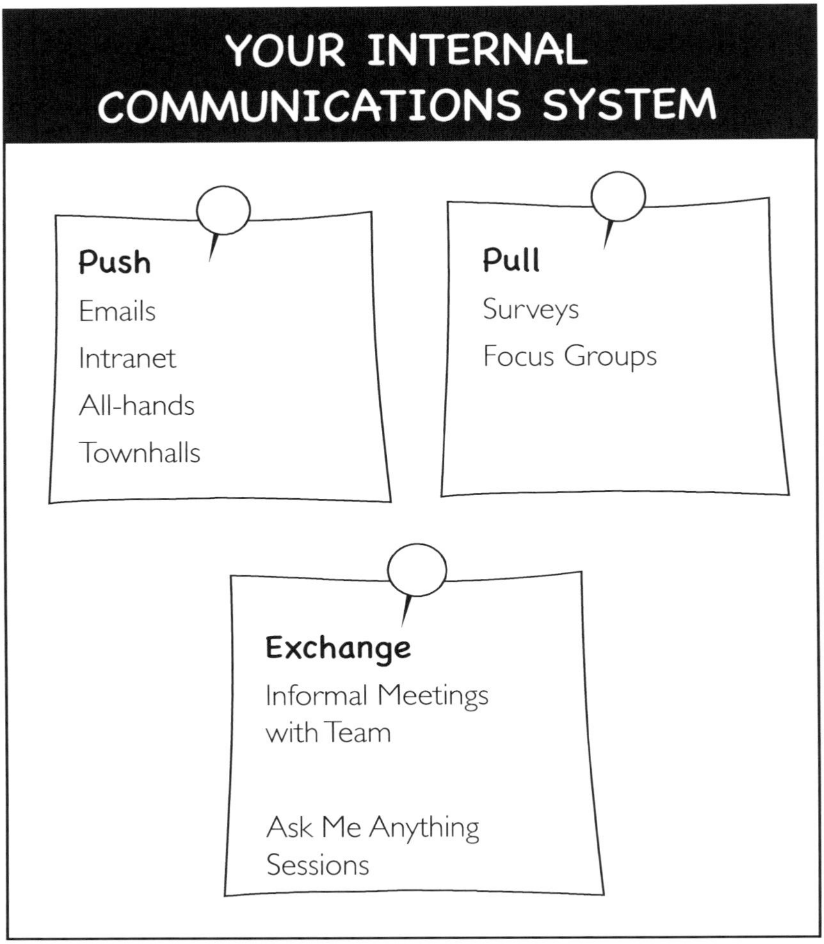

The What: Content, Messages and Style

The best system is only as good as the content you put out. Once you make the shift to treat internal communications like internal marketing and give it the attention it deserves, your content and your messages will improve as well. Whatever your content, make sure that responses are encouraged. Internal communications are no longer one-directional. They should be a multi-directional dialogue and conversational in style. You want a style that is high in emotional intelligence, authentic, simple and clear, and at the same time tailored to the audience.

Today there are more conversations happening in all directions and on many different channels. That makes it more important but also harder for founders to find the right style to guide the discussion. You want to shape the internal conversation without controlling it. Contrary to what some leaders think, employees don't want a hands-off style, because it seems like no one is steering the ship. Employees value a guided approach, where they feel led and coached. At the same time, they want to feel like they and their views are taken seriously. The upshot: you need to find the sweet spot between old school command and control, and a free-flow of unstructured conversations that happen in some places today.

Whatever your formats, give yourself and the team the license to make them short and entertaining. Internal communications can get a lot of inspiration from formats like Instagram stories or short podcasts. Having said that, you want to adapt the style to the situation. We remember the announcement when SpeedInvest brought Deepali Nangia in as a partner. Signing Deepali, a prolific angel investor and winner of the UK's Business Angel of the Year award, was a coup. The headline on the announcement read "Why a 'Brown Girl' From Calcutta Decided to Join Some 'White Blokes' From Austria on Their Venture Journey!" It conveyed a high degree of self-awareness, and levity. The message was clear – we know who we are, and we aren't afraid to change.

We have seen how internal communications can reinforce culture, foster alignment and keep motivation high. But even the best-run companies will lose people over time. To grow fast, you want to attract the best people and convince them to join your company rather than any other company under the sun. A tall order, but one that can be delivered by an outstanding employer brand.

EMPLOYER BRANDING

One of the biggest communications challenges for companies today is being seen as an employer of choice in a fiercely competitive landscape. Companies have to work harder to win and retain talent and are stepping up their employer branding game.

It is the final step in our "Employer of Choice" virtuous cycle that is made up of your Employee Experience (driven by culture), Employee Engagement (driven by internal communications) and – the topic of this section – Employer Appeal (driven by employer branding).

Let's take a step back. Startups brand themselves for a number of reasons. The first is to attract customers. So far, so obvious. The second reason is to attract investors. Like anyone else, they are attracted to strong brands, because startups with strong brands tend to become more valuable. Finally, companies brand themselves to attract and retain talent – this is employer branding. Patagonia, for example, has a great employer brand but also a great company brand that helps sell its products.

When you consider how much the survival of your business depends on attracting customers, investors and employees, taking care of your brand is just common sense. Unfortunately, employer branding is still not taken as seriously as company culture and internal communications. This is a missed opportunity. In the knowledge economy, your people are everything.

When you position yourself as an attractive employer, you are creating real value for the business. An engaged workforce and exciting company culture will radiate outside the company, and your people become your ambassadors. It's a competitive advantage, especially for high-growth ventures. People also like to buy from companies where it is evident that employees are happy. Patagonia makes it clear that they're not looking for "stars". Instead, they "seek out 'dirtbags' who feel more at home in a base camp or on the river than they do in the office." The "let my people go surfing" attitude of founder and owner Yvon Chouinard is the stuff of legends and makes the brand relatable to its core customer group.

While it has always existed, employer branding as a concept is still relatively new. Recruitment had traditionally been transactional. It was about getting bums on seats. That is no longer the case. Applicants do their own due diligence when they consider a potential employer. As a founder, you want to consider what candidates think about you and your company. Sure, money is always important, but it is by far not the only factor in the equation. Do you have a higher purpose and a positive impact on the world? Will I thrive in your culture? Will your company empower me so I can grow? These are the questions candidates may or may not ask you, but sure ask themselves.

Are You an Attractive Employer?

The point of branding is differentiation, so as a founder, you really want to think about how your employer brand and your organization can break away from convention. How can you create a situation where people look at your organization and immediately want to work there? You want prospective candidates to apply to your company because they identify with your vision, mission and values. You also want candidates to have a positive opinion about working at your company, and consider the CEO to be an inspirational leader.

Don't kid yourself though. What's most important is not you but what a candidate expects to learn and gain from the organization. Humans are driven by a mixture of altruism and selfishness, and if you can appeal to both and create a reputation for being an exciting place to work, you can win in a competitive market even without paying the highest salaries. This is why a strong employer brand is so incredibly important.

Let's establish where you stand right now. Companies that succeed in attracting top talent would agree to most of the following statements:

HOW STRONG IS YOUR EMPLOYER BRAND?

Company Culture

- [ ] Our vision, mission and values are written down and known to everyone.
- [ ] Employees know our culture code and act accordingly.
- [ ] Leadership lives and breathes our company culture.
- [ ] Our working environment reflects our culture.

Employer Branding

- [ ] Our employer value proposition is clear.
- [ ] Most of our employees would recommend us.
- [ ] We have enough high-quality applications from the right candidates to fill open positions quickly.
- [ ] We run campaigns that position us as a top employer.

Recruitment Process

- [ ] Every step of our recruitment process reflects our employer brand and company culture, including our job ads and careers page.
- [ ] We use the first interview to sell our company culture to candidates.
- [ ] We have a high offer acceptance rate.
- [ ] We have a high employee retention rate.

Total ______________________________

If you agree with nine or more statements, you are well on your way to becoming an employer of choice. If you agreed to between five and eight statements, you are on the right track, but there is room for improvement. If you agreed to four or fewer statements, you have a lot of work to do.

Be mindful that you don't know if some of these statements are true unless you ask your people. Countless studies have shown that there is a huge gap between what leaders believe is clear and what is clear to employees. Exit interviews and employee feedback sites such as Glassdoor help gain an even fuller picture. With this understanding of the status quo, you can now focus on the areas you need to improve. Is it your culture? Your employer brand? Or is it the hiring process? Likely there is potential in all three areas which together make you an employer of choice.

Activate Your Employer Brand

Since we already covered culture, here we focus on employer branding and your hiring process. Employer branding tends to be a cross-functional effort which involves the people, marketing, communications and leadership teams. Together you can take a number of actions to build or enhance your employer brand. Some are fast and free, others require some investment, but if you consider how much a high turnover and inefficient recruitment costs your company, these are in fact cheap. According to a Deloitte study, the cost of a leaver from your business is 150-200% of their annual salary due to the loss in productivity, knowledge and cost of replacement.

It's a real drain on resources. And many promising startups can't grow fast enough because of a lack of talent.

Start by crafting a convincing Employer Value Proposition (EVP) to answer the question Why should I join your company? Your EVP should be aligned with your culture and values. It also needs to talk about compensation and benefits, and of course opportunities for personal growth. Most startups do not have a convincing answer ready, or there are many different versions in people's heads and therefore no alignment. Before you go out and tell your dream employees why they should join your startup, you want to have a one-sentence EVP in place as well as a culture deck that answers all of these points.

Now that you are clear about why top talent should work for you, reach out to your target audiences. "Activation of the employer brand is as important as its creation. If you don't make sure everyone inside the company is properly aligned with the new direction, and then ensure you reach your dream candidates, all the hard work will have been in vain," says Georgiana Ghiciuc, an employer branding and recruitment marketing expert.

To activate your employer brand, you want to communicate your Employer Value Proposition through various channels. Similar to the customer journey in marketing, you want to take candidates on a journey. Package it as a story, or even hundreds of stories shared by your employees. This is what happens on the Microsoft Life Instagram account which has over 200,000 followers.

The candidate experience journey starts with the discovery phase, where they hear about your company at an event, on social media, via someone already working there or because they are a customer. Referral programs can give your team the right incentive to spread the word. A well-executed social media campaign helps to attract candidates, as long as it is authentic. Companies like Hive, a Berlin-based scale-up which offers fulfillment to e-commerce businesses, post their culture decks on LinkedIn to show what applications can expect to "Thrive at Hive".

Employee-generated content with organic reach tends to work better than a polished image video or paid ads. More and more startups empower certain employees to be ambassadors for the company. If you go down that route, ensure they get the freedom, training and logistical support they need to make a real difference.

Introduce a Brand-Led Hiring Process

Let's move on from the discovery to the consideration phase – the hiring itself. Job seekers have "lost patience with ever-cumbersome hiring processes. They know that they are in demand, and they want to see that employers recognize their value. Create a hiring process that is a positive experience for candidates to foster a good relationship from the start," urges hiring expert Brad Chambers in the Harvard Business Review.

Once a potential candidate is interested, they would normally check out your careers page and job ads. Your candidate experience is only as good as its weakest link, and job ads and careers pages often fail to inspire. Most job ads look like variations of the same grocery lists. We can probably all guess the reason, because we have all done it: we copy, paste, tweak, and are done with it. We saved five minutes, but may have lost the best candidates. Rather, customize your job ads to make them appealing to the candidate persona you are trying to attract.

Most importantly, make sure your process is transparent, fair and engaging. Whatever your webpage or job ad states needs to be delivered to avoid candidates being disappointed and your own staff becoming cynical.

Next is the conversion stage. Often this is where employer branding fizzles out, which is a gross oversight. This is the stage where top talent decides if they want to join your company. Don't leave it up to chance. Instead, make your hiring process a manifestation of your brand and your values.

Candidates are attracted by great culture, so make sure you sell yours during your hiring process. Yes, selling. Even in a buyer's market, it is the company that has to sell itself to the candidate, because A-players always have a choice. Candidates expect flexibility and autonomy. Yet, they also want more community and a shared sense of purpose. To attract top talent, offer the best of both and tell candidates about it.

Ensure that your culture and employer brand shine through all 37 touch points of a typical candidate journey. It begins with the first point of contact, be that a communication from your talent acquisition team, or a communication from your hiring agency, or even your job advertisement. The hiring process only finishes when the onboarding of the candidate is completed. **Job interviews should be conversations, not interrogations.** Think of how you schedule the interviews, how you follow up with your candidates and how you process your feedback. All of this will impact the external perception of the company and will ensure good word-of-mouth.

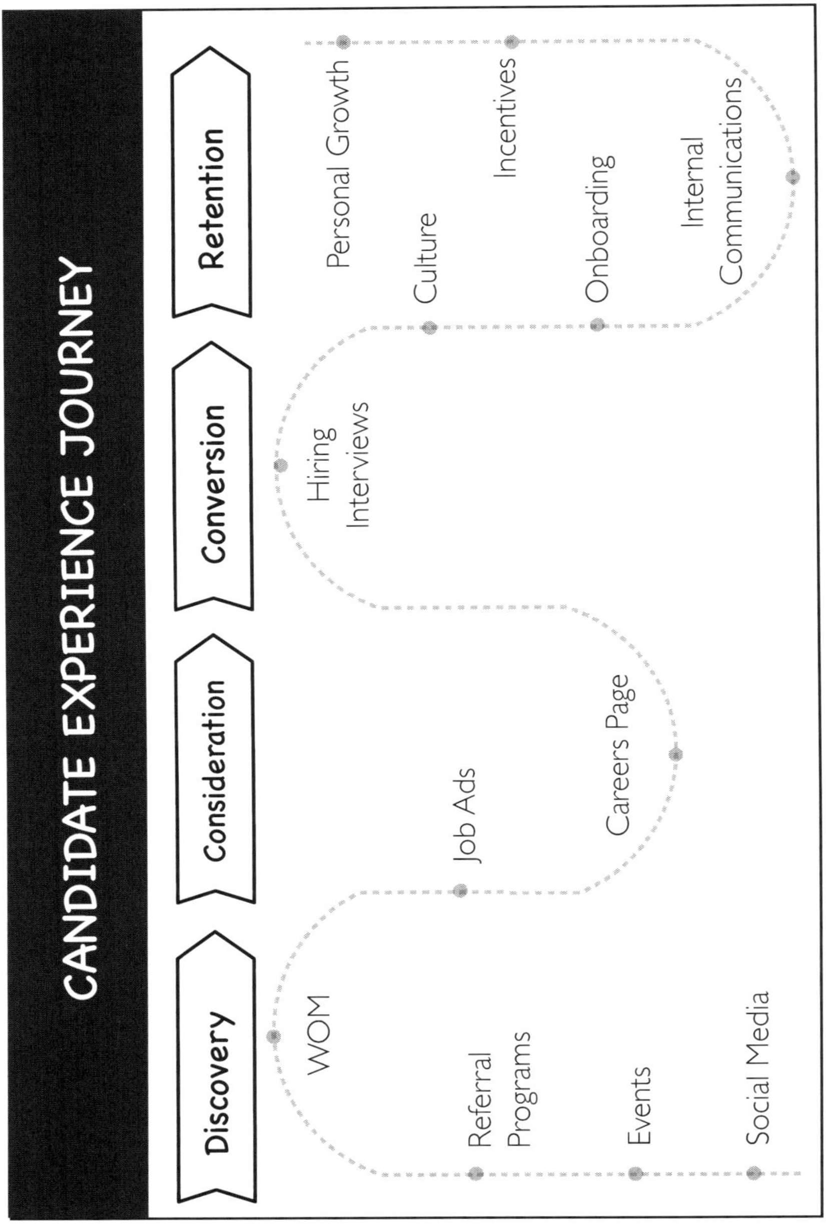
CANDIDATE EXPERIENCE JOURNEY
Discovery
Consideration
Conversion
Retention
WOM
Referral Programs
Events
Social Media
Job Ads
Careers Page
Hiring Interviews
Culture
Onboarding
Personal Growth
Incentives
Internal Communications

Once you have mapped out these three dozen steps, make sure everyone who is involved in the process sings from the same hymn sheet. If you track the data, you can even identify the exact touch points where applicants drop out of the process and fix them. There is no need to reinvent how you analyze a multi-step process. You can apply the same processes and tools your marketing team uses to track the customer journey.

The Most Damaging Hiring Pitfalls

We've observed many startup leaders overwhelmed by hiring, and subsequently delegating the whole process to the nearest HR person or even an administrator. Caution: A general HR professional is not a recruiter. They may not sell the company or its Employer Value Proposition (especially if these are unclear within the organization). As a result, candidates may get the impression that a company is not really interested in them. The solutions are to insist on a brand-led hiring process, professionalize recruitment using either internal or external expertise and have hiring managers rather than HR lead the interviews. If you use recruiters, be careful how you choose your partners. Get them to show you how they pitch the opportunity before letting them represent you.

A major pitfall for scale-ups is that they allow every hiring manager and recruiter to do it in their own way. That means that there are an infinite number of hiring processes, and leadership has no clue what actually happens, why turnover is high or why positions aren't filled with the right people. Too many HR people, recruiters and hiring managers still use the first interview to screen a candidate rather than selling the company and its culture. That is a mistake and costs them dearly in a competitive market.

Hiring is a skill, so it is important that your hiring managers are trained to interview according to your values. If they do, candidates will experience a certain type of interview that reflects the values of the organization. Your hiring managers should also be providing relevant and engaging assignments where appropriate in the hiring process. Jag had personal experience of this with Techstars, the global investment organization. One of the company's key values was respect for networks over hierarchies, and the process for hiring junior associates often involved giving them 'real work' assignments. This contrasts with many companies that hand out 'busy work' assignments to junior staff, essentially communicating that they just aren't important.

You also want your team to be trained in bias recognition and in interview best practices. Your managers should be confident to conduct various types of interviews, such as the STAR method or competency-based interviews. The STAR method (situation, task, action, result) prompts candidates to provide specific examples of how they've handled past situations or challenges. Gut feelings will always play a role in hiring, and sometimes you should listen to your instincts. But you can't bet your company's fate on guts alone. **You want a well-trained team that executes an agreed brand-led and value-led hiring and firing process. Such a process is like a magnet: it will attract the right candidates but deter those who are not a good fit.**

For most candidates, the last touchpoint with your company will be a rejection. Candidates value feedback, even if a 'no' is not what they want to hear. Feedback is so important because it allows candidates to understand how they are perceived in interviews and gives them an opportunity for improvement. Consider a creative email with valuable feedback rather than a plain, matter-of-fact rejection email. You will leave a lasting positive impression and word will get around that you are an exciting place to work.

Should I Stay or Should I Go?

This leaves us with the fourth and final stage of the candidate journey: retention. Be careful not to over-promise during your hiring process. Sometimes employer branding doesn't match reality. A study by BambooHR found that of people deciding to quit, 16% do so in their first week, and an additional 17% in their first month. Often, this is because the new job does not meet their expectations. They built up an image of what it would be like in their minds, which then turns out to be wrong. This is why it is important to live up to the expectations raised during the interview process right from day one.

Companies usually do one or two onboarding days. However, no one learns how to do a job well in such a short period. Startups with the highest retention tend to treat onboarding as an ongoing process that takes three, six or even nine months. How you onboard has a huge impact on retention. "Hiring is hard at the best of times and yet few companies put much effort into the one thing that has the single biggest impact on retention: onboarding," advises Konstanty Sliwowski, CEO of Caissa Recruitment. "Numerous studies have shown that organized and meticulous onboarding over the course of weeks and months has a significant positive impact on the ability of a business to ensure long term success and retention of their staff." How someone is onboarded sets them up for success or failure in a company. A bad onboarding experience means the person can't do their job as well as they could. This can lead to unfulfilled potential, mutual frustration and eventually an early departure.

There is a better way. For any role you are going to fill, consider who did the job before. What's the step-by-step process? What's going to make the new employee's first, second and third week successful? What would you expect after three months? Outline the process from day one. A new joiner should meet their manager, buddy and admin contact on day one, and everyone they will work with within a week. If the manager communicates the steps clearly and the new joiner knows who to ask in any situation, they will quickly feel at home and can excel in the role. None of this is probably new to you. And yet, few startups implement a thorough onboarding process. Companies don't like doing this, mostly because it's tedious and boring. That's true, but not as tedious, boring and expensive as a high resignation rate.

At some point, your new joiner is onboarded and fully integrated into the company. The question that matters most after a while is how they feel on a Monday morning. How do they feel and think about their colleagues? Do they work on interesting and exciting projects that help them grow? Or is work something they dread? The answers to these questions determine whether someone stays in a company. As we all know, retention is a prerequisite for success, as a high turnover is not just an inconvenience, but a huge expense: up to 2x the leaver's annual salary. And of course, it slows down your growth. Continuity equals speed.

Eventually someone decides to move on, which brings us to the final step of the hiring process: off-boarding. Again, most companies don't prioritize it, which is a missed opportunity. Employees will never speak more openly than during exit interviews. Are there any toxic people? Is the workload unmanageable, or management indifferent? Leavers' feedback gives you the opportunity to address any issues.

Wanting to Work for You, In Good Times and In Bad

We have seen why culture, internal communications and employer branding are not soft concepts or nice-to-haves. They are hard factors that have a massive impact on the success of your company. They attract A-players who are fully engaged, have a great experience working for you, and tell other A-players about it. That's the Employer of Choice virtuous cycle that powers your Message Machine.

Even the best employers' standing with their people, customers and investors will be tested sooner or later. We will now dissect how you can crisis-proof your startup. Because a crisis will inevitably hit you.

Chapter 9

EMERGING STRONGER FROM CRISES

Running a startup is like the early Wild West, in particular in a crisis. You didn't inherit your ranch in Wyoming from your grandparents. You got it by outmaneuvering your opponents and holding your ground. Just like the rancher who puts up a fence and practices shooting, you want to be prepared. Fail to prepare and you prepare to fail.

Communication is the foundation of any company's success. It's ridiculously more important in a crisis. We live in volatile times that require founders to be fully prepared for any eventuality and react with resolve when – not if – the next big unexpected thing happens. An important distinction: Communicating in a crisis is not the same as communicating during a time of crisis. So if you've done well during COVID-19, fantastic! But this says nothing about your preparedness for a crisis.

Crisis communications happen when your company is in trouble, and the rest of the market isn't. Either you screwed up, or an event affects only your company, like cybercriminals stealing your customers' data. It's a "hair on fire" moment.

When that happens, many people are angry and some even want you to fail. You receive a lot of unwanted attention.

In contrast, communications in a time of crisis occur when your company is in trouble, and the rest of the market is also on fire. No one has time for you, because there is a large-scale negative event going on that just happens to affect your market in a profound way, like an epidemic, a financial crisis or geopolitical conflict.

Sometimes a time of crisis turns into a crisis for your company. Urban Sports Club was on course to hit unicorn status in early 2020 when Europe announced strict lockdown rules. This was an existential threat for a startup that had thus far relied on providing physical gym, sports and wellness offers in a number of European countries. Almost overnight, the company turned its business model around and introduced online and hybrid solutions to its members. That was part one. They then communicated to all stakeholders how they were handling the crisis and why they made the choices they did. This affected investors, customers, employees and thousands of independent partners like yoga studios, whose existence was also under threat. According to co-CEO Benjamin Roth, it was mission-critical for the leadership and the communications team to make sure that the messaging was fully aligned and executed with great professionalism and empathy. This helped avoid rumors, discontent and uncertainty. By showing empathy and taking communications and crisis preparedness seriously, USC was able to overcome an existential threat.

In this chapter, we discuss how to emerge stronger from both crises and from times of crisis. You can't build a Message Machine that powers your venture to unicorn status and beyond if your reputation is in the gutter. But first, let's clarify what a crisis is:

A "crisis" is a time of intense difficulty or danger that can cause significant and lasting damage to a company, unless the right response is chosen.

The stakes are therefore extremely high in a crisis, and the wrong decisions – or the wrong response – have the potential to destroy a company. Here it is as a formula:

Event + Reaction = Outcome

So while a crisis is always bad, it does not necessarily result in a wholly negative situation. If you make the right decisions, a crisis can be turned to your advantage and become an opportunity. Oliver has helped to manage countless crises ranging from aircraft crashes to cyberattacks, from compliance issues to product screw-ups and site closures. Even in the worst imaginable situations, the outcome always depends on how the company reacts, in particular via its communications. When the volcanic ash crisis grounded Europe's air traffic in 2010, Oliver and the team at easyJet were faced with multiple crises: an economic one, because the company had no revenue coming in but huge fixed costs; and a human one, as tens of thousands of passengers were stranded far away from home. Once airspace reopened after enormous pressure by airlines on hesitant politicians, easyJet scheduled around-the-clock rescue flights to repatriate passengers and picked up the costs. It was the number one story in the media for over a week, and the public acknowledged that easyJet was the first airline to sound the alarm when the crisis started and brought customers home as soon as possible. Though that didn't solve the financial problem, because hardly anyone booked flights even after the flight ban was lifted. The CEO then went in front of the media with the head of the Civil Aviation Authority to present a technology that could detect volcanic ash in the air. Despite the fact that this "ash radar" wasn't yet fitted on any aircraft, the story was all over the television for a day and helped reassure the public.

There is everything to win and lose in a crisis. Yet most companies are ill-prepared because of a lack of training, lack of urgency or lack of commitment from leadership. In the 2021 PwC Global Crisis Survey, 95% of business leaders agreed that their company's crisis management needs improvement. As a founder, you will be the one to face the music when things inevitably go wrong. It will be both your personal reputation and the reputation of your startup that is at stake. That's why **hope is not a strategy. You need to be a prepper**. And if you think preparation is annoying and time-consuming, try facing a crisis you are not prepared for.

BECOMING CRISIS-PROOF

We have no idea what unexpected events will hit the world in the coming months or years. What we do know is that we live in crisis-prone times. Whatever sh*tstorm is brewing when you read this, it is not the first crisis. The world has ended before. And while it did, visionary founders launched some of the most successful companies ever, including Amazon and Apple and, during the huge recession of 2008-09, Airbnb, Uber, Slack, Groupon, WhatsApp, Instagram, Square and many others. (And the next generation of disruptive companies was probably founded in the 2020-22 era.)

What these companies did was to use a moment in time to aggressively attack when everyone else was scared, distracted and contracting. To play offense like that in times of crisis, you have to be great at defense. So, how do you become great at protecting your downside during a crisis or in times of crisis?

Prevent: Your First Line of Defense

Prevention is always better than the cure. Founders cannot predict the future, but with an adequate risk assessment, it is possible to detect issues that make you vulnerable or trigger a crisis in the future if left unaddressed. You want to assess market risks, geopolitical risks, technical and operational risks as well as legal and regulatory risks. Certain customers can bring risks and so can personal issues surrounding a founder. Do a no-holds-barred risk assessment and then decide on actions to minimize these risks. For instance, if all your supplies come from one country, you are very exposed if a crisis hits that market and may want to diversify your supplier base. That's why Apple recently started to produce iPhones in India in addition to China.

Prepare: Your Second Line of Defense

A solid reputation and strong relationships can protect you in a crisis. It is your reputational capital that you can draw on when times get rough. If stakeholders already trust you, it is way easier to keep them on your side. These include your investors, employees, regulators, community and journalists. Having a community and a network around you that trusts you and stands by you when things get unpleasant is invaluable. They stand by you and may even speak out for you when you are under attack, be it on social media or in quiet conversations to calm things down.

No company beyond Series A is prepared without a crisis communications plan. It determines who your crisis leader is, who does what and who speaks for the company to which stakeholders. The chain of command needs to be clear. It usually runs from the CEO – the commander-in-chief – to the crisis leader, often the chief communicator who directs the crisis team. The team tends to consist of additional communicators, HR, operations, legal and subject matter experts. The plan makes roles and responsibilities clear from the outset, so that everyone has a sense of ownership as soon as a crisis breaks. A crisis is not a democracy. It requires calm and determined leadership. The commander-in-chief needs to be able to command the room. The members of the crisis team can't crack under pressure and ideally have some experience in handling issues and crises. If you are short of experience, include external experts in your crisis team to call in when needed.

A crisis communications plan also accounts for worst-case scenarios and provides pre-agreed draft statements and countermeasures for each. Crises can be operational (e.g. a system outage that means you can't serve your customers) or reputational (as in Uber's case). It can also be a mixture of both, for instance when a cyber attack breaches your defenses and your customers' data is stolen. The Institute for Crisis Management found that 50% of crises are triggered by management behavior, so this should be one scenario that you plan for, even if it makes for an awkward discussion. Your plan should be regularly updated to account for new developments. Oliver recently helped a company in the financial industry to prepare a crisis plan, followed by a simulation of a cyber attack. Just one month later, when the company was attacked by cyber criminals over the course of several days, the team knew exactly what to do and even had the right statements ready. This wasn't because of our great foresight, but because almost every company that deals with money is targeted sooner or later.

Logistics are also part of the plan, most importantly your War Room. This is a dedicated meeting room which is fitted with all the necessary equipment that can be set up at a moment's notice. Being together in the same location has many advantages, including quick response times. If that is not possible, for instance because the team is working from home, it is better to manage a crisis fully remotely than in hybrid mode. Having part of the team on-site while others listen in via video call creates a lot of challenges. Only do that if the people on video call are not central to your crisis effort.

In addition to a crisis communications plan, you may need a crisis plan to keep everyone safe and to ensure business continuity. Drafting the plan will ensure you know what to do and have alternatives in place if all your servers fail, a production site is closed for health and safety reasons or there is a fire in your office. It answers the "what if" questions.

Make Your Training Tougher Than a Crisis

So far we've covered the theoretical part. The equally important practical part is to train those who speak on behalf of the company during a crisis. Your messengers are usually members of the leadership team and your spokespeople. They will need to be prepared to represent the company internally and externally, even under pressure and in the most challenging and emotional situations.

In addition, it is paramount that a company undertakes regular crisis training to practice your War Room muscle. The purpose is to train the crisis team and to stress-test your crisis communications plan. Some of these trainings can be basic, for example a table-top exercise in which the core team gets together in a room and thinks about how the organization would respond to a specific crisis. More advanced trainings include all relevant teams such as operations, legal, customer service and people in relevant markets. They recreate the conditions of a crisis as accurately as possible, including simulations of social media s*itstorms and devastating news reports. Of course, things will never go absolutely smoothly in simulations, but that is the point. You learn and improve until you are crisis-proof.

These steps should not be treated as one-offs, but an ongoing process to ensure you are crisis-proof, whether it is a crisis or a time of crisis. Treat this as a 12-month cycle where annual training and a simulation ensure the company is prepared for ever-changing threats. If you follow these steps and **prevent, prepare and react in the right way**, you will be ahead of most other businesses in your market. That also **means you can take advantage of times of crisis when everyone is scared and distracted**. While others figure out what to do, you can grab market share, hire their best people and emerge as a clear winner from the rubble.

WHAT TO DO IN A CRISIS

Prevention, training, a solid reputation and a watertight plan protect you against both a crisis and in times of crisis. However, there are some differences. In times of crisis such as an epidemic, you are not the protagonist but a potential casualty. A crisis that only affects you is different though. It follows the same dramatic arc as a story, because in the minds of your stakeholders it is a story that evolves in front of their eyes. The only question is: Will you be cast as the villain, or can you turn things around and get the chance to open a new chapter? A crisis unfolds as a three-act story:

Setup: the moment when the crisis unfolds; it can be sudden or slowly emerging.

Confrontation: things come to a head, accusations are flying around, it's messy, all sides struggle to shape the narrative.

Resolution: either a happy ending for the company because it rose to the challenge, or a dramatic ending for the company as the villain who goes down.

Let's look at an example: In 2017, accusations against Uber CEO Travis Kalanick reached a tipping point (The Setup). Clearly, his reputation had tarnished the business, and both Uber and its CEO were cast as villains. In a boardroom showdown (The Confrontation) the company's backers decided they no longer wanted Uber to be a villain. They removed Kalanick as

CHECKLIST: CRISIS-PROOFING YOUR COMPANY

Prevent

- [ ] Carry out risk assessment
- [ ] Put mitigating measures in place

Prepare

- [ ] Build solid reputation
- [ ] Maintain strong network
- [ ] Draft crisis communications plan
- [ ] Draft business continuity plan
- [ ] Ensure fully functional War Room
- [ ] Organize crisis media training
- [ ] Execute a simulation with the crisis team

Review and repeat at least once a year.

CEO and replaced him with a new CEO with a more amicable leadership style. This gave the company a fresh start and the possibility to tell a new story: We have listened and we are changing for the better (The Resolution).

This example shows how crucial the narrative is in a crisis. This is often overlooked in the midst of the business equivalent of a category 5 hurricane. When the debate in the situation room focuses on legal and operational technicalities, you need to take a step back and reflect: Where are we, and how do people think and talk about our company right now? In Uber's case, it may have been "The boss is a douchebag, and they don't care about anyone but themselves. I don't like them, and I don't want to use them anymore." You can easily see how a reputational problem with the CEO filters down to customers, and if they go somewhere else, investors and employees will be pretty unhappy. In Uber's case, replacing the CEO was the only move that allowed them to reach a conclusion, protect revenue and move on. Any other action would have fallen into the category of "too little, too late," and the crisis would have continued.

This example shows that a key objective in a crisis tends to be to minimize revenue loss. There will always be some impact on revenue – otherwise it would not be a crisis but an issue, and issues pop up every day.

As mentioned, to pause and reflect is crucial in a crisis. Ask yourself: What are our three top priorities right now? Is it to:

- clarify what happened?
- reassure your employees?
- reassure customers to protect revenue?
- (re-)gain trust?

- maintain productivity?
- convince investors?

Keep it simple and address your top priorities with a simple, consistent message to control the narrative.

Controlling the Narrative

A crisis is an unfolding story, and your job is to control the narrative to avoid becoming the villain. This is becoming more important every day. Because today there are more crises, affecting more businesses, and they spread faster. The first step in crisis management is identifying the crisis, and recognizing its existence. A crisis can emerge slowly or break out unannounced from one second to the next. If it breaks slowly, a good indication is that the public starts to become aware of your issue. It can also be that members of your team alert you that a potential crisis is brewing. Once you've identified that there may be an issue, take immediate action to address it so as not to exacerbate the situation further or risk losing control completely over time if left unattended. You need to know where you stand, who the stakeholders are, what issues to address and how you can best manage the situation—all before taking any action.

Sometimes a crisis breaks without warning and you may only have minutes to react before it blows up. That's why the first 60 minutes are crucial for the outcome of the crisis. This period is called the Golden Hour in crisis communications. The business must respond quickly and get the message out or risk losing control of the narrative. Like Starbucks CEO Kevin

Johnson, who apologized after two African American men were arrested for 'loitering' in a store in 2018. He closed thousands of cafés for two days to ensure all staff attended racial bias training, and was quick to communicate externally. Silence creates an invitation for others to frame the crisis. Remember: Whoever shapes the story gets to decide who the villain is. But don't lose your head. It's easy to get swept away when everyone panics. Be strategic, and focus on your priorities.

Once a crisis breaks, time is against you. On Twitter, false stories are 70% more likely to be retweeted than true ones and spread six times faster, according to an MIT study. Digitalization brings countless benefits, but also cyber attacks and misinformation spreading like wildfire. And with increasing numbers of employees now working remotely, there are even more points of attack for cybercriminals. The larger and more visible you are, the more you may become a target, both as an organization and as an individual.

You win the Golden Hour in three phases. In phase one, the pre-appointed crisis manager puts the crisis plan in motion, convenes the team and identifies who needs to know what immediately. The second phase is about analyzing the situation, gathering all available information, creating a stakeholder map and considering scenarios of how the crisis may unfold. Finally, in phase three you have your initial response ready to go out internally and externally, assigning who speaks on behalf of the organization and who is responsible for which stakeholder group such as regulators, shareholders, customers and the team. All of these steps as well as the chain of command, roles and responsibilities are clearly outlined in your crisis plan.

With a solid crisis plan and regular training, everyone knows what to do and you have a good chance to shape the narrative.

Your key objective during those first 60 minutes is to not lose control over the crisis. It is easy to see why pre-agreed holding statements greatly improve response times while unprepared companies struggle to get their response out quickly and lose control of the narrative as a result. If you are invisible when a crisis unfolds, the information vacuum will be filled by others – trolls, competitors and the rumor mill – and you won't like it. More importantly, you give the impression to your customers and the world that you don't care. And that's the worst thing you can do in a crisis. Teddy Roosevelt had it right: "People want to know that you care before they care what you know."

Admittedly it can be hard to find the right words in the midst of battle. As a principle, **in a crisis, "Acknowledge, Apologize, Act" (AAA); don't "Deny, Diminish, Deflect" (DDD).** In the latter case, when companies use the DDD approach, this means that they:

Deny fault
Diminish the crisis or their involvement in it
Deflect the situation to shift the blame to someone else

In a crisis situation, we must never underestimate the intelligence and perceptiveness of the public and our stakeholders. Most can detect when companies are trying to pass the buck or weasel themselves out of a mess they created. As a result, these businesses undermine their long-term value and ultimately their survival – like Boeing following the first 737 MAX crash in 2018. First, the company tried to shift the blame to pilots and the airline, and allegedly intimidated journalists. They desperately tried to make someone else the villain in the story. But once the truth came out about the technical fault after the second crash the following year, Boeing's leadership completely lost control of the situation and were eventually forced out. The manufacturer and its ousted leadership team were cast as the villains by the media, the public and regulators around the world. Four years after the crisis started, Boeing was still losing billions while trying to rebuild its reputation.

Compare this with the AAA approach:

Acknowledge: Regardless of who is at fault, immediately acknowledge a critical situation. Don't stay silent when the news breaks, or better still, be the one who breaks the news on your terms.

Apologize: In oftentimes tragic, convoluted and complex situations, apologies are always in order. Make sure you show genuine care and empathy. This is not to be confused with admitting guilt.

Act: The crisis will not go away by itself. Act fast to remediate the situation. Reassure your stakeholders that you will do your utmost to prevent it from ever happening again.

Once the initial response is clear, the company's messengers should contact the various stakeholders, in line with your crisis communications plan. One founder may focus on investors, another on employees. Other members of the leadership team would keep customers informed and would ensure that you shape the message via the media and on social media.

All regular social media, PR and marketing communications should be put on hold until the crisis is over.

While everyone communicates the same message, it is tailored to the audience and channel. A customer email sounds different to a statement to investors or regulators, but the message needs to be the same, usually: *We are aware, we are sorry, we are working tirelessly to solve it. It won't happen again.* Remember: Your customers don't care about your company's financials — they just want answers! When something goes wrong, honesty is key. Communicating transparently with customers will help ensure that this trust between company and consumer isn't broken in future experiences together. Remember the pillars of trust outlined in Chapter 1: competence, integrity and benevolence. We all make honest mistakes, but lying, withholding or selfish behavior when things go wrong are much harder to forgive. It may be tempting to bend the truth a little in a crisis, but this seldom ends well.

Not all audiences are created equal when it comes to timing your response. You want to inform your investors and employees before you go external, or at least at the same time. Otherwise you risk your most important stakeholders hearing about your crisis from the media or on Twitter, and they won't be pleased.

Working with the media is critical to effective crisis communications. Ideally you already have strong relationships with key journalists in your sector. They can be your allies, or at least neutral observers. Situations where the media become intrusive or hostile often occur because an organization has withheld legitimate information or tried to intimidate journalists (don't, it always backfires). In refusing to effectively cooperate with the media, you lose a valuable opportunity to shape the narrative. Others will tell the story for you and it can backfire badly if your organization comes across as arrogant or indifferent to the crisis.

Dealing with Lawyers, Politicians and Regulators

Crisis situations require advice from lawyers, and they undoubtedly have a vital role to play. Lawyers are not, however, communications professionals, and your organization will find itself in the court of public opinion long before it finds itself in a court of law. Given the likelihood that a crisis will result in lawsuits, your lawyers will rightly advise that the organization should not admit guilt during a crisis. But that does not mean that CEOs should remain quiet or read out lawyer-like statements. What may sound like a zero-risk approach is in fact fraught with danger. It is possible to express deep regret and empathy for the individuals affected by a crisis without accepting guilt in the legal sense. In fact, it has been done many times, so do not listen to the "say nothing" school of thought if you value your reputation and the valuation of your company.

Of course, a showdown between lawyers and communicators in the heat of a crisis is the last thing a company needs. It may even lead to a rift in management, at a time when unity is of the essence. The way out of this dilemma is to find common ground before a crisis strikes. Ideally, the heads of legal and communications should reach a general understanding that a "say nothing" response would be incredibly harmful to the company. Based on this understanding, their teams can draft a number of pre-approved statements and lines to take that would serve a company well in a crisis situation.

In a crisis, unwanted attention comes from all corners, including from politicians and regulators. Ideally you have an existing relationship with them when a crisis hits and can pick up the phone and explain the situation. If not, at least make sure you know who the relevant players are. Reaching out to them and keeping them informed tends to make a big difference in a crisis. If you show regulators that you take them seriously, they don't feel the need to grab you by the throat to get noticed. And politicians are much less likely to put the boot in on Twitter or in the media when you are in dialogue with them.

Managing a crisis ultimately comes down to trust. We are generally willing to forgive an honest mistake if a company comes clean about it and puts counteractions into place. And that's where it gets interesting: **Doing the right thing tends to enhance a company's reputation, despite a crisis.** You show that you are reliable, no matter what.

MANAGING BAD NEWS

For most companies, scaling is a bumpy road, not a smooth ride. Chances are you will be forced to make difficult announcements at some point, such as laying off 20% of your staff. Handled incorrectly, this could alienate the other 80%, negatively impact your reputation for a long time and prevent top talent from applying when you are ready to hire again.

In March 2020, a well-known scale-up announced that it would be laying off about 30% of its staff in response to the financial uncertainty of the coronavirus pandemic. Here's their justification for the announcement which went down like a ton of e-scooters: "We purposefully and intentionally did not have any video on to protect privacy as we delivered the news live to individuals. A live speaker delivered the news in real time over the web-based call and a slide was projected outlining additional information including four weeks of pay, three months of medical coverage and an extended timeframe to exercise options."

Here's what actually happened at e-mobility company Bird, according to those on the call. It's April 2020. One of the regular biweekly all-hands (referred to as Birdfams) was canceled, and all employees were expecting an update from the CEO. Some employees received a calendar invite to a webinar with no participation list, unlike their usual Zoom calls. They realized not everyone had been invited, and started trading frantic messages on Slack. The call starts, no one can hear anything, just a slide on the screen saying 'COVID 19 Update'. After five minutes of dead air, a woman is heard saying "this is a suboptimal way to deliver this message. COVID-19 has also had a massive impact on our business, one that has forced our leadership team and our board of directors to make extremely difficult and painful decisions. One of those decisions is to eliminate a number of roles at the company. Unfortunately your role is impacted by this decision."

Bird managed to turn a time of crisis into a crisis of its own making. It wasn't the layoffs themselves, which were understandable and happened at many companies when the lockdowns started. It was the way it was announced that led to a furious reaction and significant damage to the company's reputation.

If you need to reduce headcount, you will need to explain the reasoning and show empathy with the affected, as well as providing reassurance to the rest of the team. What could Bird have done better? First of all, an announcement like this needs to come from the CEO. The CEOs of many other affected companies did exactly that during COVID and faced the music rather than cowardly sending a messenger to do their dirty work. Second, news like this is better delivered personally, rather than in a mass video call. If that isn't possible, show your face and be prepared to answer questions on the call. Third, you want to shape the external narrative to prevent your reputation taking a hit. When presentation software startup Pitch had to part ways with 30% of its staff in 2022, CEO Christian Reber posted an empathetic announcement on LinkedIn, outlining the reasons for the decision and what the company was doing to help those affected. He followed up with an alumni list to ensure each affected colleague would quickly find a new position.

While Pitch protected its reputation in a critical phase, Bird's way of handling the situation pretty much guaranteed a backlash against the company. It shouted "we don't care" – not a great message to the remaining 70% of employees. The main reason for this is an astonishing lack of empathy. We are not saying that the leadership had no empathy. But it sure looked that way to everyone inside and outside the company. In a crisis, you have to show that you care.

Turning Customer Feedback Around

There are many critical situations that do not meet the definition of a crisis and may not warrant a full-scale response from a company. However, you still want to address these, in particular negative customer feedback. It can be a huge liability for fast-growing companies. You get word-of-mouth alright, but not the right kind. And the transparency of the web means an indefinitely small number of negative experiences can be seen by an indefinitely large number of potential customers. To neutralize negative feedback on social media, respond quickly with an apology and an offer to help the customer offline. Empower your community managers and customer service team to turn things around so that the customer feels compelled to post a *thank you*. To counter negative reviews on Google or Trustpilot, ensure that you have enough positive reviews in the first place.

You can even make negative customer experiences a selling point. Sometimes it's okay to be vulnerable, as it can help turn around a brand or a critical situation, provided that the company outlines a plan of action to address the shortcoming – acknowledge and act! You can sell the fact that you're listening to your customers, as Carlsberg did. In the spring of 2019, Danish beer brewer Carlsberg launched a campaign on TV and social media sharing that they had changed the recipe of their Pilsner. Carlsberg's slogan had until then been 'the best beer in the world.' The problem: Beer drinkers disagreed. The TV ad depicts employees of Carlsberg reading the meanest tweets about the taste of Carlsberg, such as "It's like drinking the bath water your nan died in", and finishing with the new slogan

"Probably not the best beer in the world. So we changed it." By acknowledging that the old beer recipe was not as good as they claimed it to be, taking action to change it, and adding humor to the mix, Carlsberg managed to turn a negative customer experience into a selling point.

So you can turn negatives into positives, if you play your cards right. But can negatives be good in themselves because they raise your profile?

No Such Thing as Bad Publicity?

Oscar Wilde said: "There's only one thing in the world worse than being talked about, and that is not being talked about." Is that also true for a startup?

In *Antifragile,* Nassim Nicholas Taleb invites us to consider a scandal that affects a politician, a construction worker and a writer. The politician's career could be utterly ruined by a scandal or another kind of Black Swan event. He is therefore *fragile*. The construction worker may lose his job but chances are he can find another construction job somewhere. He is relatively *robust*. The writer, however, is *antifragile* because even a storm of negative publicity raises her profile which is going to lead more people to check out her book. She gains from a negative event, a Black Swan, that wipes out the politician.

For a business, a degree of controversy can actually make it stronger, as we have seen with challenger brands like low-cost airlines. What they may not survive, however, is a crash. That is a new airline's or urban air mobility startup's single point of failure. It can completely wipe them out. For other companies, it can be that cyber criminals steal customer data which destroys trust in a fintech, or a health food business that uses inferior ingredients. As a general rule, the younger the company and the less trust capital it has accumulated, the harder it will be hit by a crisis.

So clearly, there is such a thing as bad publicity — in business. It therefore won't surprise you that the person who coined the phrase "There's no such thing as bad publicity" made his money in entertainment. It was Phineas T. Barnum, a 19th century American showman and circus owner.

Be a Prepper

A crisis does not end once the immediate fallout has passed. On the contrary, the following days, weeks and months are essential to rebuild trust in your organization and ensure that everything possible will be done to ensure that a similar crisis can never happen again. Constant communication, internally and externally, can help rebuild your brand and reputation. You may want to go on a charm offensive like Travis Kalanick's successor as Uber CEO, Dara Khosrowshahi. Or you may want to inform your customers of the actions you have taken since the crisis.

Even if crisis communications have been largely successful, there are always lessons that can be learned. It goes without saying that the leadership and the communications team need to do a proper post-mortem and reflect on its crisis communications strategy and amend it for future use.

Communications are about promoting and protecting your Message Machine. Out of all aspects of communications, crisis communications is arguably the most important, since a crisis can make or break the company. Once your company reaches a certain size or has been around long enough, it is not a question of if a crisis will hit, but when. Managing a crisis is different from living through times of crisis. But whatever happens, it is your job as a leader to ensure that your company and yourself are prepared so that the end of the story is a happy one. At all times,

Be strategic. Be a prepper. Be consistent. Keep it simple.

CONCLUSION

In an article entitled "The Soul of a Start-up", Harvard Business School professor Ranjay Gulati writes:

There's an essential, intangible something in start-ups – an energy, a soul. Company founders sense its presence. So do early employees and customers. It inspires people to contribute their talent, money, and enthusiasm and fosters a sense of deep connection and mutual purpose. As long as this spirit persists, engagement is high and start-ups remain agile and innovative, spurring growth. But when it vanishes, ventures can falter, and everyone perceives the loss – something special is gone.

He's right! As a startup, you feed off that energy. That energy, that soul is precisely what many large companies have lost along the way and are trying to get back. The big idea of this book is that communications should be your number one priority, because they impact all other priorities in your business. You become an unstoppable founder when you build your Message Machine, unlocking the full potential of your startup. What's more, **your communications keep the soul of your startup alive**.

Now it's time to take action to turn your business into a Message Machine. Your actions will depend on where you are on your founder's journey. We will therefore briefly sketch out the most relevant milestones for you personally and for your company before giving you a framework to think about your next moves towards becoming a master communicator and building a Message Machine.

Personal Milestones

Your first funding round stands out as a personal milestone, particularly the first investor presentation that leads to someone committing a chunk of money to your venture. It means that you communicated clearly, presented with impact and listened to feedback. You told the story of your startup to great effect.

Then, your first media interview. This is a rite-of-passage. Journalists are skeptical by nature, and what you say will be online forever. Positive media coverage therefore shows a whole new level of awareness about how you communicate. Similarly, your first time speaking on stage shows that you can capture the attention of a room full of strangers. Your story lands, your message resonates.

As your startup grows, you increasingly inspire your team and ensure that everyone is aligned and focused on executing your vision and strategy. It's not all fun and games though. At some point there is likely to be conflict among the founders, with an investor or an employee. Things could turn ugly or dysfunctional. Fortunately, you understand exactly how to turn such conversations around and ensure a positive outcome. No one builds a great company without going through some drama. But your leadership steers the ship through the first crisis as well. You ensure that your company communicates with empathy, fast. You acknowledge, apologize and act so whatever happened won't happen again. As a result, your company emerges stronger.

Whenever you pass a personal milestone towards becoming a master communicator, you take a beat and acknowledge the moment. And you do the same for every milestone you pass as you build your Message Machine.

Message Machine Milestones

In the early days, each additional employee, each round of funding and each new customer can be a milestone for your startup. The first customer you lose or the first employee who quits – these are also milestones. They point to the fact that a company is mature enough to afford to lose customers or employees who weren't a good fit.

Your company's milestones allow you to tell your story with a fresh hook, highlighting what this milestone means for the company and its internal, external and financial stakeholders. Customers care about one set of milestones; employees care about another. People within the leadership team care about different sets of milestones. For investors, important milestones tend to be achieving a certain amount of revenue, a certain amount of customer and employee satisfaction, reducing churn rates and beating external or industry benchmarks. The messages vary. When hiring the first employee, the message to the customer is that this employee is going to allow you to provide the customer with a greater amount of services. The message to investors is that this employee will make the team productive.

You set the agenda and define which milestones are important to whom and which ones should be celebrated with the whole team. Then you deliver exactly the right news to your internal, external and financial audiences at the right time using the right medium. Here are the most important rites-of-passage for a startup, and how communication shapes them.

Milestone 1: First Customer

Your first customer is your first milestone. You put out the message that "we are learning from this first customer and we will be applying what we learned to our messaging, our sales process, our marketing process, and our customer onboarding process." You signal to the broader world that you are ready for more customers, and ensure that the organization is in fact ready for them. Your first customer even becomes your first third-party endorsement.

Milestone 2: First Funding Round

Securing funding is a sign that you have done a few things – but not everything – right. Externally and internally, your funding round is perceived as proof of your idea and the team. Early-stage investors generally understand that they're playing the odds game, and fully expect you to still fail. In fact, they've probably already written off the investment in a spreadsheet somewhere. Your first angel investors will still think that it took you twice as long as it should have to achieve this, or they might think that you should already be capable of raising three times the amount. Your competitors might think that you have already reached a ceiling and will not be able to go any higher.

There are clear-cut examples of companies, like WeWork, almost destroying their reputations because they over-celebrated a milestone that some or all of their stakeholders did not perceive as a relevant milestone. More money does not need to mean lavish parties or new MacBooks for everyone.

This will not happen to your venture. You are aware of these concerns because you listen and are able to lead these difficult conversations to positive outcomes. As always, it is not about what you say, but about how you say it. Everyone can say "we are on track", but you make that message stick by giving yourself a pat on the back, and then setting your focus on to the next hurdle.

Milestone 3: From Startup to Scale-Up

You have validated the vast majority of assumptions your business is built upon. You have hired the right people who now power your Message Machine. As the business grows and complexity inevitably increases, you manage to keep communications simple and effective. You build a communications system that maximizes results while minimizing the time and energy it takes.

You are able to convey to your investors that for every $1 they put in they are going to get a certain amount back. The question here is no longer whether the idea works. Instead, it's reframed to ask "Can we make the scale-up happen?" as you start to define the limits of your market. The narrative shifts from the idea to the execution and the resources needed to get there. A scale-up requires you to communicate in a far more mature manner. Your investors are now more likely to include bankers – the corporate type – or ex-bankers. Your biggest customers are likely to be large enterprises. And each of them has their own multiple stakeholders to deal with.

Our friend, John von Berenberg-Consbruch, a former banker and now Partner at Angel Invest focuses on such later-stage investments. He often tells founders who have already hit the $1 million recurring-revenue milestone that he "still has to determine whether they'll actually get to the $10 million mark, which unfortunately won't mean much to our institutional investors; or $100 million in revenue, which means investors in our fund might actually have a shot at getting some money back."

As you start to think about international expansion, you are aware of the need to localize your messages rather than simply translating them. Cultural context matters, and each region is different. You empower your local leadership to be able to communicate instead of being a bottleneck.

Milestone 4: First Crisis, and Emerging Stronger from It

The bigger you get, the more of a target you become. Competitors, labor unions, regulators, reporters, cyber criminals – no one gets a free pass from everyone. Fortunately you are well prepared and know exactly how to handle a crisis, and how to maneuver in a time of crisis. You emerge stronger from it, which gives you and the team more confidence and credibility. Others admire how you deal with a challenging situation.

Milestone 5: Exit

At some point, there is likely to be a sale or an acquisition. This involves some form of exit and requires your communications to evolve. The story you tell is no longer one about a scrappy startup, nor a scale-up that's crushing it. It is a story about a company that is set up for long-term success. You position your business in the sweet spot between the new and innovative on the one side and the stable and predictable on the other. Because for an exit, you need to attract an even wider portfolio of investors.

There is a limited number of people you should be speaking to about selling. Lawyers, existing investors and advisors are realistically the only ones who are aligned with your interests. While there is always a case for expanding the number of people who may be able to help, there are risks associated with communicating with too many people. For one, it poses a reputational risk in case the deal does not go through. In addition, the simple principle that "anything you say can and will be used against you" to potentially block or prevent the deal from going forward applies here.

Companies are not sold, they're bought. An acquisition signals that someone sees value in whatever you've built. It is usually the acquiring company that wants to talk about the acquisition because it achieves a certain goal with it. They will have their own communications plan, however. If you are the acquired company, you are aware that the acquiring company is the one that's going to be setting the terms for who communicates what and how. Your job is to continuously reassure customers that their services will still function, employees that they will still have a place to work and investors that you are trying to extract the highest amount of value to provide them with the highest returns possible. This might entail convincing your investors that the acquisition is the only way for them to secure a return on their investment. Many investors have blocked acquisition offers when they felt the price was too low.

Boards are the most relevant body of an organization when it comes to communicating how an acquisition is playing out or will play out in the future. Your Board communicates with a clear, united voice about the implications of the acquisition for the various stakeholder groups.

Not every exit is a happy ending. If an exit is involuntary, you handle it with grace. Similarly, imminent bankruptcy presents an important opportunity to communicate to your investors, customers and employees. You see what is coming, you take the right decision and then you communicate openly with all relevant stakeholders, wrapping it up as a professional. Your reputation is intact. People actually laud you for the way you handled the situation. Investors get some of their money back because you did not burn through it until the very end. Customers have time to find a new supplier. Your employees feel respected because you are open with them and give them some time to think about next steps.

Milestone 6: Going Public

Exciting times! Your PR successfully builds a narrative arc towards your IPO. However, you are aware that there are new constraints and that saying too much or the wrong things violates regulatory requirements and compliance. Your CFO, one of the most valuable people in the organization, is a seasoned professional who helps to navigate this high-stakes situation.

You have a full grasp of the regulatory landscape and are in dialogue with your regulators on a regular basis. You reassure your investors – from the earliest investor who put in $15,000 in your seed round to the large institutional pension fund that invested $15 million in your most recent funding round. At the same time, you galvanize your employees and customers towards your mission. Customers tend to find milestones exciting because they like winners. But it also presents an opportunity to large customers to renegotiate contracts because they know you are vulnerable to losing them. You manage to walk that tightrope.

An IPO brings an increase in visibility and transparency. You are required to report on your activities much more openly. The increased scrutiny and transparency mean that you need to disclose potentially doing business in parts of the world or with certain governments, companies or individuals that you did not need to disclose before. This factors into your milestone communication strategy.

Milestone 7: The Post-Exit

At some point you exited, whether it was a success or a failure. But your life or your career is not over. You are thinking about the next opportunity. Timing matters here. If your company fails before it even gets started then no one else was on that journey with you yet. You know that it is your job to communicate what you did right and what you did wrong. You shape that story to fit your own agenda.

If your business already had employees, customers and investors, you take your responsibility towards them seriously. You ensure that they come out of this not only with their reputations intact, but hopefully enhanced, whether the business was a success or failure. What your former stakeholders communicate about your last venture affects others' perceptions of you. Because you have been truthful and worthy of their trust, their stories match up to yours. This matters because you may build another company and raise money again.

Following the exit, the story of your venture is now incorporated into your personal story. The story is nuanced. Even if your company was hugely successful, you are humble and highlight that there was an element of chance. You were lucky to be the right person at the right time. You stress how much you have learned along the way. On the flip side, if you fail, the narrative is not all negative, either. You have learned and will use that knowledge in your next venture. Personal stories are never all black or white.

Determining Your Next Moves

As you shift from a 'communications last' to a 'communications first' approach, you want to consider ways to tie your background and past experiences together. In other words, your reputation. Warren Buffet, in his 2010 letter to Berkshire Hathaway shareholders, wrote: "We can afford to lose money – even a lot of money. But we can't afford to lose reputation – even a shred of reputation." We've been taught that reputation is perhaps the most important single asset that any company has, and perhaps it equally applies to individuals as well. This reputation, as well as that of your company, is what will likely propel you forward into your next venture.

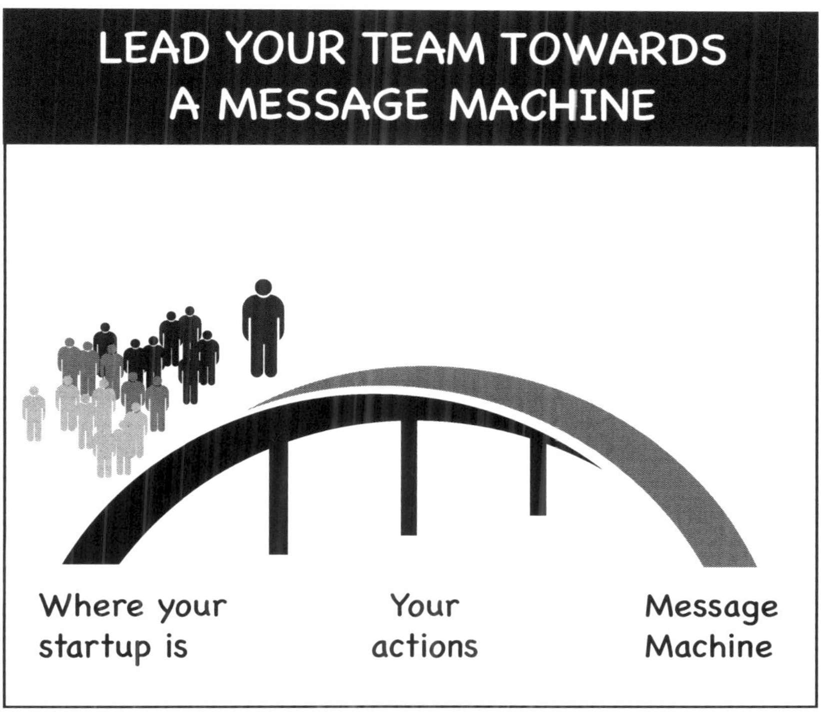

The personal and company milestones we just outlined give you a strong indication of what you want to focus on next. We encourage you to find at least one trusted partner for this, whether it is a shareholder, advisor or mentor. The easiest place to start is with one of your existing investors or a founder who's already 'crossed this metaphorical bridge' before. You probably need more than one, but one is a great start. You can then lead your team over the metaphorical bridge towards the Message Machine that empowers you to fulfill your mission.

Now ask yourself this: Which of the areas covered in this book do you want to tackle next? Pick the highest priorities for you personally and for the company. These should be the ones which are currently holding the organization back, or may do so shortly. Once you have singled out your focus areas, decide on your immediate actions to ensure rapid improvement. For your execution, circle back to the relevant chapters and principles in this book, as they will give you guidance and help you turn insights into actions.

Do not fret about stepping on someone's or your team's toes. If you see an urgent need to improve internal communications, you could decide to ensure that the right person is driving it, review all channels with the communications team, and schedule regular coffee or 'getting to know you' sessions with employees. The cost of inaction here could have profoundly catastrophic consequences. Before even thinking about your employees, customers and shareholders, you owe it to yourself.

DETERMINE YOUR NEXT MOVES

Actions Personal

1) ______________________________

____

2) ______________________________

____

3) ______________________________

____

Actions Company

1) ______________________________

____

2) ______________________________

____

3) ______________________________

____

Building Your Message Machine

As a founder or CEO, you ultimately own communications, so delegation is fine, but not abdication. Your company, your communications strategy. Nina Pütz, the CEO of Berlin-based fintech Ratepay echoes this principle:

I consider myself not only as CEO but as Chief Communicator. Why? Because motivation, reputation, valuation, engagement, productivity, and performance all start with our communication at the top. How we as leaders communicate sets the tone for communication throughout every department and every level of a company. Throughout my career, I have learned that communication externally and internally is everything but a soft skill; it's an objective, quantifiable strategy.

Developing personal communication skills never ends, and internal, external and financial communications are constantly evolving. Yet, we believe the communications principles on the following pages will remain true and relevant to every founder's journey. Please also head over to the book's website at **https://messagemachine.io** for bonus content and to get in touch with us. We are grateful for any feedback, and will strive to address the inevitable shortcomings in any future edition. You can also check out our episodes on the *Speak Like a CEO* podcast in which we discuss the topics of the book.

Communications can make you an unstoppable founder. It is now up to you to make that happen. Now is the time to build your Message Machine.

CONCLUSION

NINETY-TWO COMMUNICATIONS PRINCIPLES FOR UNSTOPPABLE STARTUP FOUNDERS

This list entails every single principle of this book with corresponding page numbers.

1. As a company grows, its biggest challenge always becomes communications. (p. 1)
2. If you don't communicate, you don't exist. (p. 1)
3. All the key tasks of a startup founder require high proficiency in communications. (p. 5)
4. Poor communications are the underlying reason why startups fail. (p. 5)
5. Companies don't rise above the communication skills of their founders. (p. 7)
6. Great communications accelerate growth. (p. 8)
7. All communications are audience-specific. (p. 9, p. 80)
8. Effective communication always feels like a one-to-one conversation. (p. 10)
9. The hierarchy of communications: the most basic level is data, above that comes information, then knowledge, and finally wisdom at the top. (p. 14)

10. Communications can be planned, but they can't be controlled. (p. 19)
11. Clarity trumps complexity. (p. 21)
12. Clear thinking precedes clear communication. (p. 23)
13. Repeat what is important so it sticks. (p. 39)
14. No one cares about the company or product. People care about what they get out of it. (p. 24, p. 87)
15. Every conversation or piece of communication has two dimensions: the explicit content dimension and the relational dimension. (p. 26)
16. Humans put a lot of value on authenticity in communications. (p. 27)
17. Your fear of looking stupid is making you look stupid. (p. 28)
18. Creating a meaningful distinction between you and the competition is what branding and marketing is all about. (p. 32, p. 112)
19. Companies move at the speed of trust. (p. 34)
20. No visibility, no trust. (p. 35)
21. Words matter because they activate frames. To persuade someone or change someone's mind, activate the right frame. (p. 37)
22. Communication is a hard skill for founders. (p. 43)
23. The better you communicate, the more intelligent you appear. (p. 47)
24. Focus on one idea. (p. 49)
25. Hearing is passive. Listening is active. (p. 49)
26. The company story is the company strategy. (p. 55)
27. The CEO is the chief storyteller. (p. 56)
28. The customer is the hero, never the company. (p. 58)

29. Even a single story makes a talk, interview or presentation more impactful. (p. 58)
30. As a founder, it is not your job to inform; your job is to inspire. (p. 60)
31. Highly charismatic people exhibit the perfect blend of warmth and competence. (p. 65)
32. Energy is vital in leaders. Be an energy-giver, not an energy-taker. (p. 66)
33. Your business succeeds or fails one conversation at a time. (p. 68)
34. Direct communication equals speed. (p. 68)
35. Your pitch deck is as strong as your thinking is clear. (p. 77)
36. Build it and they will come does not work. (p. 79)
37. Every successful company needs to achieve both product-market fit and message-market fit. (p. 79)
38. In a startup, everything depends on selling, and selling depends on the right messaging. (p. 82)
39. Focusing on your biggest differentiator can be very powerful. (p. 86)
40. You have to make them care. (p. 87)
41. Customers don't buy what you are selling, they buy the outcome. (p. 88)
42. Your positioning leads you to the right answers. Your messaging gives you the right words. Together they underpin your branding and marketing. (p. 91)
43. Identify what is working and double down on it. (p. 96, p. 141)
44. People don't buy the product, they buy what it stands for. The brand. The values. The status. (p. 108)

45. Your brand is the personality of your business. (p. 108)
46. Your brand is partly created by how you present your company to the world, and partly earned through consistent action. (p. 108)
47. No one remembers what you told them, but everyone remembers how you made them feel. (p. 109)
48. If you do not have a strong brand, you have to compete on something else. (p. 109)
49. Communications are the opposite of one-and-done: you iterate, iterate, iterate. (p. 116)
50. To build a brand, find its organizing idea and make it matter. (p. 115)
51. Your customers will not think consciously about your brand. It needs to be immediately obvious. (p. 121)
52. In branding, perception is reality. (p. 126)
53. People want to hear from people, and they trust people more than companies or brands. (p. 128)
54. Money follows attention. If you are visible as a founder, you attract more investors, customers and talent. (p. 128)
55. If you build a personal brand, do it in the service of the company and your own reputation will flourish. (p. 129)
56. To build a personal brand, you have to stand for something. (p. 130)
57. Everyone wants to be helped, but no one wants to be sold to. (p. 140)
58. The aim of marketing is to ensure that you build trust and an emotional connection with your ideal customers. You want to attract, not chase. (p. 141)

59. If the first rule of marketing is 'no one cares' and the second is 'know your customer', the third surely is 'don't be boring'. (p. 142)
60. Take your prospects on an emotional journey at the end of which they would feel stupid not to buy from you. (p. 143)
61. Successful businesses tend to scale thanks to one core channel. (p. 147)
62. Your customers don't buy because they understand you. They buy because you understand them. (p. 148)
63. Word-of-mouth is the most powerful marketing tool there is. (p. 148)
64. Effective marketing is the result of long-term thinking and excellence in execution. (p. 155)
65. Communications take time to build and can't be turned on and off at will. (p. 159)
66. PR's role is to establish the company's narrative and to build and protect the brand. (p. 164, p. 191)
67. In an interview, be a spokesperson, not an answer-person. (p. 166)
68. The most common mistake startups make is to assume that they are the story. Existing is not news. (p. 167)
69. Content is a meritocracy – consisting of credibility, interestingness and value. (p. 175)
70. Proper preparation prevents poor performance – the five Ps. (p. 182)
71. All major communications functions – internal, PR, marketing, employer branding – should report to one person to prevent friction and duplication. (p. 189)

72. The key to making your relationship with external advisers a success is to treat them as partners, not service providers. (p. 198)
73. Culture is destiny. (p. 199)
74. Culture is about creating shared beliefs, values and behaviors that lead to extraordinary results. (p. 201)
75. As a founder, you can't enforce results. (p. 201)
76. You influence culture directly by the way you communicate. (p. 204)
77. Culture is never done. It's always a work in progress. (p. 206)
78. Hire people with common values. You can train for skills, but you can't train for culture. (p. 214)
79. A high-achieving work environment is the result of strong technical skills AND strong communication skills. (p. 216)
80. Internal communications have three central goals: promote alignment and focus, reinforce culture and keep motivation high. (p. 225)
81. Think of internal communications as you think of marketing: deliver the right message to the right person, at the right time, on the right channel. (p. 228)
82. To maximize engagement, get information and inspiration across (push), gather feedback (pull) and exchange views with the team. (p. 230)
83. Job interviews should be conversations, not interrogations. (p. 243)
84. A brand-led and value-led hiring process is like a magnet: it will attract the right candidates but deter those who are not a good fit. (p. 246)

85. Communication is the foundation of any company's success. It's ridiculously more important in a crisis. (p. 251)
86. Hope is not a strategy. A crisis will hit you. (p. 254)
87. Prevent, prepare and react in the right way and you can take advantage of times of crisis when everyone is scared and distracted. (p. 259)
88. A crisis is an unfolding story, and your job is to control the narrative to avoid becoming the villain. (p. 262)
89. In a crisis, "Acknowledge, Apologize, Act", don't "Deny, Diminish, Deflect". (p. 264)
90. Doing the right thing tends to enhance a company's reputation, despite a crisis. (p. 268)
91. Your communications keep the soul of your startup alive. (p. 275)
92. As a founder or CEO, you ultimately own communications, so delegation is fine, but not abdication. Your company, your communications strategy. (p. 288)

THANK YOU!

We would be lying if we said this was an easy book to write. Before we wrote this book, both of us had searched for the seminal book on startup communications, and realized that there was little structured, timeless advice out there for founders, especially for the post-seed years that make or break a company. We then both independently had the urge to write that book ourselves. When we met for coffee in the summer of 2021, we decided to do it together. You have now seen the result of that endeavor. Jag comes from the world of startups and investing and has brought plenty of strategic communications experience. Oliver is an entrepreneur, communications expert and author with two decades of startup, scaleup and post-IPO experience. We have brought different perspectives, and our hope is that this unique combination has made this book and its principles more valuable to you.

Writing a book is a team sport, and this book would have never seen the light of day without the support of an incredible group of people who contributed their insights and expertise throughout the genesis of Message Machine. A massive thank you goes to our book-writing mastermind gang, our friends

Gerrit McGowan, Rebecca Schween and Christian Poensgen. Their feedback throughout the whole process ensured that we didn't lose motivation, momentum or direction while writing this book.

A huge thank you goes to our editor Gabriella Williams, as well as Beatriz Saab, Diane Vitry, Katja Vogel, Sarah Fuchs and Sophie Sternberg who all helped to turn seventy thousand words into a coherent text.

We always thought that this book deserved a strong design language in line with our message, and we are indebted to Bianca Amorim for the visual identity of this book, as well as to Dan Iowe who designed the striking cover.

Our first readers provided priceless feedback and were instrumental in whipping the manuscript into shape. Thank you Akash Bajwa, Bettina Hausmann, Catherine Thomas, Chelsea Blacker, Chris Murphy, Declan Kelly, Deepali Nangia, Fabian Leipelt, Francis Goodenday, Desi Tech Mafia, Diljit Singh, Georgiana Ghiciuc, Hilary Klassen, Holger Weiss, Julia Singh, Katia Yakovleva, Konstanty Sliwowski, Linda Broschkowski, Liz Stefan, Madeline Lawrence, Margaux Wehr, Marie Fabiunke, Michael Kirch, Niraj Dattani, Peter Botting, Pranav Ahuja, Rani Singh, Robert Ermich, Ren Yi Hooi, Sameer Singh, Simon Stodieck, Shilpika Gautam, Swarnali Mitra, Vera Montacuti! We feel very privileged that such an accomplished group of investors and founders gave us their unfiltered advice on how to turn the text from good to great, or at least mediocre to decent.

Most importantly, our heartfelt gratitude goes to our partners in life and crime, Linda Broschkowski and Julia Singh. Their insights, contribution and no-holds-barred feedback at various stages of the manuscript proved invaluable. Their love and support kept us going even if that meant many early mornings, late nights and weekends spent writing rather than with our families. Thank you! We could never have done it without you.

In the spirit of full disclosure, we would also like to mention that we have or had personal ties to a number of startups mentioned in the book as either investors, advisors or mentors. These are Eversend, Ratepay, SALT Global, Twilio, Urban Sports Club and Zenhomes. To be clear: This is not the reason we chose to highlight them in the book. We gave these companies and their founders shout-outs and included their quotes and stories because they deserve it.

Finally, we would like to thank you. We do not take it for granted that you stayed with us until the very end of this book. We sincerely hope that Message Machine will be a valuable guide on your journey that you keep close to your desk. The world needs you to innovate, solve problems and improve lives. Now more than ever. Let's venture forward.

Oliver & Jag

Printed in Poland
by Amazon Fulfillment
Poland Sp. z o.o., Wrocław
24 September 2024

4d8546a2-e6fd-4faf-b2ce-66a53d53d9a1R01